Science fiction movies are on the rise again...Right now they rank at the top of the box office in revenue, so I was thinking to myself, "Wow, everyone must really like sci fi..." and then I realized I'm one of those people too!

—Masashi Kishimoto, 2002

Author/artist Masashi Kishimoto was born in 1974 in rural Okayama Prefecture, Japan. After spending time in art college, he won the Hop Step Award for new manga artists with his manga **Karakuri** (Mechanism). Kishimoto decided to base his next story on traditional Japanese culture. His first version of **Naruto**, drawn in 1997, was a one-shot story about fox spirits; his final version, which debuted in **Weekly Shonen Jump** in 1999, quickly became the most popular ninja manga in Japan.

NARUTO
3-in-1 Edition
Volume 5
SHONEN JUMP Manga Omnibus Edition
A compilation of the graphic novel volumes 13–15

STORY AND ART BY MASASHI KISHIMOTO

Translation & English Adaptation/Mari Morimoto
Touch-up Art & Lettering/Inori Fukuda Trant
Additional Touch-up/Josh Simpson (Manga Edition)
Design/Sean Lee (Manga Edition)
Design/Sam Elzway (Omnibus Edition)
Editor/Joel Enos (Manga Edition)
Managing Editor/Erica Yee (Omnibus Edition)

Printed in the U.S.A.

Published by VIZ Media, LLC
P.O. Box 77010
San Francisco, CA 94107

10 9 8 7 6 5 4
Omnibus edition first printing, May 2013
Fourth printing, November 2015

www.viz.com

PARENTAL ADVISORY
NARUTO is rated T for Teen and is recommended for ages 13 and up. This volume contains realistic and fantasy violence.
ratings.viz.com

SHONEN JUMP MANGA

VOL. 13
THE CHÛNIN
EXAM,
CONCLUDED...!!

STORY AND ART BY
MASASHI KISHIMOTO

SAKURA サクラ

Smart and studious, Sakura is the brightest of Naruto's classmates, but she's constantly distracted by her crush on Sasuke. Her goal: to win Sasuke's heart!

NARUTO ナルト

When Naruto was born, a destructive fox spirit was imprisoned inside his body. Spurned by the older villagers, he's grown into an attention-seeking trouble-maker. His goal: to become the village's next *Hokage*.

SASUKE サスケ

The top student in Naruto's class, Sasuke comes from the prestigious Uchiha clan. His goal: to get revenge on a mysterious person who wronged him in the past.

Kazekage 風影

The shadowy leader of Sunagakure (the Village Hidden in the Sand) within the Land of Wind.

Gaara 我愛羅

Mysterious, bloodthirsty Gaara may be the scariest ninja competing in the Chûnin Exams.

Rock Lee ロック・リー

First, Lee seemed weak, only able to perform physical taijutsu. But he's got powerful tricks and unrivaled super speed.

Might Guy マイト・ガイ

The flamboyant Master Guy is Lee's idol...and Kakashi's rival!

Hokage 火影

The leader of Konohagakure. He was retired, but stepped back into the position when the fourth Hokage was killed by the nine-tailed fox spirit.

Kakashi カカシ

Although he doesn't have an especially warm personality, Kakashi is protective of his students.

THE STORY SO FAR...

Twelve years ago, a destructive nine-tailed fox spirit attacked the ninja village of Konohagakure. The *Hokage*, or village champion, defeated the fox by sealing its soul into the body of a baby boy. Now that boy, Uzumaki Naruto, has grown up to become a ninja-in-training, learning the art of *ninjutsu* with his teammates Sakura and Sasuke.

During the Second Chûnin Exam, in the Forest of Death, Naruto and the others were attacked by the mysterious shinobi Orochimaru, who left a curse mark on Sasuke and vanished...

Now it's the Chûnin Exam finals! But Sasuke is missing! To prevent Sasuke from losing to Gaara by forfeit, the next two scheduled matches were moved up. Things went downhill from there: Kankuro withdrew from his match against Shino to reserve his secret moves for the coming coup. Shikamaru almost beat Temari, but called it quits at the last minute. But now, at last, it's the fight you've all been waiting for...!

NARUTO

VOL. 13

THE CHÛNIN

EXAM, CONCLUDED...!!

CONTENTS

Number 109:
Tree Leaves Dancing...!!
しるこ

VICTOR, TEMARI!!

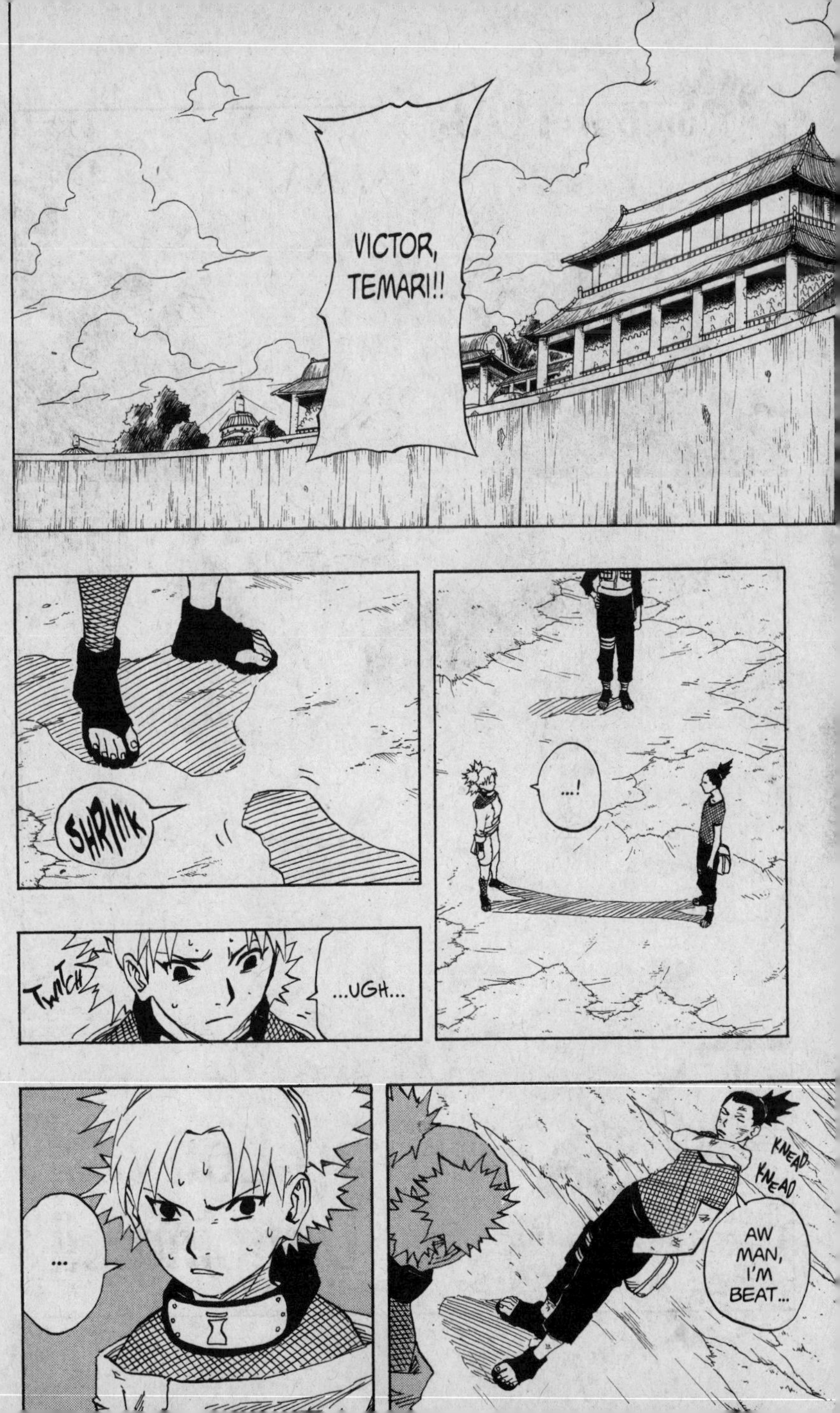

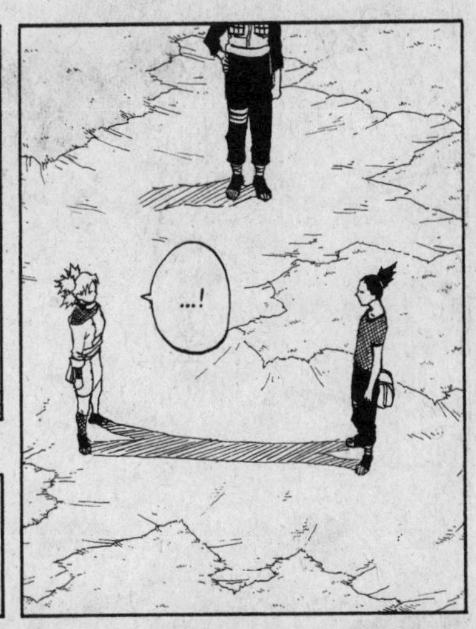
...!

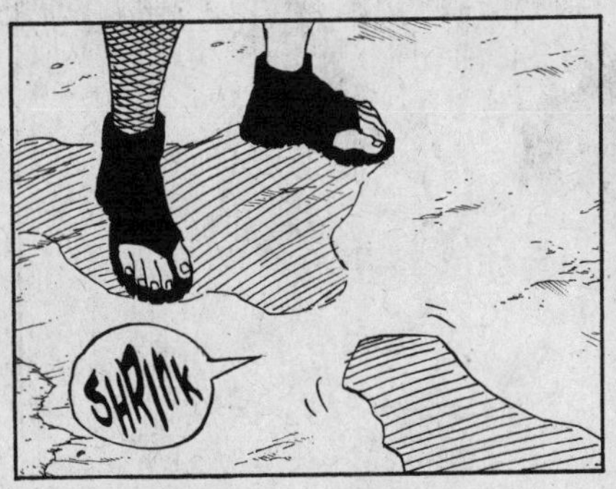
SHRINK

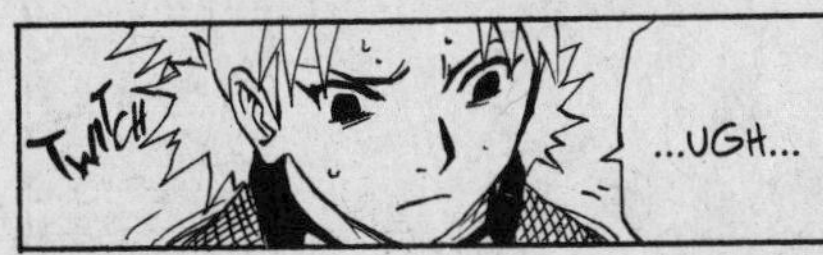
TWITCH
...UGH...

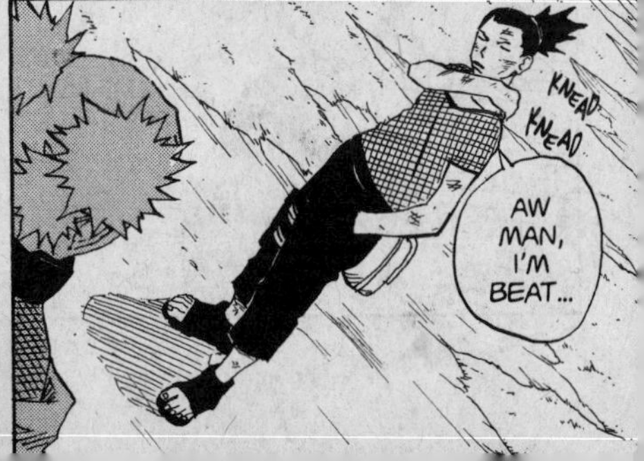
KNEAD
KNEAD
AW MAN, I'M BEAT...

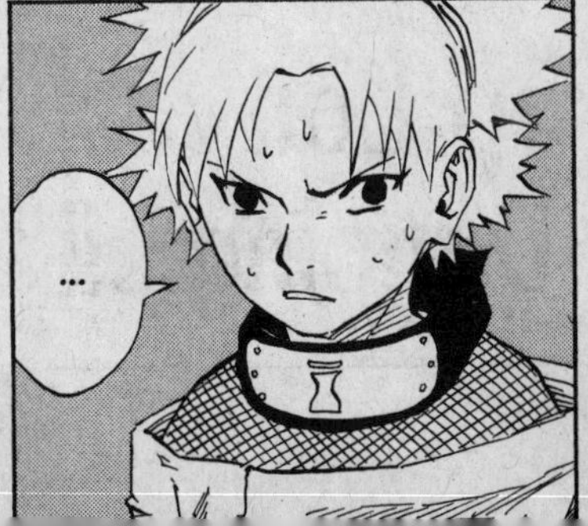
...

READ
THIS
WAY

ARGH! WHAT A WASTE. WHY...? HE COULD HAVE BECOME A CHÛNIN!!

SHIKAMARU'S SHIKAMARU.

SHEESH...
DOES HE HAVE ANY WILL TO FIGHT...?
I REALLY DON'T KNOW... IT'S A MYSTERY.

IF THIS HAD BEEN AN ACTUAL MISSION WITH HIM AS A MEMBER OF A BASIC 4-MAN PLATOON, SHIKAMARU'S VICTORY WOULD HAVE BEEN ASSURED WHEN HE CAPTURED TEMARI.
AND YET, THAT KID'S KNOWLEDGE AND STRATEGY ARE ALREADY DEFINITELY BEYOND GENIN LEVEL...
IT'S A CASE OF WINNING THE BATTLE BUT LOSING THE MATCH.

IT'S DISAPPOINTING THAT HE DOESN'T SEEM EAGER TO FIGHT, BUT...
...YOU COULD SAY THAT IT'S BECAUSE HE HAS THE ABILITY TO COOLLY ANALYZE ANY AND ALL SITUATIONS.
BECAUSE HE IS THOROUGHLY AWARE OF HIS OWN KNOWLEDGE AND SKILLS, HE DOESN'T PANIC OR BECOME HOTHEADED IN THE MIDST OF BATTLE. AND THAT IS HOW, EVEN IF HE FINDS HIMSELF IN THE WORST FIX, HE CAN CALMLY RETREAT.

I SUSPECT, IN TERMS OF THE PSYCHOLOGICAL PROFILES DEEMED ESSENTIAL IN CHÛNIN...

...SHIKAMARU'S GOT THE MOST IMPORTANT ONE...

KNEAD

...THE DISPOSITION OF A NATURAL LEADER!

IF WE ASSESS HIM AS A PLATOON LEADER...
...THE ABILITY TO PROTECT AND SAFELY GET ONE'S SOLDIERS OUT OF DANGER IS EVEN MORE IMPORTANT THAN CARRYING OUT ONE'S MISSION...

IN THE CASE OF INTELLIGENCE GATHERING, COMPLETING THE MISSION BUT GETTING WIPED OUT IS NOT A VIABLE OPTION...
UNLESS YOU CAN BALANCE RISKS AND SAC-RIFICES AGAINST THE MISSION AND PROCEED WITH SURVIVAL AS YOUR FOREMOST CONCERN...
...YOU DON'T HAVE WHAT IT TAKES TO BE A CHÛNIN...

ALONG THOSE LINES, NEITHER HYUGA NOR NARUTO ARE QUALIFIED...

...ALTHOUGH THEY MAKE PERFECTLY GOOD GENIN!

WHY'D HE GIVE UP?! IS HE STUPID OR SOME-THING?!

THAT REALLY MAKES ME MAD! I'M GONNA GO GIVE HIM A LECTURE HE WON'T EVER FORGET!

CLAMBER

WELL, I STILL THINK SHIKAMARU GAVE UP TOO EARLY TOO, BUT...

WHAT DO YOU THINK?

LEAP
LECTURING IS DIFFICULT.
ONE MUST NOT ANGER THE AUDIENCE.

WHAT DO I THINK...?
I THINK HE DEFINITELY HAS MORE PROMISE THAN NARUTO...
...TO BECOME A CHÛNIN...
STRETCH

SHUT IT, MEGA-DORK!!
STUPIDHEAD!!!
JAB

!
THUMP

LET'S GO WATCH THE NEXT MATCH, OKAY?

WHY'D YOU GIVE UP?!
AT THIS POINT, WHAT DOES IT MATTER...?

!
OH...!
NEXT IS...

...SASUKE!!

READ THIS WAY

CRUNCH
!

OH! YOU'RE...

OH WELL! I GUESS IT'S JUST LIKE HIM--
GLANCE GLANCE

HE'S...
...STILL NOT HERE...

SASUKE...

GOOD TO SEE YOU, SIRS!
NOW, PLEASE COME IN!

ROGER !!
ALL RIGHT! LET'S GO, LEE!
OH! YES SIR.
HIKE

READ THIS WAY

ALMOST ALL OF THE FIRST ROUND BATTLES HAVE CONCLUDED...
THE ONLY ONE REMAINING IS UCHIHA SASUKE VS. GAARA!

!
...
WH-WHAT ABOUT NARUTO AND NEJI'S BATTLE...?!

THAT'S THE INTERESTING THING...

NARUTO DEFEATED NEJI...

...

...
I SEE...

NICE WORK...
...NARUTO!!

LEE, YOU ARE SUCH A GREAT KID...

READ
THIS
WAY

WHAT'S UP WITH THE NEXT MATCH?!
WHERE'S UCHIHA?!

!
SHUF

WE'VE FINALLY RECEIVED WORD FROM KAKASHI...
MUTTER
MUTTER

...

...

...

!

BOUNG

...

H-HEY, IT'S ALMOST TIME...
IS HE REALLY GOING TO COME?!

HE'LL COME...
...I'M SURE OF IT!

READ THIS WAY

HMM... WHAT IS THAT FOOL DOING? HE'S STILL NOT HERE?!
GLANCE
GLANCE

FLUTTER

!

!!
SWIRL

READ THIS WAY

READ THIS WAY

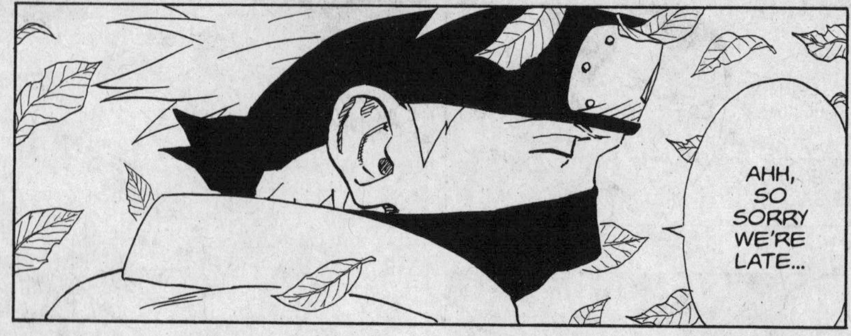

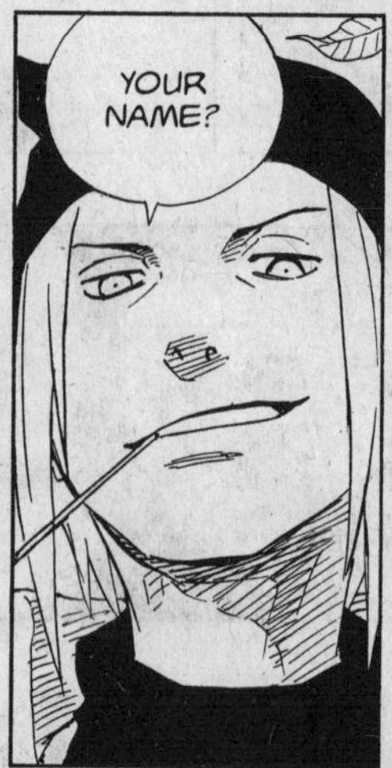

S...
SASUKE...!!

HEH... ACTING ALL HIGH AND MIGHTY...
...EVEN THOUGH HE'S INCONVE-NIENCED EVERYONE!

HEY...
ISN'T THAT...

IT'S SASUKE, ALL RIGHT!
!!

LEE!

READ THIS WAY

HEY! YOU'RE REAL LATE, HUH?!
I WAS WONDERING IF YOU GOT COLD FEET ABOUT FIGHTING ME!

SHEESH... YEAH, RIGHT.
AND WHO WAS THE ONE INSISTING HE WAS GOING TO SHOW UP?!

HEH... CHILL OUT...
...YOU BIG DORK...

GULP

SEE...
HE CAME.

THE WORLD OF KISHIMOTO MASASHI
MY PERSONAL HISTORY, PART 16

IN HIGH SCHOOL I WAS DRAWING MANGA ALL THE TIME, AND EVEN THOUGH I WAS IN THE PROGRESSIVE TRACK, MY HOMEROOM TEACHER TOLD ME I WOULDN'T GET INTO ANY COLLEGE BASED ON MY GRADES IN THE STANDARD SUBJECTS. "..." "...HEH..." "SO WHAT!!" I DIDN'T PANIC! I'D ALREADY THOUGHT IT OUT AND PLANNED AHEAD FOR THAT! AND WHAT WAS IT THAT I HAD IN MIND...?

SINCE I WAS IN ELEMENTARY SCHOOL, FOR SOME UNKNOWN REASON, MY GRADES IN ART HAVE ALWAYS BEEN EXCELLENT! ..."THAT'S RIGHT! IF IT'S AN ART COLLEGE, I THINK I CAN GET IN!" THIS COMPLETELY GROUNDLESS CONFIDENCE HAD SECRETLY ALLAYED MY FEARS!

(P.S. BECAUSE IT WAS A PROGRESSIVE TRACK, THERE WERE NO ART CLASSES AT ALL!) MOST ART SCHOOLS ONLY TEST ART ON THEIR APPLICATION EXAMS.

IN ANY CASE, TO BE HONEST, DESPITE THE FACT THAT I WAS CONSTANTLY DRAWING IN HIGH SCHOOL, I WAS PAINFULLY AWARE THAT I DIDN'T HAVE GOOD SKETCHING SKILLS. SO I SAID TO MYSELF, "I'LL HONE MY SKETCHING ABILITY IN COLLEGE!" AND PRACTICED SKETCHING THE SAMPLE PLASTER MODELS BEFORE HEADING OFF TO THE ACTUAL EXAM!

WHILE DEEPLY REALIZING THAT HUMANS ARE CREATURES OF CONVENIENCE WHO ONLY OFFER PRAYERS TO THE GODS WHEN FACED WITH CRISES, I WAITED SEVERAL WEEKS FOR THE RESULTS!
A-AND THEN... THE GODS HADN'T YET ABANDONED ME...

I PASSED!!
"YES!! NOW I CAN DRAW MANGA ALL I WANT!! YEAH!!"

SO AMIDST HIGH STRESS, I WENT OFF TO ART SCHOOL!

AND THEN, BRIEFLY REFLECTING ON MY HIGH SCHOOL YEARS, I WONDERED THUSLY: FOR THREE YEARS, I HAD DESPERATELY STRUGGLED THROUGH MATH, ENGLISH, GRAMMAR, CHEMISTRY, AND HISTORY... TO WHAT END?

Number 110: At Long Last...!!

FROM THAT LOUDMOUTH ATTITUDE OF YOURS...
...I TAKE IT YOU WON YOUR FIRST ROUND BATTLE?

WELL, UH, FLASHY ENTRANCE NOTWITH-STANDING...
...DON'T TELL ME...

...SASUKE LOST BY FORFEIT?

SEE... I TOLD YOU WE'D BE LATE, SASUKE.
MAYBE YOUR TARDINESS IS CONTA-GIOUS?!
SHEESH!

...
SO... WHAT'S THE DEAL?

DON'T WORRY, YOU'RE SAFE!
SASUKE'S MATCH WAS POSTPONED.
HIS MATCH WASN'T FORFEITED.

READ
THIS
WAY

AH HA HA...
OH, GOOD! GOOD!

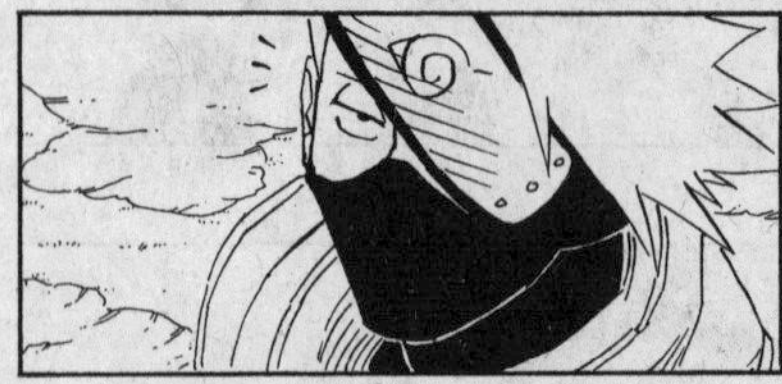

...

GLANCE

DON'T YOU DARE LOSE TO A GUY LIKE HIM!

YEAH...
...

YOU'RE ONE OF THE ONES I WANT TO FIGHT...

SASUKE!

...

I...
...WANT TO FIGHT YOU TOO...!

READ THIS WAY

WHEE! SASUKE!
A FEW MINUTES AGO SHE WAS ALL FOR SHIKAMARU, AND NOW SHE'S ALL FOR SASUKE... POOR SHIKAMARU.

MUTTER
MUTTER
HEY! IS THAT THE LAST OF THE UCHIHA CLAN?!
MUTTER
UCHIHA'S MATCH IS STARTING!!

WELL, I'VE GOTTA ADMIT, I'VE KINDA BEEN LOOKING FORWARD TO THIS TOO...
... SO I CAN'T GET TOO UPSET OVER BEING THE OPENING ACT...

HEY, SAKURA!
YOUR TEAM'S KINDA PRETTY AWESOME--!
HUH?

I MEAN...
...I NEVER IMAGINED NARUTO WOULD BEAT UP HYUGA NEJI...

READ THIS WAY

HUH?

...

...AND SASUKE'S AN UCHIHA ELITE...
...WITH EVERYONE ITCHING TO WATCH HIS MATCH!

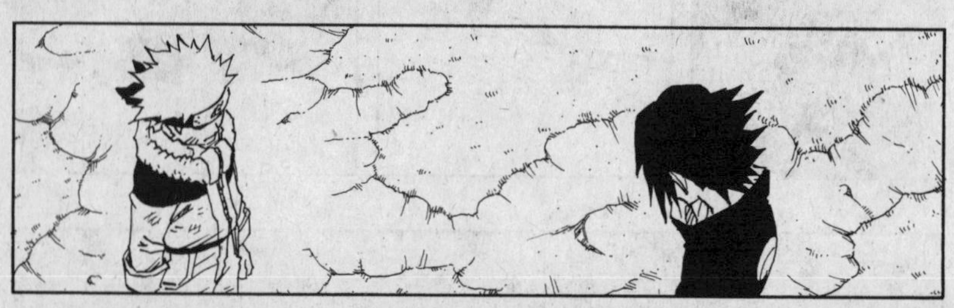

SASUKE IS FIGHTING THAT SAND NINJA GAARA, WHOM I WAS POWERLESS AGAINST...
AND NARUTO WON AGAINST NEJI, WHOM I HAVE ALWAYS WANTED TO DEFEAT...

CLENCH
WHY...
SEEP
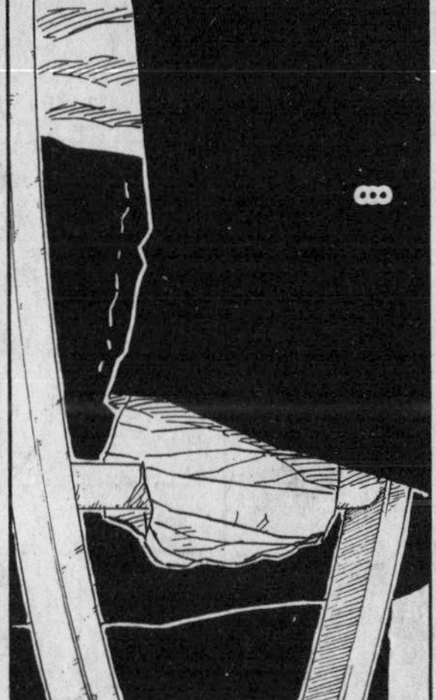
...

DRIP
WHY AM I SO...
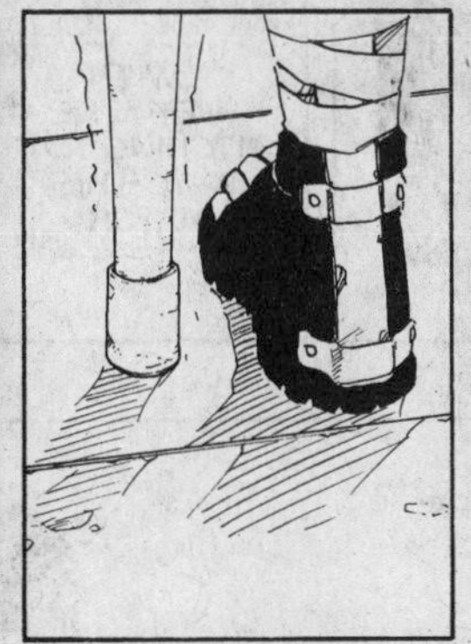

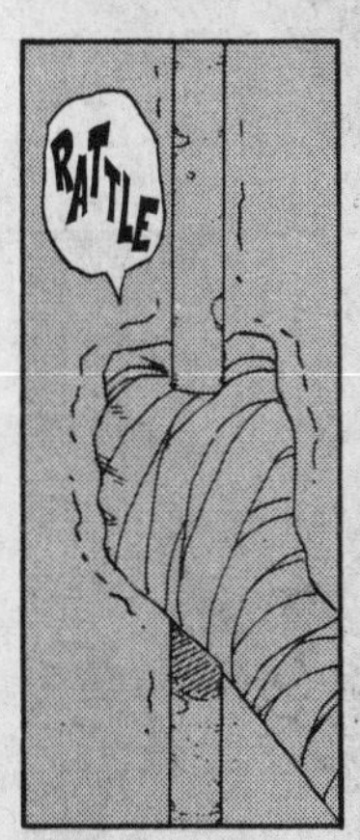
RATTLE

...JEALOUS?!

...
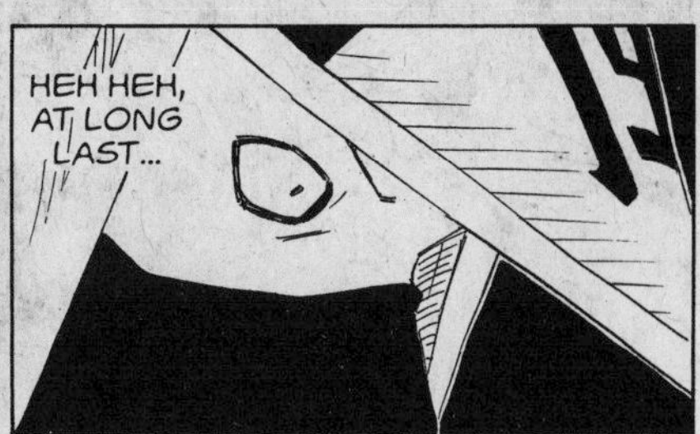
HEH HEH, AT LONG LAST...

READ THIS WAY

GAARA, COME DOWN.

NARUTO! LET'S GO BACK UPSTAIRS.

AND LET'S JUST TAKE THE STAIRS THIS TIME, OKAY?!
TURN
WHAT! ARE YOU STILL HOLDING IT AGAINST ME THAT I SHOVED YOU?!

SH-SHOOT... I HAVEN'T SEEN GAARA THIS BAD IN A WHILE...

...H-HEY, GAARA... DON'T FORGET ABOUT THE PLAN, ALL RI--
WHIP

!!
SMAK

DON'T TALK TO HIM RIGHT NOW...

...!

READ THIS WAY

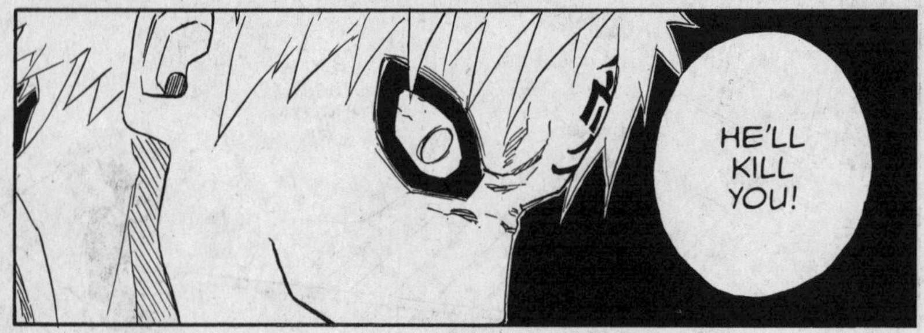
HE'LL KILL YOU!

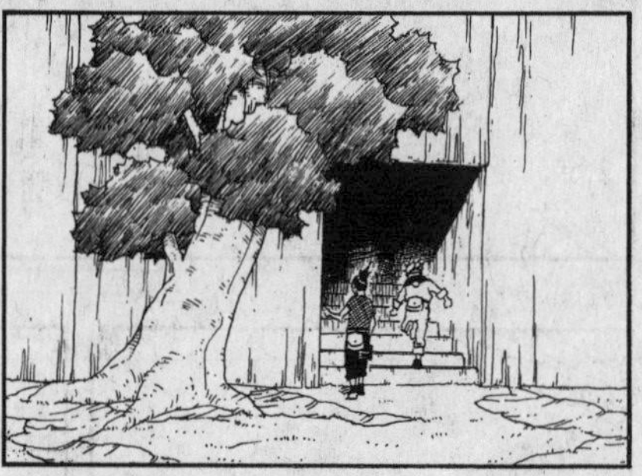

STEP

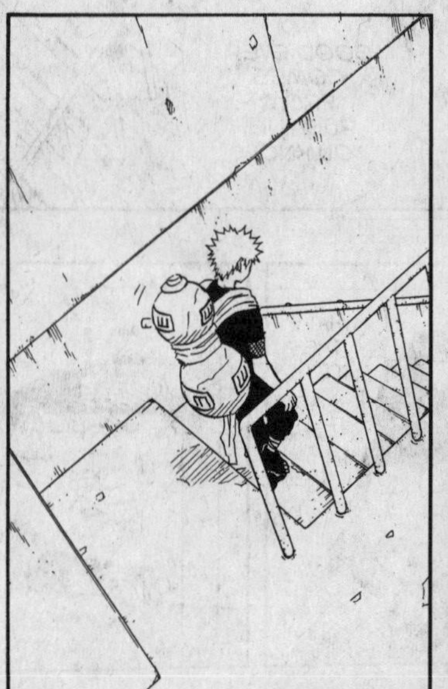

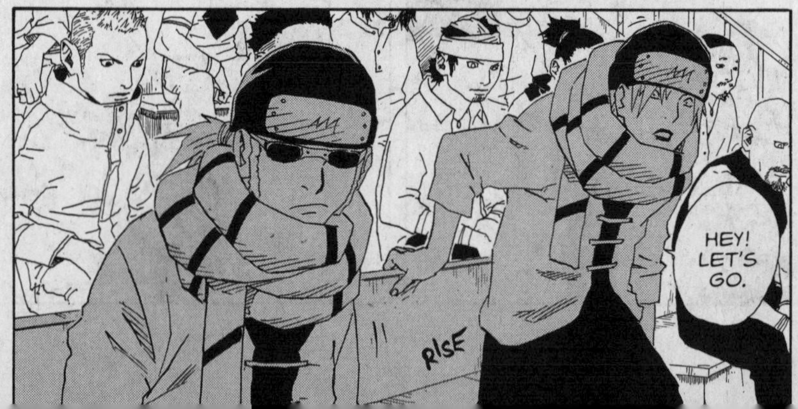
HEY! LET'S GO.
RISE

HEY! C'MON, HURRY UP!
NO GOOD EVER COMES FROM RUSHING, YOU KNOW.

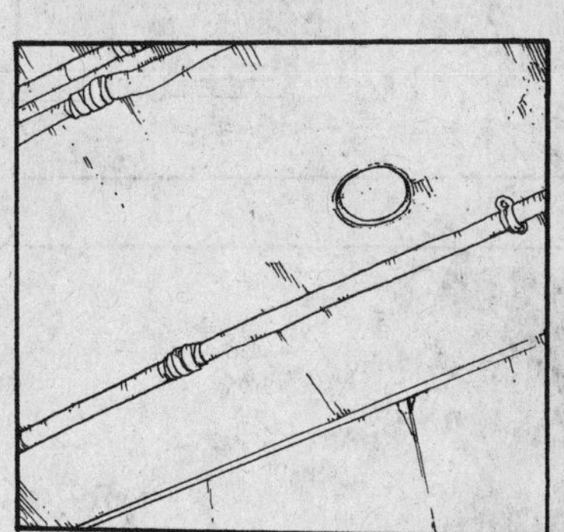

WHAT'S THE MATTER...?

!

HALT!

CRUNCH
CRUNCH

READ
THIS
WAY

LOW-LEVEL TOURNAMENTS LIKE THIS CHŪNIN EXAM ARE IDEAL FOR GAMBLING, YOU KNOW...
THERE ARE A NUMBER OF LORDS WHO HAVE COME JUST FOR THAT REASON.

AND SO...
...THIS MATCH... WE WANT YOU TO LOSE IT...

愛

SQUELCH
SQUICH
!!!
!!!
RRRR RROAR
RRROAR
FSSSH
SSSH
SQUILCH

FSSH
SQUILCH

...
TROMP
TROMP
TH-THUMP

TROMP
TH-THUMP

TROMP
TH-THUMP

...!

READ
THIS
WAY

CRUNCH

...IF IT HADN'T BEEN FOR THOSE TWO... WE PROBABLY WOULD HAVE BEEN KILLED.
WHEW...
HUF
HUF
HUF

I'VE NEVER MET ANYONE WHO KILLED SO AUTOMATICALLY.
...EVEN SASUKE BETTER WATCH IT... YIKES...

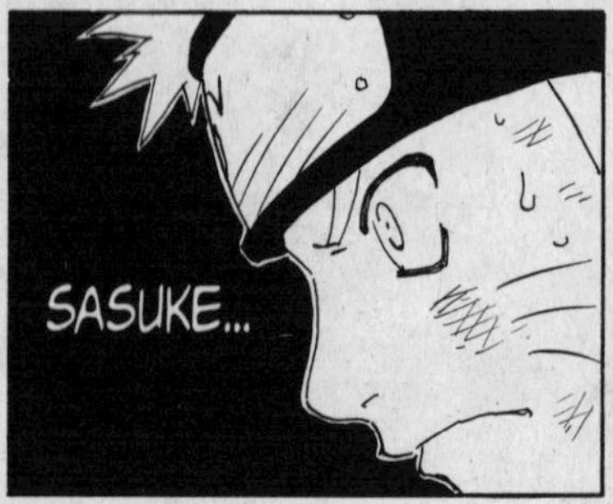
SASUKE...

NOW THEN...
AT LONG LAST...

Number 111: Sasuke vs. Gaara!!

HEH
HEH
HEH...

?!

!
SHOOM

!

READ THIS WAY

YO, GUY!
AND YOU TOO, LEE... ARE YOU ALL RIGHT NOW?

KAKASHI!
!

MASTER KAKASHI!

OH! SORRY, SORRY.
YOU WERE WORRIED, WEREN'T YOU...?
SORRY I DIDN'T KEEP IN TOUCH...

OH YEAH. SHE'LL GET MAD... SAKURA WILL...

...IT'S ALL RIGHT.
!
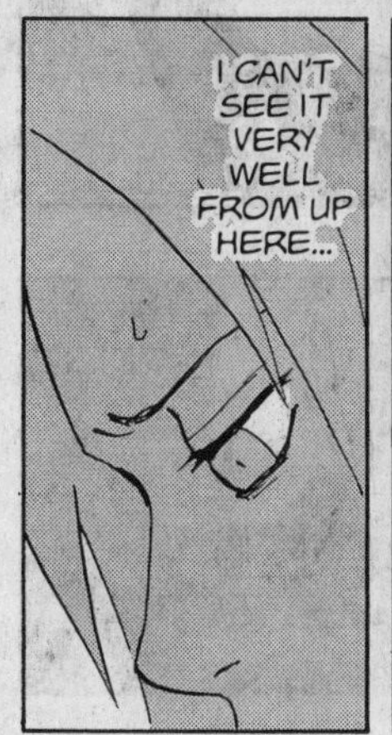
I CAN'T SEE IT VERY WELL FROM UP HERE...

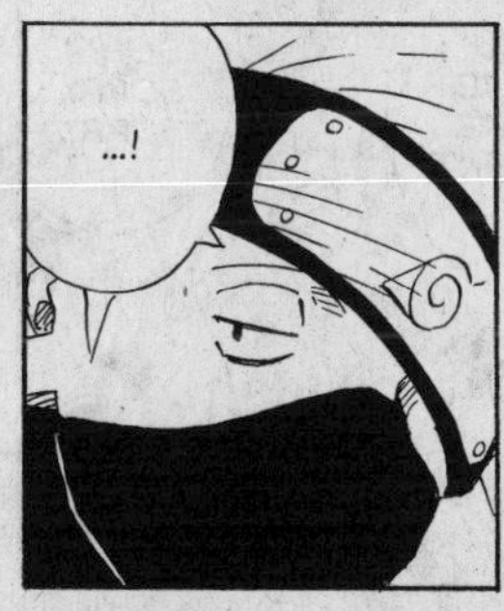
...!

...MASTER KAKASHI...

...

READ THIS WAY

THAT MARK...
...ON SASUKE'S NECK... IT'S STILL...
IT'S NOTHING TO WORRY ABOUT.

!

MARK?

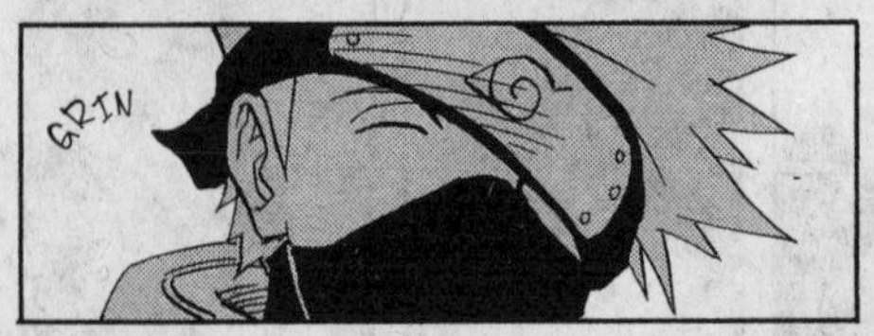
GRIN

...

...

ONLY EIGHT BLACK OPS FOR THIS HUGE STADIUM...? TWO PLATOONS AREN'T ENOUGH... WHAT IS LORD HOKAGE THINKING...?
WELL... NOT KNOWING HOW THE ENEMY IS GOING TO ACT...
...THE BLACK OPS HAVE PROBABLY ALSO BEEN DISPERSED AND STATIONED AROUND THE KEY PARTS OF THE VILLAGE.

MUTTER MUTTER

BEGIN!

LEAP
SO THIS IS THE SAND KAKASHI WAS TALKING ABOUT...

FSSSH

THROB
UGH...!

?
FSSSH

PLEASE... DON'T BE SO ANGRY...
?

...
MOTHER...
HUF
HUF
HUF
HUF

?!
WHAT IS HE TALKING ABOUT...? WEIRD.

FSSSSSS
I... GAVE YOU BAD-TASTING BLOOD EARLIER, DIDN'T I...?
I'M SORRY...
BUT... DON'T WORRY... THIS TIME...

I'M SURE IT'LL BE REALLY TASTY...

READ THIS WAY

THE "CONVERSATION" HAS STARTED ALREADY...
...THIS IS NOT GOOD.
I'VE NEVER SEEN GAARA SO WORKED UP BEFORE A BATTLE EVEN STARTED...
THAT'S HOW MUCH OF AN OPPONENT SASUKE IS...

THROB
UGH!

...
IT SEEMS TO HAVE SETTLED DOWN.

HUF
HUF

愛
COME.

REMEMBER THE TIME WE RAN INTO HIM AT THE HOSPITAL?

THAT TIME, HE SAID...
I WILL KILL YOU ALL...
...JUST YOU WAIT.

BUT... HE DIDN'T.
EVEN THOUGH IT WAS HIS BEST CHANCE...
WE DON'T EVEN REGISTER IN HIS SIGHT.

...NOW...
HELP ME FEEL ALIVE!

WE'RE...
...NOT ENOUGH FOR HIM.

RIGHT NOW, THE ONLY ONE WHO CAN SATISFY HIM...

...IS SASUKE!

I WOULD FIGHT ONLY FOR MYSELF AND LOVE ONLY MYSELF.

IF ALL OTHER PEOPLE EXIST TO MAGNIFY THAT LOVE, THEN THERE IS NO MORE SPLENDID WORLD THAN THIS ONE.

HERE I COME.

SHK
SHK

KWIP

SHOOM

THWOCK
THWOCK

SSSH

SHHFF

HIS SAND SHIELD TRANSFORMED INTO A SAND CLONE...!!

DASH
SHHH

!
LEAP
!!
SHOOM
FWIP
CHAK
CHAK
!
FWIP

CLENCH
THWAP
TAK
SHA
SHKKSH
FWP
KA
SHUNK

KOO
SSH

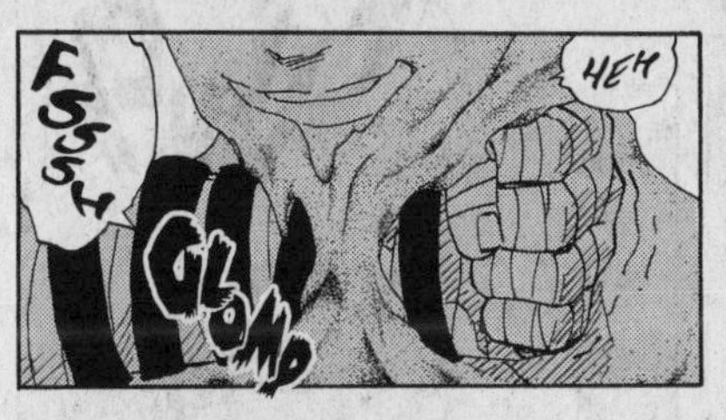
HEH
FSSSSH
GLOMP

UGH!

SHUP

FWOONK
YAH!

SPURT

READ THIS WAY

DASH

VOOSH

HEH

SHF

!

FAST!
JUST LIKE... HIM...

SLAM

READ THIS WAY

HE'S QUICK!! HE'S ALMOST AS FAST AS LEE'S AVERAGE SPEED...
AND...

...HIS STANCE MATCHES...
...MY TAIJUTSU IMAGE!!

愛
SSSSH

IS THAT YOUR SAND ARMOR?

COME!
SHUP SHUP

THE WORLD OF KISHIMOTO MASASHI
MY PERSONAL HISTORY, PART 17

HAVING BRILLIANTLY ACHIEVED COLLEGE STUDENT STATUS AND HAVING ALL OF MY CLASSES REVOLVE AROUND DRAWING MADE FOR A DREAMLIKE, HAPPY EXISTENCE FOR ME.

AND NOW THAT I WAS A FIRST-YEAR COLLEGE STUDENT, I WAS ABOUT TO TURN 19 YEARS OLD! I STARTED FURIOUSLY DRAWING MANGA, WITH *JUMP'S* HOP ☆ STEP AWARD AS MY GOAL. "I FEEL A SAMURAI MANGA COMING ON RIGHT NOW!" I THOUGHT, SO I STEADILY DREW A SAMURAI MANGA, BUT THEN, JUST AS I WAS ABOUT TO COMPLETE IT, AN UNBELIEVABLE THING HAPPENED...!!

YIKES! A DOUBLE PUNCH OF NEWCOMERS WHO WERE BOTH THINKING THE SAME THING AND HAD GOOD ART SENSE--I COULDN'T BELIEVE THERE WERE SO MANY!! AND IN THIS WORLD, THE EARLY BIRD REALLY DOES GET THE WORM...!

IN THE STAND-ALONE STORY SECTION OF *JUMP* APPEARED A MANGA BY *RUROUNI KENSHIN* AUTHOR WATSUKI NOBUHIRO-SENSEI! AT THE TIME, THE TITLE DID NOT YET HAVE "KENSHIN" IN IT, BUT IT STILL HAD A HUGE EFFECT ON ME. IN ADDITION, AROUND THE SAME TIME, SAMURA HIROAKI OF THE IMMORTAL SAMURAI *BLADE OF THE IMMORTAL* FAME ALSO WON THE GRAND PRIZE AND FOREVER CHANGED THE STANDARD FOR *AFTERNOON'S* RISING ARTISTS' CONTEST!! SAMURA'S ART AND STORY WERE WAY ABOVE THE LEVEL OF A NEWCOMER, ALMOST THAT OF A FULL PRO!

I RECEIVED THE BIGGEST SHOCK OF MY LIFE SINCE *AKIRA*!

WHEN I CAREFULLY REREAD MY OWN SAMURAI MANGA WITH THOSE TWO AMAZING WORKS IN FRONT OF ME, I FELT MY OWN PUNINESS MORE THAN I CARED TO... OF COURSE, I STILL ENTERED THAT SAMURAI MANGA INTO THE CONTEST, BUT IT DIDN'T EVEN MAKE A MARK... MY PATH TOWARDS BECOMING A MANGA-KA STILL STRETCHED FAR BEFORE ME, WROUGHT WITH PERIL!

Number 112: Sasuke's Taijutsu...!!

IF YOU'RE NOT GOING TO COME TO ME, I'LL GO TO YOU!

!
FSSH
SHOOOOM
!!
...HE'S SO FAST!
FSSHT
FSSSSH
VOOSH

SLAM
THUD

THAT ARMOR OF YOURS...
HUF
I'LL RIP IT OFF OF YOU.
HUF
SHOOM
ZHOOM ZHOOM

THAT'S PRACTICALLY THE SAME SPEED...
...AS LEE WITHOUT HIS WEIGHTS.

I-IT LOOKS... JUST LIKE LEE'S TAIJUTSU...
EVEN HIS SPEED IS A LOT GREATER THAN BEFORE!

!!
!!
FWUMK
GRAB
YANK
BOOF

READ THIS WAY

SASUKE... YOU REALLY ARE AN AMAZING GENIUS.
IT TOOK ME YEARS TO ACHIEVE THAT LEVEL OF SPEED...
BUT YOU ATTAINED IT IN JUST ONE MONTH...

HOWEVER... MAINTAINING THAT SPEED STILL EXPENDS QUITE A LOT OF ENERGY, DOESN'T IT...

WHAT ARE YOU GOING TO DO, GAARA...? THE SAND ARMOR USES TOO MUCH CHAKRA...
YOU CAN'T KEEP IT GOING THAT LONG...

...

...EXACTLY WHAT KIND OF TRAINING DID YOU PUT HIM THROUGH...
...TO HONE HIM TO THAT EXTENT IN JUST ONE MONTH?!

SASUKE MIMICKED LEE'S TAIJUTSU USING THE SHARINGAN ONCE BEFORE...
...SO DURING HIS TAIJUTSU TRAINING, I JUST HAD HIM VISUALIZE LEE'S MOVEMENTS.

!

READ THIS WAY

BECAUSE SASUKE KNEW LEE...
...HE WAS ABLE TO MASTER THOSE MOVES.
OF COURSE, IT WAS STILL EXTREMELY DIFFICULT.

BUT... IF THAT'S IT...
...YOU CAN'T DEFEAT THAT SAND SHINOBI WITH TAIJUTSU ALONE.

GLANCE

KAKASHI...
I KNOW HE WATCHED THE MATCH BETWEEN THAT DETESTABLE GAARA AND MY CHARMING LEE...
HE'S GOT TO KNOW THAT HASTILY ACQUIRED TAIJUTSU ALONE WON'T WORK AGAINST GAARA, WHOM EVEN LEE COULDN'T DEFEAT...
THEN...

WHY DID HE HAVE SASUKE HONE JUST HIS TAIJUTSU?!

!
KSSSH

FZZZT
FSSHT
愛

READ
THIS
WAY

FOR WHAT PURPOSE DO I EXIST? WHY AM I ALIVE?
...

WHILE I CONTINUE TO LIVE, I NEED A **REASON.**
I EXIST TO KILL ALL HUMANS OTHER THAN MYSELF.

!
SHUP

SHIKA-MARU ...
LET'S GO UP TO MASTER KAKASHI!

WHAT ARE YOU THINKING...?

DASH
HEY!

I'M GOING TO...

...STOP THIS MATCH!!

ZHOOM

READ
THIS
WAY

DON'T TELL ME GAARA'S INITIATING **THAT** JUTSU?!?!

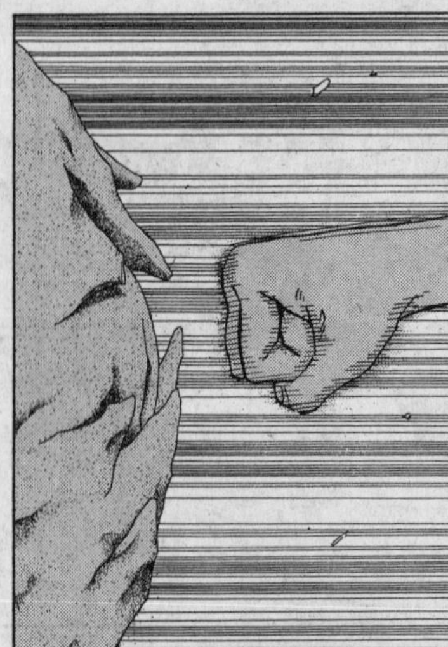

KSSSSH

SSSH

FWUNK

!!!

HUF
HUF
DRIP

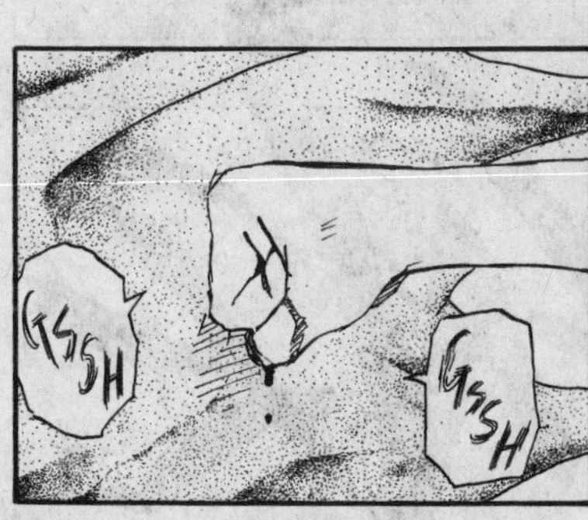
GSSH
GSSH

READ THIS WAY

FSSSSSH
SHUP
UGH...

HUF
PLIP
HUF

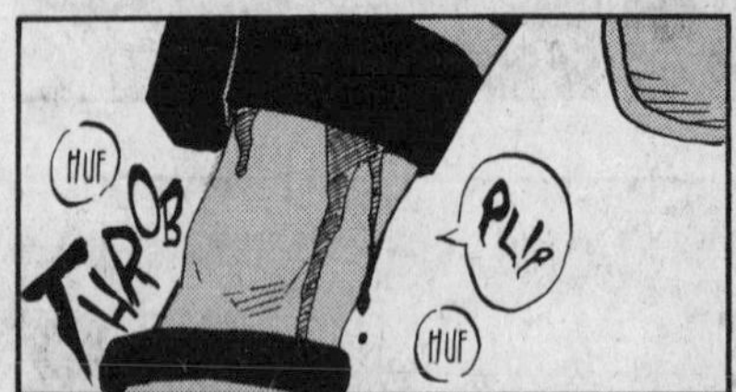
HUF
THROB
PLIP
HUF

HE'S MOBILIZED HIS SAND INTO DEFENSIVE MODE...
BECAUSE OF SAND'S DENSITY, I DIDN'T THINK HE COULD CREATE SOMETHING THIS SOLID...

TWITCH
TWITCH

SO THIS IS THE MEANING OF AN ABSOLUTE DEFENSE, HUH...?
HUF

MASTER KAKASHI!!

!

!

NARUTO!

READ THIS WAY

YO!
WHAT'S UP?

MASTER!
PLEASE STOP THIS MATCH RIGHT AWAY!

HE'S COMPLETELY DIFFERENT FROM THE REST OF US!
HE'S NOT NORMAL!

NARUTO...
...WHAT ARE YOU TALKING ABOUT--?

AND...
HE LIVES TO KILL OTHERS!

JIN* MONKEY SNAKE MONKEY...
...IF THEY KEEP GOING, SASUKE'LL DIE!!

* *Jin* means Yang Water, one of the elemental influences in the Chinese sexagenary cycle. -Ed.

THERE'S NO MISTAKE, IT'S THAT JUTSU!
NO! GAARA'S SO WORKED UP THAT HE'S NOT REMEMBERING THE PLAN...

READ THIS WAY

MASTER KAKASHI!!

...

WELL!
DON'T WORRY ABOUT IT!

!

THERE WAS A REASON...

SWIP
...WHY WE WERE SO LATE GETTING HERE!

THE WORLD OF KISHIMOTO MASASHI
MY PERSONAL HISTORY, PART 18

I DIDN'T WIN THE CONTEST, SO I ENDED UP SPENDING MY FIRST YEAR OF COLLEGE PRETTY DISGRUNTLED.

ONE DAY, SOMEONE APPROACHED ME SAYING "I DRAW MANGA TOO" AND PROFFERED THIS: "IF YOU'LL DRAW MANGA FOR MY NEW COLLECTION, I'LL PAY YOU." "WELL, IF I CAN GET MONEY FOR MY OWN PIECE, MIGHT AS WELL," I THOUGHT, SO I QUICKLY PUT TOGETHER ROUGHLY EIGHT PAGES OF A RANDOM STAND-ALONE SHORT AND GAVE IT TO HIM. HE WAS PUTTING TOGETHER A DÔJINSHI [SELF-PUBLISHED WORK] WITH ABOUT FIVE PEOPLE IN TOTAL, AND HAD COME TO COMMISSION ME TO BE ONE OF THE FIVE, HAVING HEARD A RUMOR THAT I DREW MANGA. SINCE THE DEAL WAS THAT I WOULD GET AN EQUAL SHARE OF THE PROFIT, I PLEASANTLY LOOKED FORWARD TO THE BOOK'S COMPLETION. BUT NO MATTER HOW LONG I WAITED, NO BOOK!

AFTER I HAD WAITED A LONG WHILE, I ASKED THE FELLOW "SO WHEN IS THE BOOK COMING OUT?" BUT HE ANSWERED, "THREE OTHER MANGA, INCLUDING MY OWN, ARE STILL NOT DONE..." I REALLY WANTED TO SHOUT BACK, "HOW CAN IT TAKE YOU MORE THAN FOUR MONTHS TO COMPLETE EIGHT PAGES!" BUT INSTEAD I JUST MUTTERED "AH, I SEE" AND ENTERED A STATE OF RESIGNATION. THE NEXT TIME I SAW HIM HE HAD HIS BACK TO ME, FURIOUSLY PLAYING VIDEO GAMES AT THE ARCADE. THAT'S WHEN IT FINALLY HIT ME (AAH! HE'S A SHAM MANGA ARTIST).

HOWEVER, THIS WORLD IS NOT MADE UP OF JUST SHAM MANGA ARTISTS! A CERTAIN PAIR OF SENPAI [UPPERCLASSMEN] WOULD END UP TRANSFORMING MY DISGRUNTLED LIFE WHEN I ENTERED MY SECOND YEAR OF COLLEGE! THOSE TWO COMPETED AGAINST EACH OTHER, COLLECTING NEWCOMER AWARDS LEFT AND RIGHT, AND WERE VETERANS ENOUGH TO ALREADY HAVE ASSIGNED EDITORS, EVEN CUTTING BACK ON SLEEP TO INCREASE THEIR TIME SPENT DRAWING MANGA. "YES! FINALLY, I'VE MET GENUINE MANGA ARTISTS!" I JOYFULLY SAID TO MYSELF, FREQUENTLY RUNNING OVER TO MY SENPAI'S HOUSES TO HANG OUT AND LEARN ALL ABOUT MANGA PRODUCTION! THEY WERE ALSO WILLING TO READ MY MANGA AND GIVE ME ALL SORTS OF CRITIQUES SO THAT MY SKILLS WERE HONED! I AM SO ETERNALLY GRATEFUL TO THOSE TWO. EVEN NOW, THEY LET ME CALL THEM ON OCCASION... HOWEVER, I FEEL BAD ABOUT BOTHERING THEM, SO IT'S STILL HARD FOR ME TO PICK UP THE PHONE. FOR THEY'RE BOTH SLEEP-DEPRIVED PROFESSIONAL MANGA ARTISTS LEADING IRREGULAR LIVES!

Number 113:

The Reason He Was Late...!!

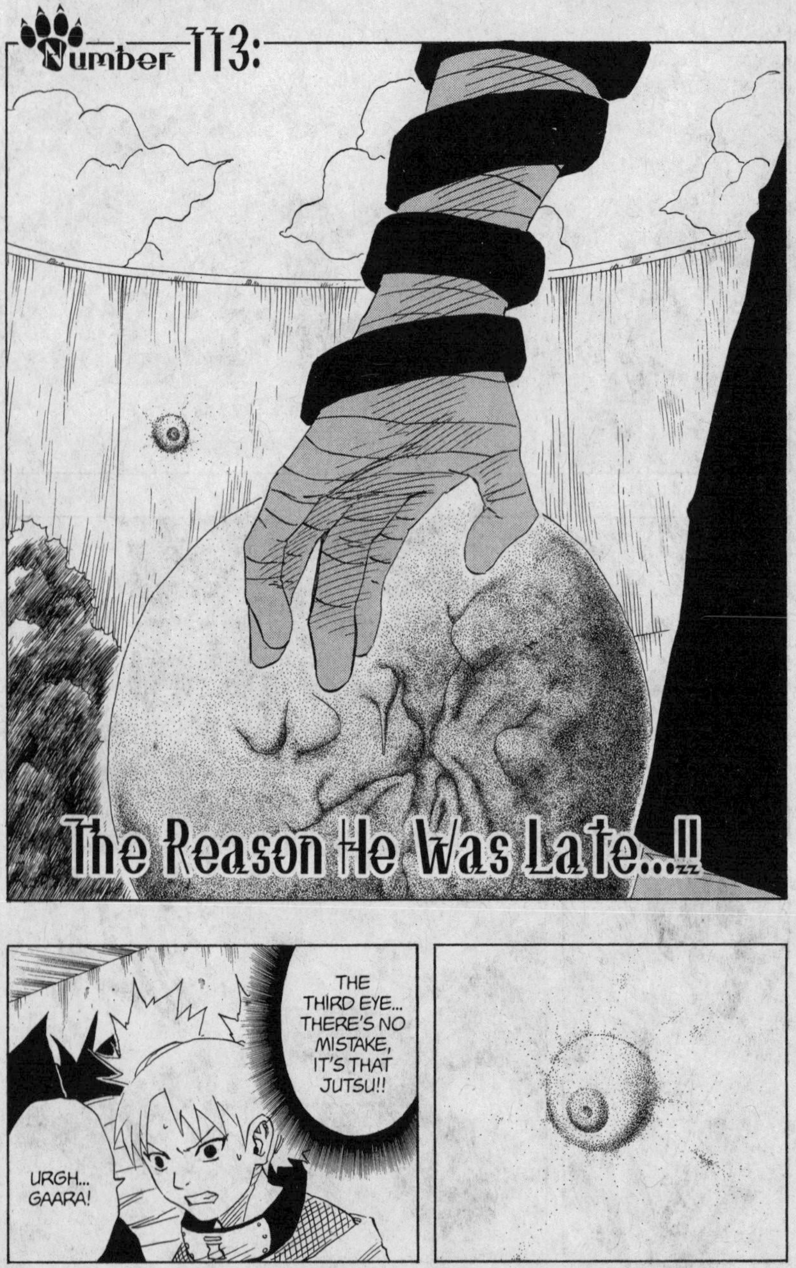

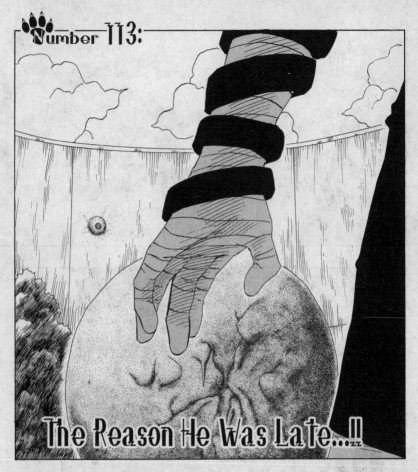

THE THIRD EYE... THERE'S NO MISTAKE, IT'S THAT JUTSU!!
URGH... GAARA!

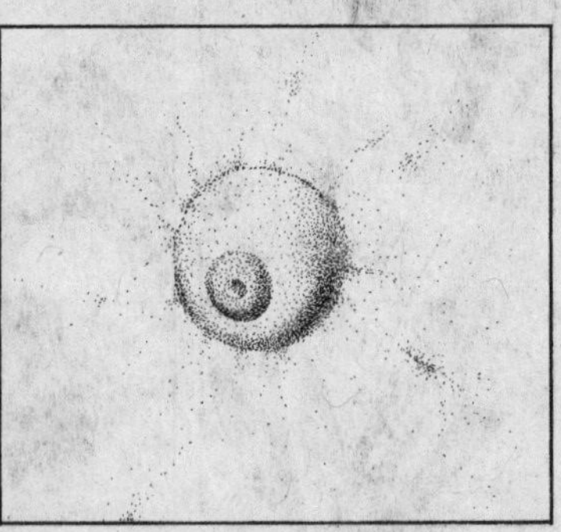

SWAY

JIN MONKEY BIRD DRAGON...

ZAA

TH

SWING

WAP

READ THIS WAY

SHUP

IT'S NO GOOD...
...JUST AS I FIGURED...

!

MUTTER
RAT MONKEY JIN RAT RABBIT TIGER BIRD JIN...
MUTTER

HE'S SHUT HIMSELF INSIDE... I DON'T KNOW WHAT HE'S UP TO, BUT...
...IT'S FINE BY ME. THIS THING OF MINE...

...IS GOING TO TAKE TIME TOO...
CHAK

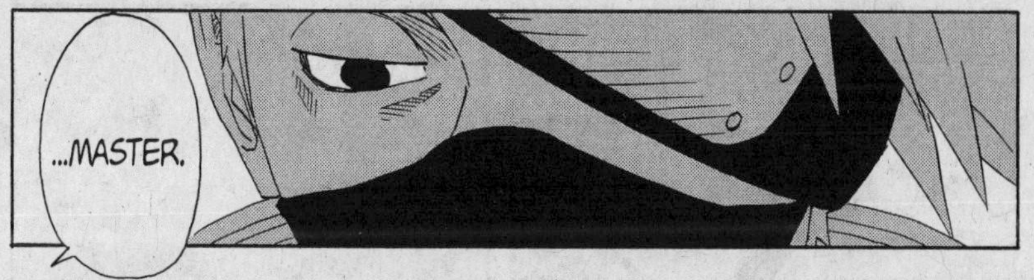
...MASTER.

WHAT DO YOU MEAN BY "THERE WAS A REASON WE WERE SO LATE GETTING HERE"?!

HMM...?
YOU REALLY WANT TO KNOW?

I'M TELLING YOU, THIS ISN'T THE TIME TO BE CHATTING!!

JUST BE QUIET AND WATCH HIM...

!

!

!

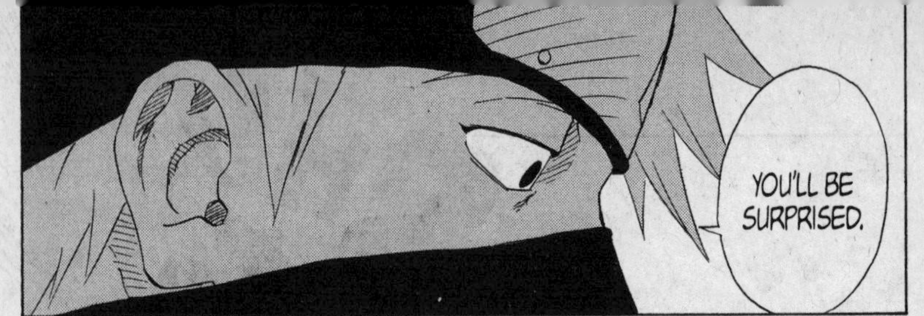
YOU'LL BE SURPRISED.

FWISH
FWISH

SKKSH

GSSH
SHUP

TUNK

SHUNK

NO... GAARA, THAT FOOL...
WE DON'T KNOW WHEN THEY'RE GOING TO GIVE THE SIGNAL!!

FEH... AT THIS POINT, THERE'S NOTHING WE CAN DO.
NEVER MIND THE PLAN, IS HE GOING TO GO ON A RAMPAGE?! UGH, GAARA...
HEY... WE PROBABLY SHOULD GET AWAY FROM HERE...

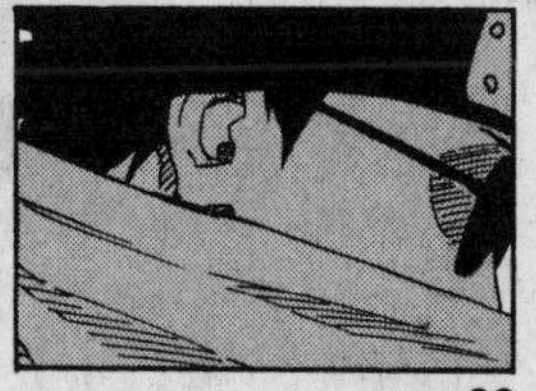

...PLAN...?

READ THIS WAY

GOOOSH

!
D-DON'T TELL ME THAT'S...

THE REASON I TOOK SASUKE UNDER MY WING...
...IS BECAUSE HE'S...

...VERY SIMILAR TO ME.
KOOSH
KOOSH
SNAP

READ THIS WAY

TOOM
CHIRP
SHUP
CHIRP CHIRP

CHIRP
CHIRP

CHIRP
CHIRP
FLESH ACTIVATION?!

I SEE, SO THAT'S WHY YOU HAD HIM FOCUS ON TAIJUTSU...
...AND INCREASE HIS SPEED SO MUCH...!

YUP!

CHIRP

CHIRP
CHIRP

CHIRP
CHIRP
CHIRP
CHIRP

I CAN'T BELIEVE... HE'S MASTERED THAT JUTSU...
SO THIS IS WHAT THE UCHIHA CLAN IS CAPABLE OF...

W-WOW... I CAN TOTALLY SEE HIS CHAKRA... WHAT IN THE WORLD IS THAT ABOUT?!

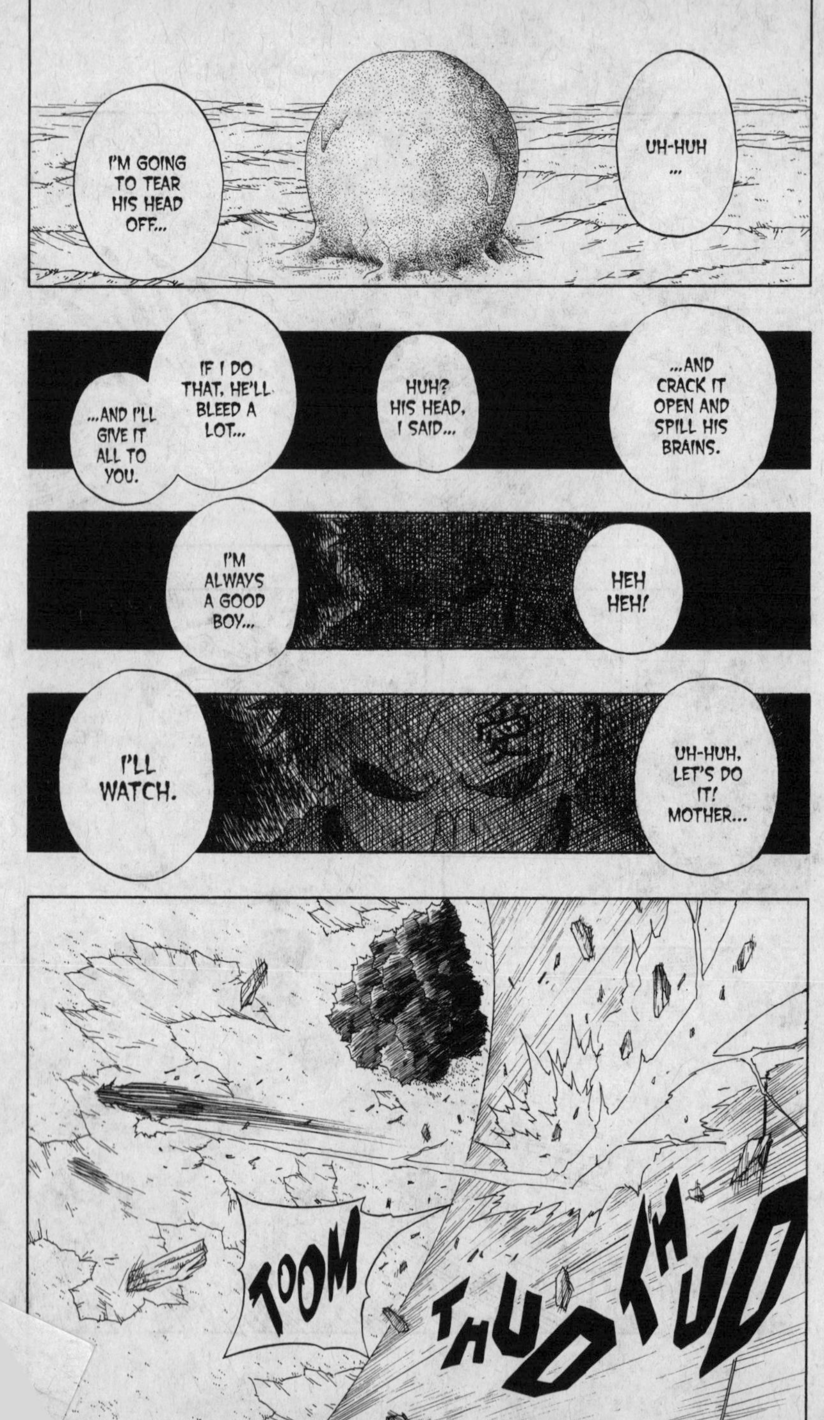
UH-HUH ...
I'M GOING TO TEAR HIS HEAD OFF...
...AND CRACK IT OPEN AND SPILL HIS BRAINS.
HUH? HIS HEAD, I SAID...
IF I DO THAT, HE'LL BLEED A LOT...
...AND I'LL GIVE IT ALL TO YOU.
HEH HEH!
I'M ALWAYS A GOOD BOY...
UH-HUH, LET'S DO IT! MOTHER...
I'LL WATCH.
K'THUD
THUD
TOOM

THUD

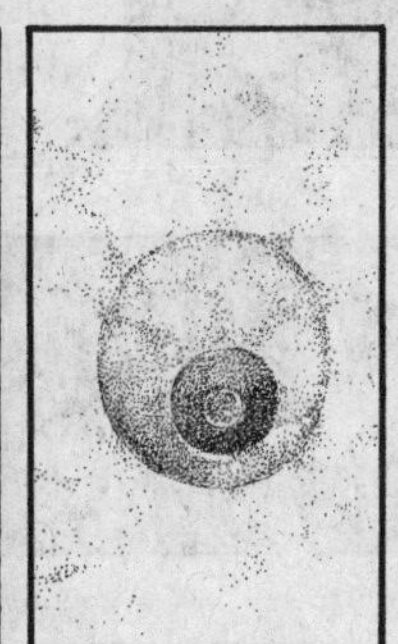

WH-WHAT THE...?!
WHAT IS THAT...?!

ZHOOM

TRULY...

SWAY...

SLUMP

CHIRP
CHIRP
CHIRP CHIRP

WHAT MOVE IS THAT...?!
AND THAT INCREDIBLE NOISE...

IT'S **JUST** A HAND CHOP...

READ THIS WAY

HUH?

HOWEVER, IT'S A UNIQUE **ORIGINAL** MOVE...
...CRAFTED BY KONOHA'S TOP JUTSU MASTER, COPY NINJA KAKASHI.

?!

IT'S A MOVE RESERVED FOR ASSASSINATION...
THE SECRET IS IN THE SPEED OF THE THRUST...
...AND THE IMMENSE CHAKRA PRODUCED BY SUPER-ACTIVATING ONE'S FLESH.

BY NARROWLY FOCUSING MASSIVE AMOUNTS OF CHAKRA FROM THE DOMINANT HAND, A PULSING FLUCTUATION FORMS IN THE THRUST...
CHIRP CHIRP CHIRP CHIRP...
...RESULTING IN A UNIQUE ATTACK SOUND THAT RESEMBLES THE CRYING OF A THOUSAND BIRDS.

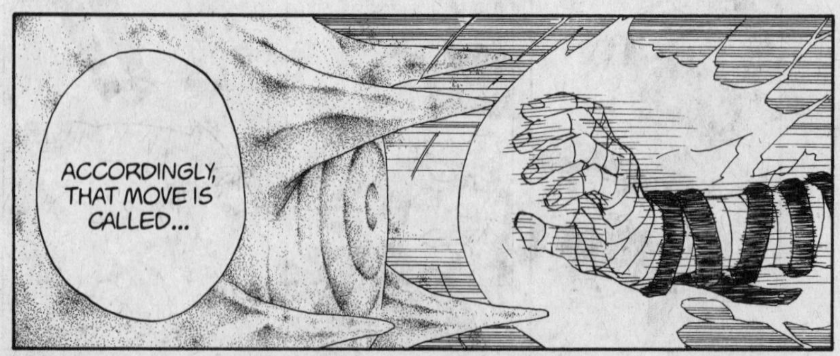
ACCORDINGLY, THAT MOVE IS CALLED...

CHIDORI: 1000 BIRDS!!!

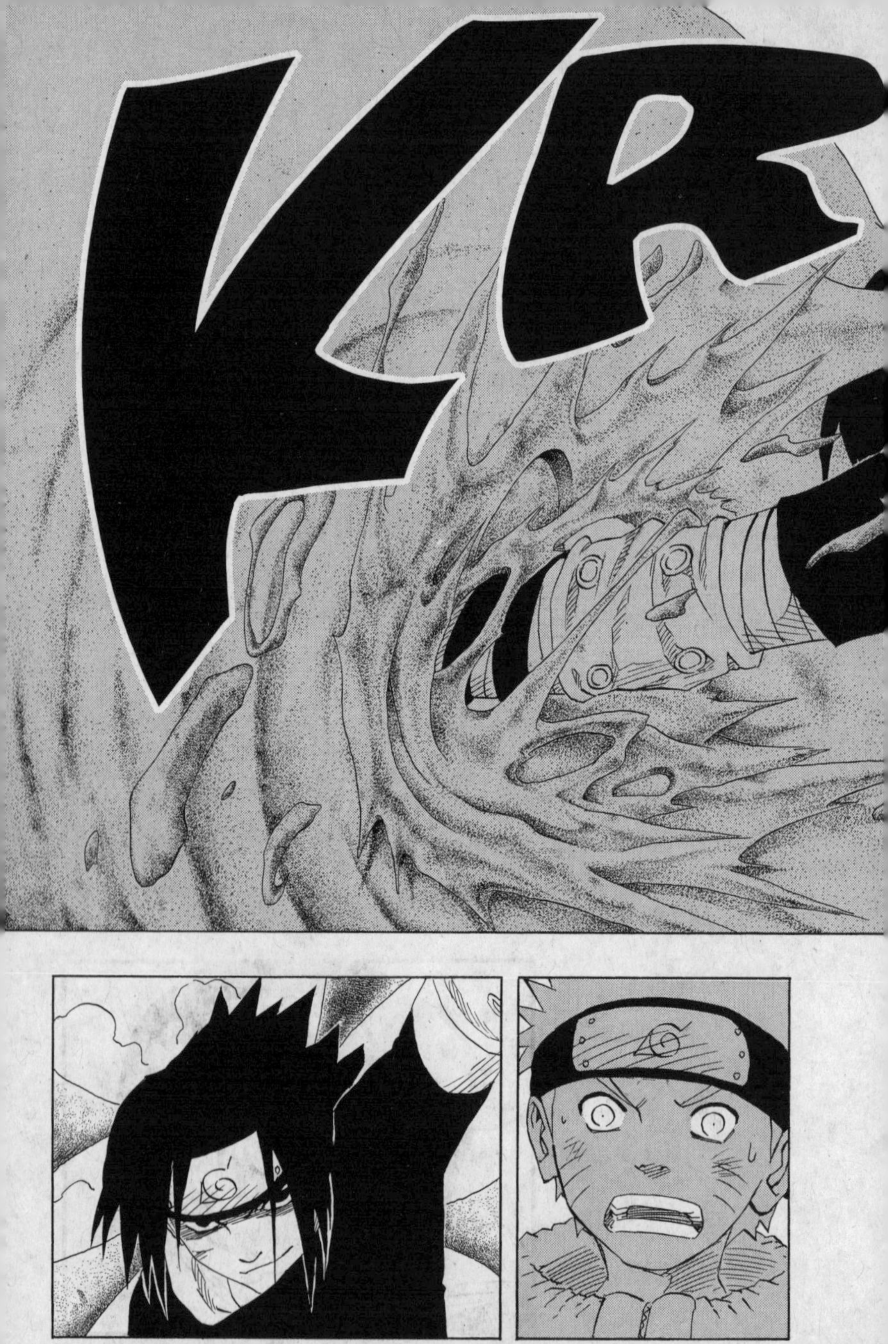

Number 114: Violent Assault...!!

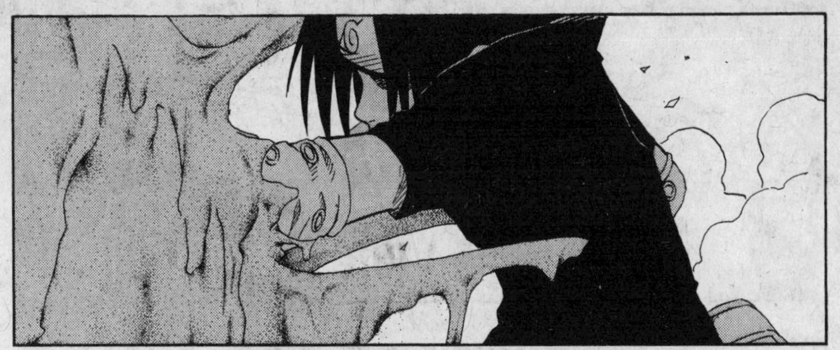

YOU MUST BE JOKING...!
HE COULDN'T HAVE PENETRATED GAARA'S "ABSOLUTE DEFENSE"!!

IT CAN'T BE...

NOT POSSIBLE ...

READ THIS WAY

THAT IS KAKASHI'S...

LIGHTNING BLADE...?

THE LIGHTNING BLADE...

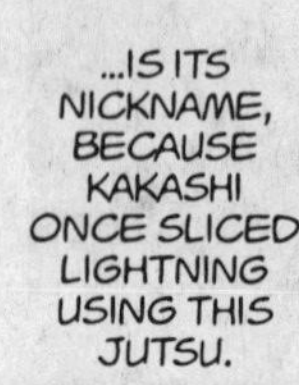

...IS ITS NICKNAME, BECAUSE KAKASHI ONCE SLICED LIGHTNING USING THIS JUTSU.

HUH? SLICED LIGHTNING...? WHAT?!
SOUNDS SO HOKEY...
W-WOW...
ITS FORMAL JUTSU NAME IS CHIDORI, AND ITS SECRETS LIE IN THE ALMOST IMPOSSIBLE SPEED OF ITS STROKE AND THE IMMENSE CHAKRA FOCUSED IN THE ARM...

...THAT TRANSFORMS IT INTO A BLADE THAT CAN CUT THROUGH ANYTHING.

BUT... HOW COULD YOU HAVE TAUGHT HIM SUCH A RECKLESS MOVE...?
LIKE YOU REALLY HAVE THE RIGHT TO CRITICIZE ME...
RIGHT, LEE?!

THIS IS ALL KIND OF BEYOND THE LIMIT OF MY COMPRE-HENSION, BUT...
...EITHER WAY, IT'S AN INCREDIBLE MOVE...!!

...

I UNDERSTAND... IF THAT HAD BEEN ME, I WOULDN'T HAVE LAUNCHED A HEAD-ON FULL-SPEED ATTACK ON MY OPPONENT LIKE THAT...
OR RATHER, I **COULDN'T** HAVE!!
A BEELINE ATTACK IS EASY TO COUNTER OR AVOID...
...AND I DON'T HAVE THE EYE TO PERCEIVE AND SEE THROUGH THAT COUNTER...

READ THIS WAY

I TRULY ENVY YOUR GENES...
...SASUKE!

ONCE, WHEN WE FACED OFF AGAINST EACH OTHER, I SAID TO YOU THAT...
... "IT DOESN'T MATTER WHAT YOUR EYE CAN SEE IF YOUR BODY'S TOO WEAK TO ACT!" I WAS BASKING IN A SENSE OF SUPERIORITY BACK THEN.

BUT NOW...

CLENCH
YOU'VE ATTAINED A HIGH-SPEED BODY JUST LIKE MINE...

AND YOU POSSESS THE SHARINGAN AS WELL...!!
GOTCHA!

HUH... YOU WERE SO WORRIED ABOUT SASUKE EARLIER...
AND NOW, YOU'RE JEALOUS OF HIM...

!

WHAT...
...IS THIS... WARM MOIST-NESS...?

MOTHER... WHAT HAPPENED...?

SPLISH

THROB
UGH...!
!!

GSSSH

GRRRR...!
KSSH
KSSH

HAH!!

FSSK

AAARRGH!!

D-DON'T TELL ME...
...GAARA'S... BEEN WOUNDED?!

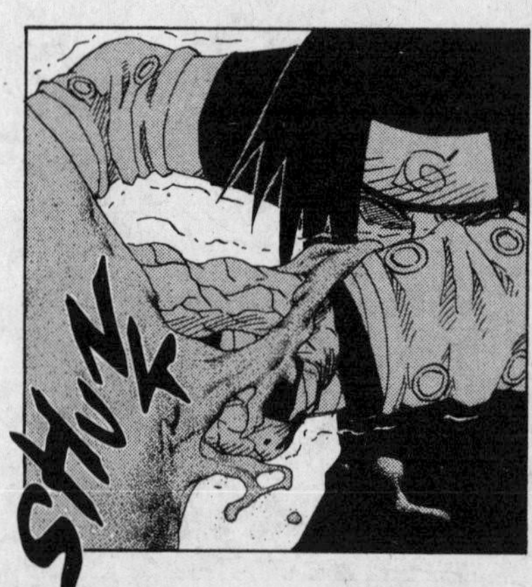
SHUNK

GSSH

KOOSH

THOOM

UGH!

FWAK

SKKSH

!!

THAT'S **ITS** ARM...!!

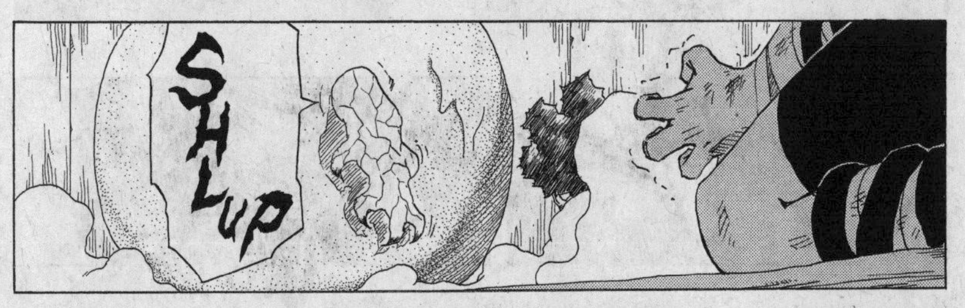

!!
WHAT IS THAT?!
DID HE MORPH INTO THE PERFECT POSSESSION FORM?!
I DON'T KNOW...?
IT LOOKS LIKE HE'S INJURED. NOTHING LIKE THIS HAS EVER HAPPENED BEFORE...

READ THIS WAY

WHAT IS GOING ON INSIDE...?

JUST THINKING ABOUT IT GIVES ME THE SHIVERS...
WHEN I SAW IT FOR THE FIRST TIME, I LOST MY APPETITE BECAUSE OF THE WAY IT LOOKS...

DARN... WHAT HAS HE GONE AND DONE NOW...

...!

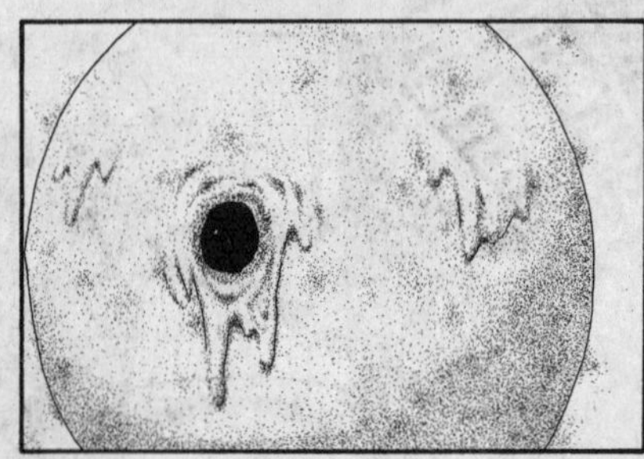

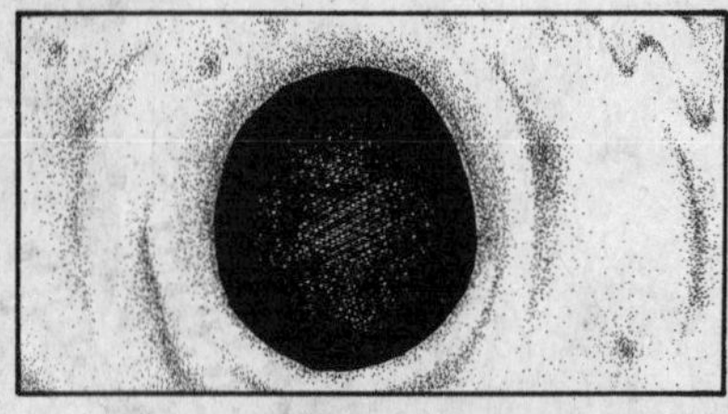

READ THIS WAY

!!
SIZZ
SIZZ
WHAT IS THIS SENSATION ...?

!!

CRACK
FSSH

FSSSH...

FSSSSH...

...!

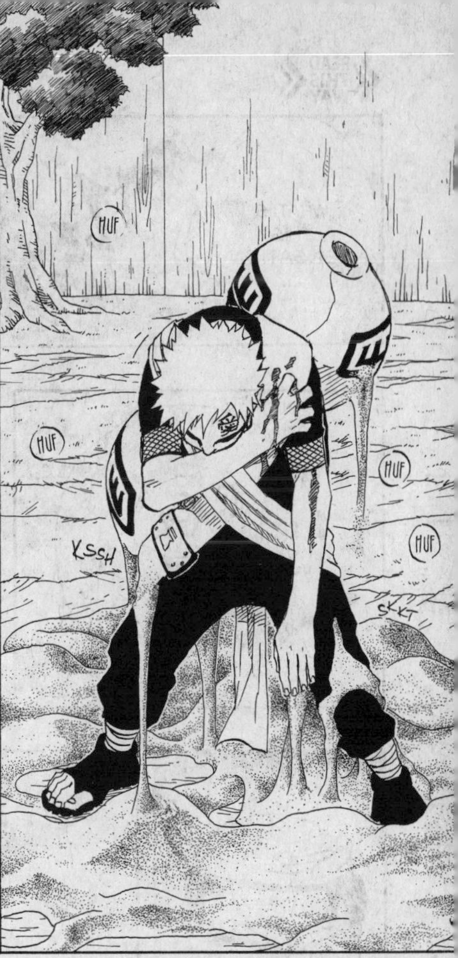
HUF
HUF
HUF
HUF
KSSH
SKKT

愛
HUF
HUF

HE IS INJURED...
!!
HIS SHELL WAS BREACHED BEFORE HE COMPLETED TRANSFORMING!!

...?!

NO... THOSE WEREN'T HIS EYES!
WH-WHAT WAS THAT... THAT I SAW EARLIER...?

SHA

!!

HUH... WHAT THE... WHY DO I SEE FEATHERS...?

KAKASHI! THIS IS...!
YEAH... GENJUTSU!!

CLENCH
CLENCH
KAI! RELEASE!!

HEH... LEAVE IT TO THE KONOHA ELITES...
THEY WOULD NOTICE AND REVERSE THE GEN-JUTSU...
ZZZ
ZZZ

WHAT IS GOING ON?!
KAI! RELEASE!

READ
THIS
WAY

GENJUTSU...!
KABUTO'S MAKING HIS MOVE ALREADY, HUH...?
THEN IT'S ALMOST...
...TIME!!

SHOOM

SHALL WE GET GOING...?

SHOOM

PIK

BOOF!!

!
!
!
PUSH
COMMENCE OPERATION!!!

NARUTO IS IN ITS THIRD YEAR. AND ASSISTANTS HAVE COME AND GONE. ASSISTANT NO. 1, THE DUMB-ACTING SUPER-COOL KYUSHU NATIVE TAKAHASHI-SAN, WHO WAS THERE FROM THE VERY BEGINNING OF *NARUTO* (SEE VOLUME 6, PAGE 26) HAS LEFT OUR OFFICE, AND TWO NEW ASSISTANTS HAVE STARTED. AND SO...
MEET KISHIMOTO MASASHI'S ASSISTANTS
PART 5
ASSISTANT NO. 5: NISHIYA KOUICHI
KISHIMOTO-SAN. CONGRATULATIONS ON YOUR SECOND ANNIVERSARY!
PLEASE KEEP WORKING HARD IN GOOD HEALTH!
PROFILE
° YOUNGEST PERSON IN THE OFFICE.
° BUT LOOKS LIKE THE OLDEST ONE IN THE OFFICE.
° VERY KIND-HEARTED FELLOW.
° HAS AN AMAZING PHYSIQUE (LIKE THE INCREDIBLE HULK). IN OTHER WORDS, HUGE!
° HAS INHERITED THE PREVIOUS ASSISTANT TAKAHASHI-SAN'S ULTRA-COOL DUMB ACT.
° PROBABLY THE BIGGEST METAL-HEAD IN THE WORLD (SERIOUSLY. I WAS REALLY SURPRISED!)
JOBS: BETA [COLORS IN THE BLACK AREAS (HAIR, CLOTHING, ETC.)], TONING, BACKGROUNDS.

Number 115: The Chûnin Exam, Concluded...!!

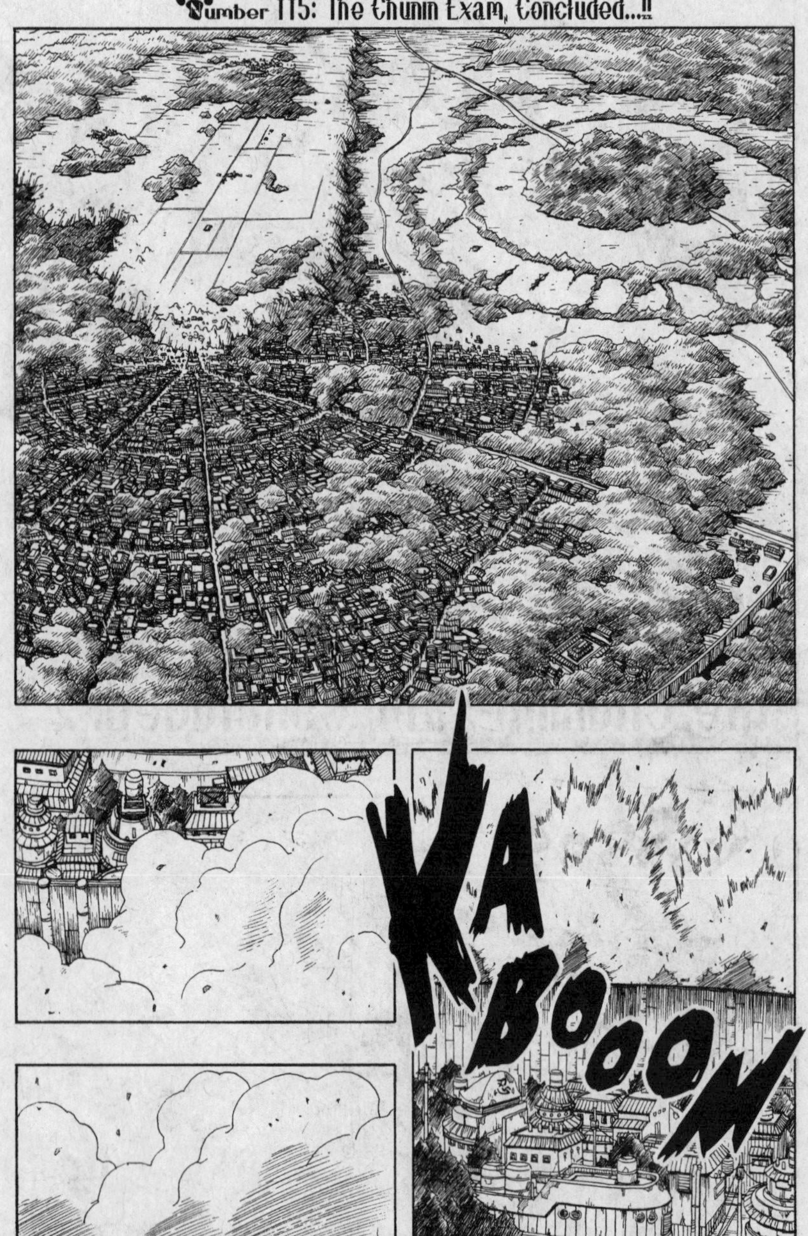

Number 115: The Chûnin Exam Concluded...!!

READ THIS WAY

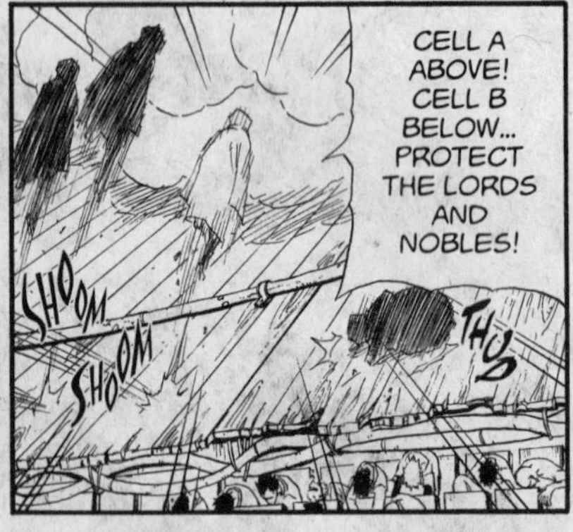
CELL A ABOVE! CELL B BELOW... PROTECT THE LORDS AND NOBLES!
SHOOM
SHOOM
THUD

FOOSH
FOOSH
FOOSH

!!
BOOF
BOOF

SH
!!
OUT OF THE WAY...
!!
SLA

READ
THIS
WAY

!

CLANC
THUD
ARGH!!

!!

BOOM
!!

!
!!

!!

風
火
THUMP
THUMP
THUMP
SHP
SPLAT
SPLAT
SPLAT
SPLAT
FSSH
FSSH
FSSH
FSSH

!!
SHOOM
SHOOM
AFTER THEM!!
SHOOM
SHOOM

THUMP
THUMP
THUMP
THUMP

DO IT...

HAH!
FOOSH
NINJA ART: SHISHIENJIN! FOUR FLAMES FORMATION!

READ THIS WAY

SO HE'S THE ONE WHO PERFORMED THE GENJUTSU...
SO IT WOULD APPEAR...

SHEESH...
THERE WAS A NINTH TRAITOR...

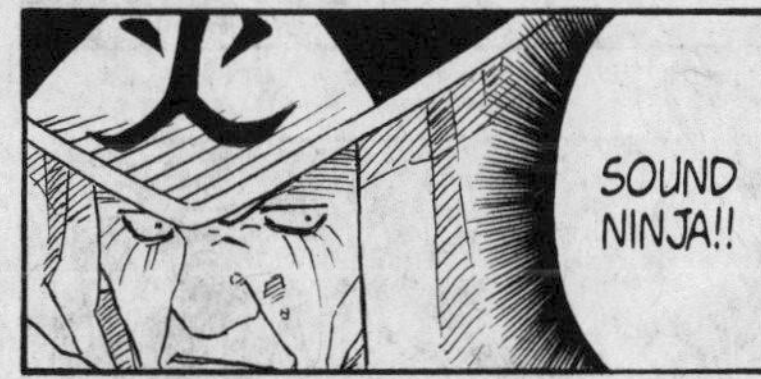
SOUND NINJA!!

SHOOM
SHOOM
SHOOM

I NEVER IMAGINED SAND WOULD BETRAY KONOHA...
TREATIES ARE MERELY SMOKE-SCREENS TO LULL THE OTHER PARTY INTO RELAXING THEIR GUARD.

THIS PITIFUL PRETEND COMPETITION IS NOW OVER...
FROM HERE ON OUT, HISTORY WILL BE MADE...

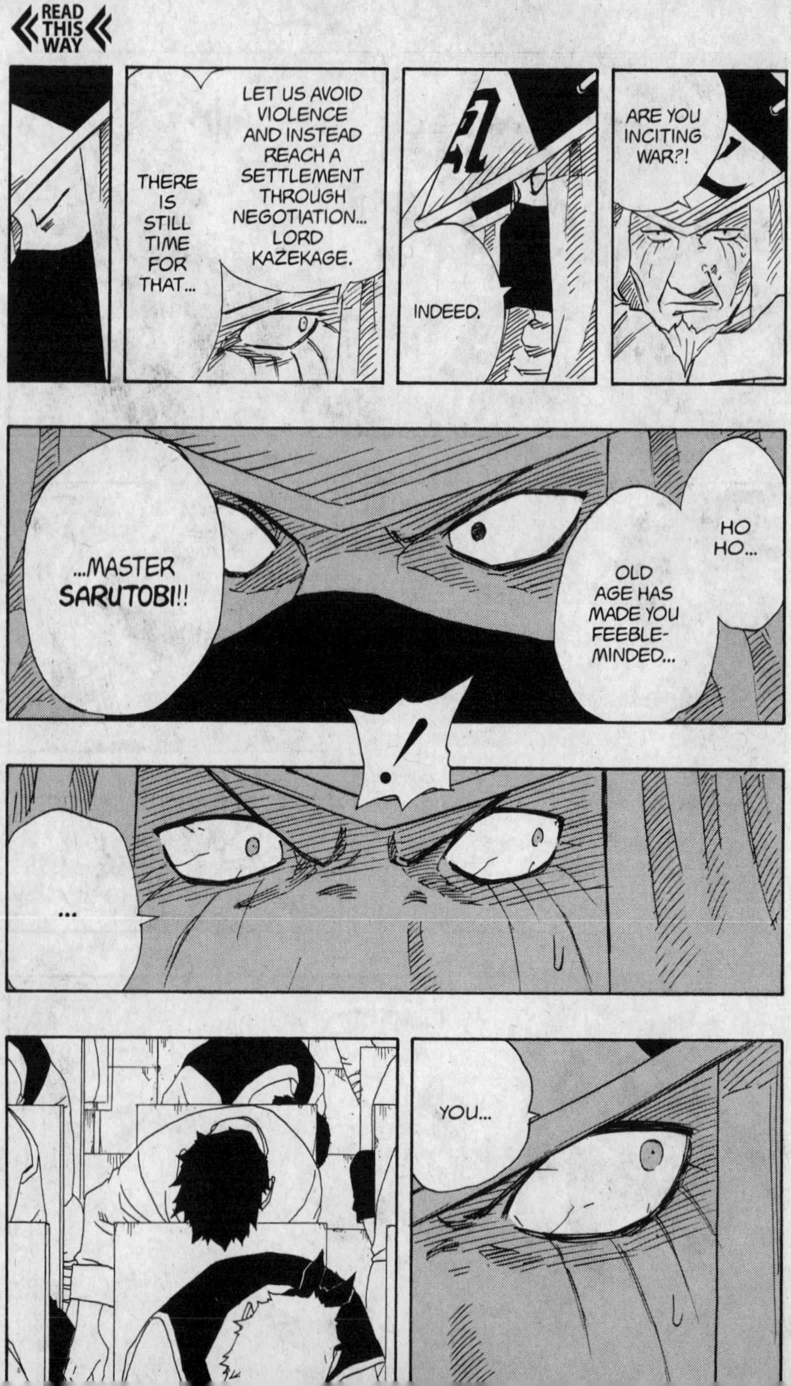

READ THIS WAY

ARE YOU INCITING WAR?!

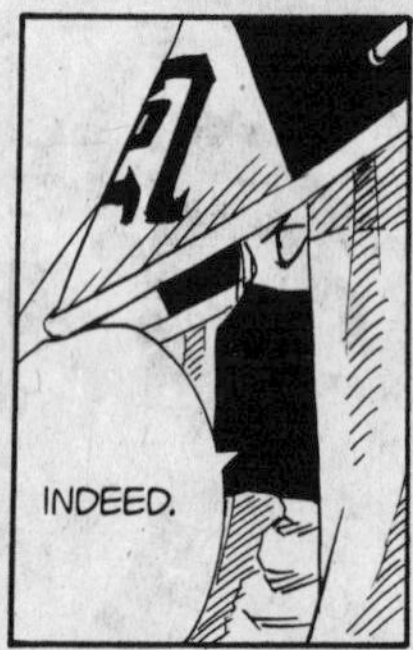

LET US AVOID VIOLENCE AND INSTEAD REACH A SETTLEMENT THROUGH NEGOTIATION... LORD KAZEKAGE.
THERE IS STILL TIME FOR THAT...

HO HO...
OLD AGE HAS MADE YOU FEEBLE-MINDED...
...MASTER SARUTOBI!!

!
...

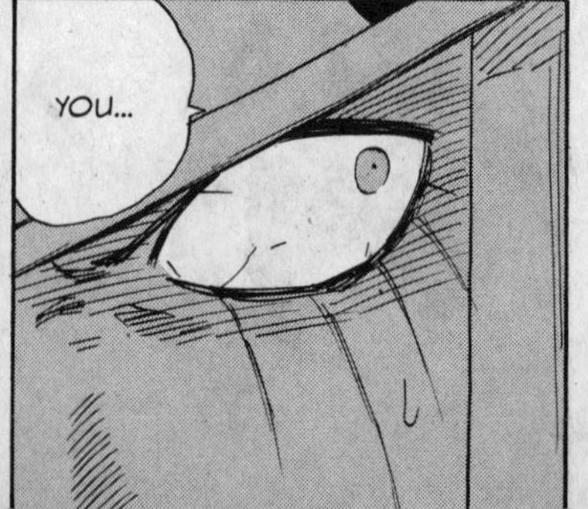

SHF
!

GAARA, THE PLAN...

HEY...
WHAT'S WRONG...?

...!

UNH...
UNH...

READ
THIS
WAY

IDIOT!!
I CAN'T BELIEVE HE WOULD TRY TO UNDERGO COMPLETE POSSESSION WITHOUT WAITING FOR THE SIGNAL...!

HE'S SUFFERING A REACTION.
HE CAN'T DO IT ANYMORE!!

THEN WHAT ARE WE SUPPOSED TO DO?!
YOU WANT US TO GO AHEAD WITHOUT GAARA?!

?!

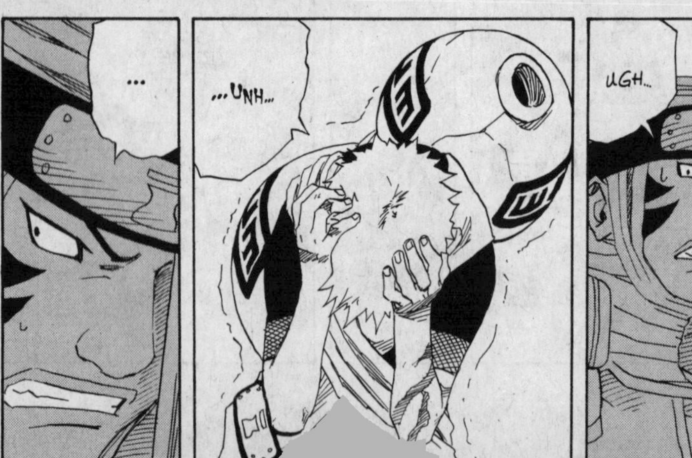
UGH...
...UNH...
...

I'M
CALLING
IT OFF!

!!

WHAT
ABOUT
YOU,
MASTER?!
CRUD...

YOU TWO
TAKE GAARA
AND
WITHDRAW
FOR NOW!

I'M
GOING
TO HELP
FIGHT.
GO!!

Y-YES,
SIR!

!

SHOOM
SHOOM

IS THE HOST OF THIS LITTLE PARTY...
...OROCHIMARU?

WHO KNOWS...?
LET'S JUST AMP THINGS UP A BIT, SHALL WE...?

HEY! WH-WHAT'S GOING ON?!

SORRY, BUT THE CHÛNIN EXAM IS OVER.
YOU GO AFTER GAARA AND THE OTHERS, RIGHT NOW!

!!

YOU'RE ALREADY AT CHÛNIN LEVEL. IF YOU CONSIDER YOURSELF A KONOHA SHINOBI, DO SOMETHING USEFUL...

...!

SHEESH...

WHAT THE HECK'S GOING ON...?

SHOOM

READ THIS WAY

!

SASUKE...!!

GAARA WASN'T OF ANY USE, HUH...?

HEH HEH HEH...
...

...I SEE... SO THAT'S WHAT'S AFOOT...

YOUR FOOLISHNESS HAS STALLED, PERHAPS EVEN STAGNATED, KONOHA...
IT'S MY VICTORY.

HUMPH...!
I THOUGHT I TAUGHT YOU NOT TO COUNT YOUR CHICKENS BEFORE THEY'RE HATCHED...

GSSH

... OROCHIMARU.
SHLUP

READ THIS WAY

風
I THOUGHT THIS DAY WOULD EVENTUALLY COME...

HOWEVER, MY HEAD WON'T COME OFF AS EASILY...!

I THOUGHT I WARNED YOU TO HURRY UP AND NAME THE FIFTH HOKAGE...

...

BECAUSE THE THIRD...
LICK
...IS GOING TO DIE RIGHT HERE...

Number 116:
Operation Destroy Konoha...!!

NARUTO
-ナルト-

しるこ

SO... WHAT SORT OF FELLOW IS THIS OROCHIMARU?

HE WAS FORMERLY ...
...THE THIRD HOKAGE'S STUDENT...

HOW DID HE END UP A ROGUE SHINOBI...?
YOU SEE, BACK IN THE DAY...WHEN THEY WERE SELECTING THE FOURTH HOKAGE...
...OROCHIMARU SUPPOSEDLY PUT FORTH HIS OWN NAME FOR CONSID-ERATION...
...THOUGH ULTIMATELY HE WASN'T CHOSEN...

SHORTLY AFTER THAT, HE RAN FROM THE VILLAGE...
OROCHIMARU'S PROBABLY RESENTED THE THIRD LORD...
...EVER SINCE.

A VENDETTA...?!

MOST LIKELY.

LONG AGO, BACK WHEN I WAS STILL A BRAT, I LOOKED AT HIM AND HAD...
...JUST ONE THOUGHT.

...

READ THIS WAY

THAT HE WASN'T HUMAN... MERELY SOMETHING THAT HAD HUMAN FORM...
...HE SCARED ME.

JUST... SCARED ME...

...

SHOOM

REPORTING IN!!
GIANT SNAKES HAVE APPEARED IN THE VICINITY OF THE EAST GATE! FOLLOWING THEM, ROUGHLY 100 SAND SHINOBI HAVE INFILTRATED THE VILLAGE!

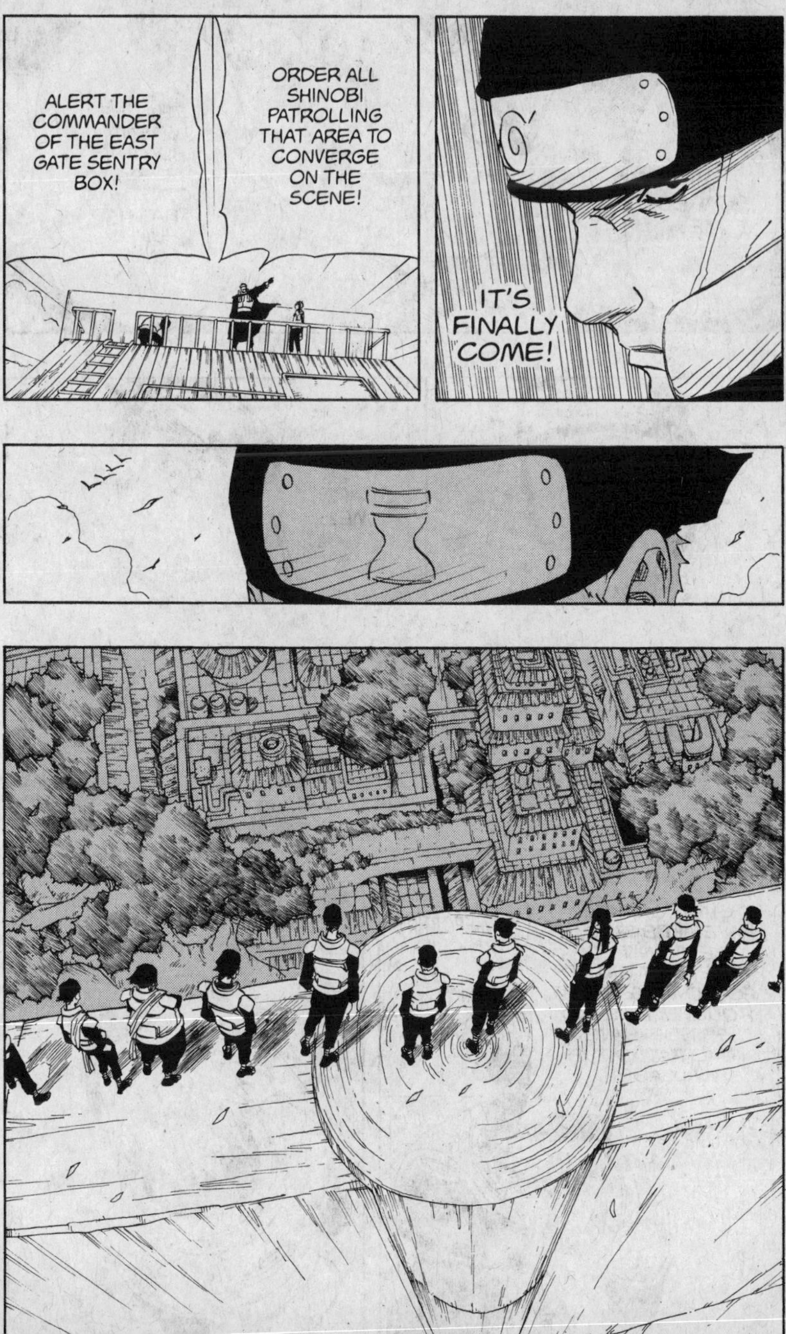

IT'S FINALLY COME!

ALERT THE COMMANDER OF THE EAST GATE SENTRY BOX!
ORDER ALL SHINOBI PATROLLING THAT AREA TO CONVERGE ON THE SCENE!

READ THIS WAY

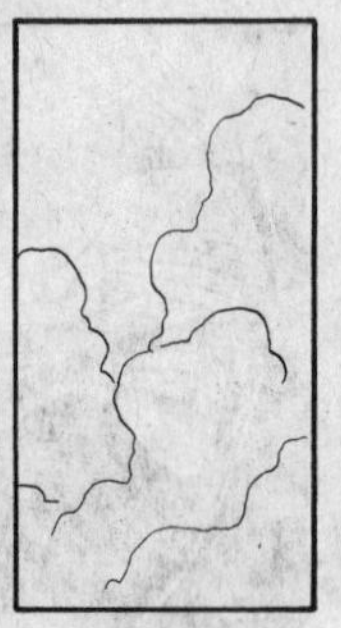

IT'S QUITE A CROWD ...

THAT'S NOT ALL. THERE'S SOME-THING EVEN WORSE.
LOOK OVER TOWARD THE ROOF OF THE CENTRAL VIEWING TOWER.

THAT'S A BARRIER-NINJUTSU...!
!

WH-WHAT IN THE WORLD IS GOING ON?!

KAKASHI, LOOK CLOSELY INSIDE THE BARRIER!
!

...

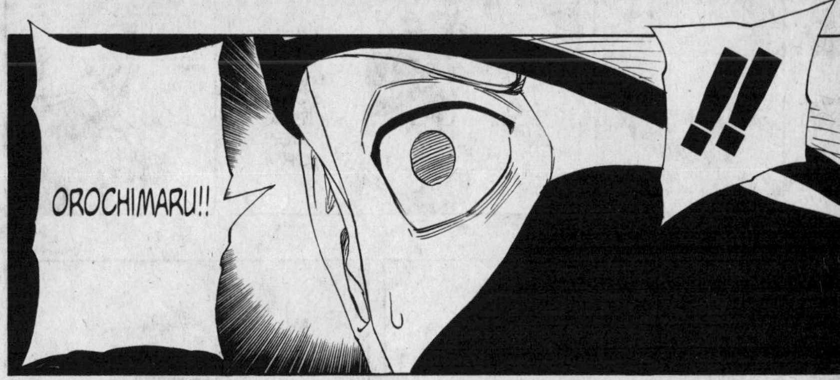
!!
OROCHIMARU!!

OROCHIMARU?!

WH-WHAT'S HE DOING HERE...?
DON'T TELL ME HE'S AFTER SASUKE AGAIN...!!

SASUKE...!

READ
THIS
WAY

OH...
WHERE'S SASUKE...?!

FSSH
HUH?
FSSH

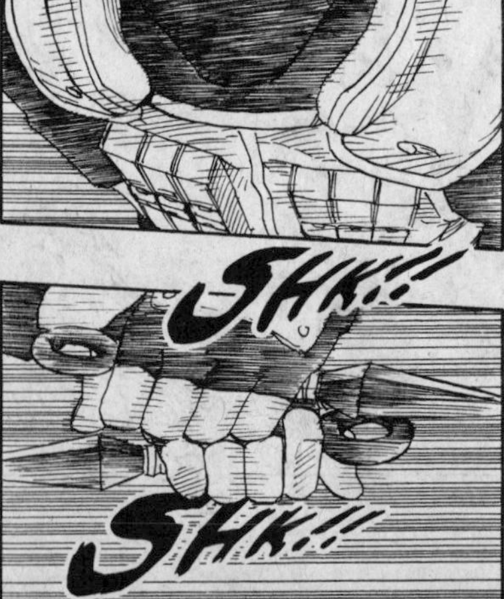
SHK!!
SHK!!

SHUN
SHUNK

THUD
THUD
...

...
PEEK

SAKURA, STAY THERE FOR A LITTLE WHILE... I'LL GO THIN OUT THE ENEMY RANKS.

KACHINK
KACHINK
WHOOSH

SHUNK
THUMP
ARGH!

KBOOSH

KACHINK
DARN IT...
I'M CONCERNED ABOUT LORD HOKAGE, BUT...
SHUP

LEAVE THAT TO THE ANBU BLACK OPS AGENTS. BESIDES...
...LORD HOKAGE ISN'T THE TYPE TO BE TAKEN DOWN SO EASILY...
BUT...

FOR HE IS...
KONOHA VILLAGE'S...
...HOKAGE.

!

PLIP

ARE YOU THAT OVER-JOYED...?
OR IS IT...
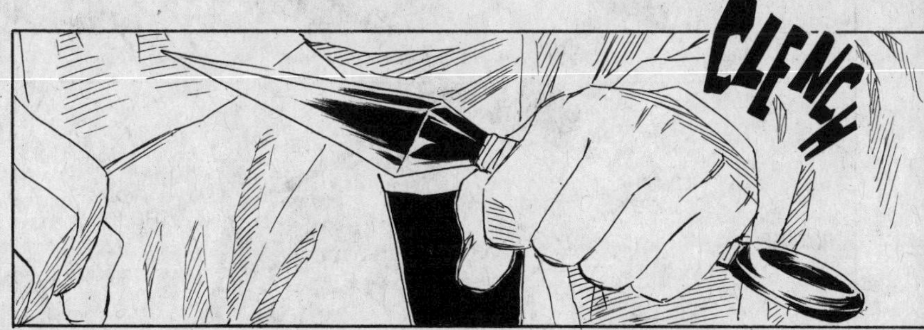
CLENCH

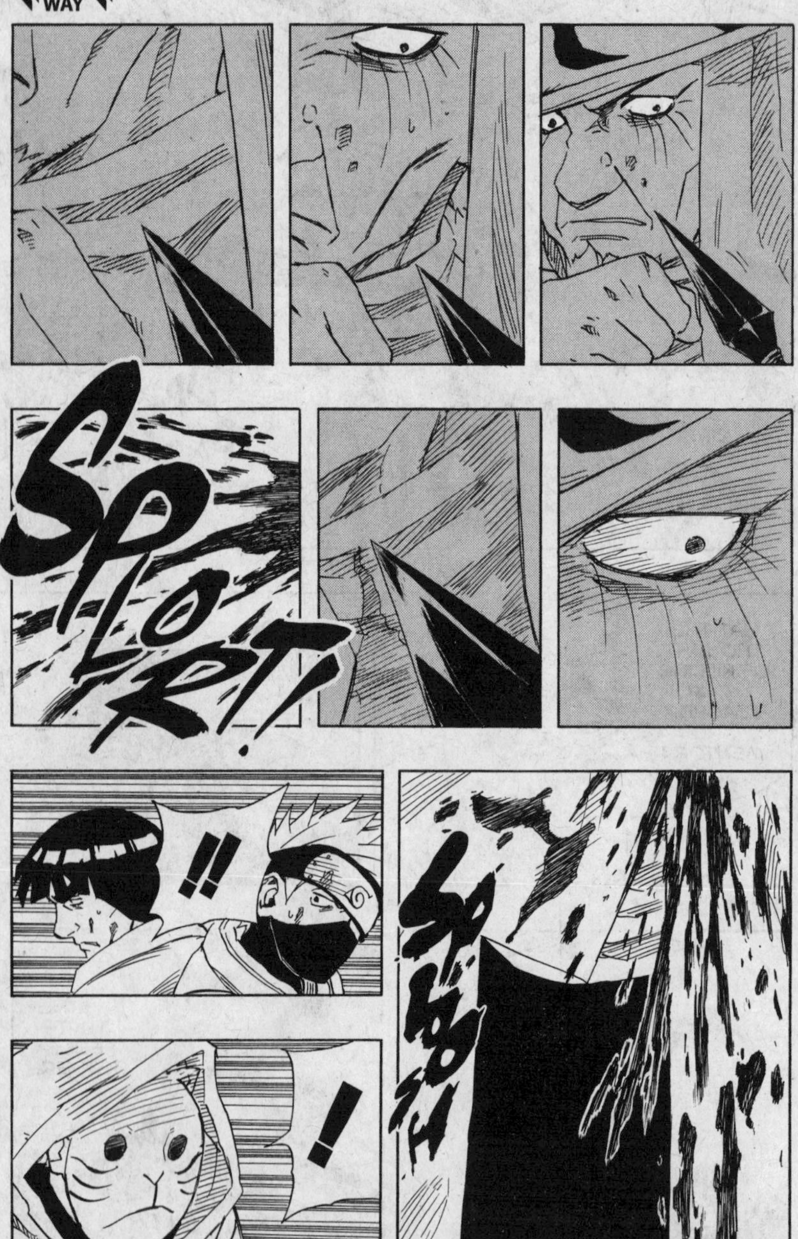
READ THIS WAY
SPLORT!
!!
SPLOOSH
!

PLIP PLIP

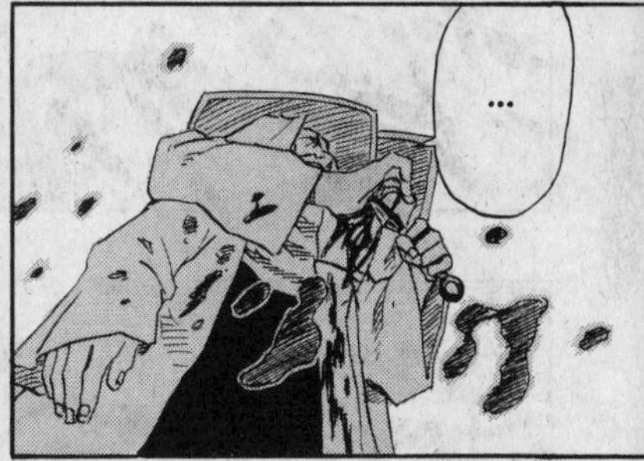
...

...THAT YOU ACTUALLY POSSESS SOME REGRET...
...AT THE THOUGHT OF KILLING YOUR TEACHER AND MENTOR?

THERE... THAT FEELS BETTER.

PLIP

NAH... JUST A BIT SLEEPY...
SOME TEARS WELLED UP WHEN I YAWNED, THAT'S ALL...
RUB

...!

...!

EXACTLY AS I SUSPECTED...

TMP

I KNOW YOU'RE NOT A MAN TO BE MOVED BY HATRED...
YOU HAVE NEITHER MOTIVES NOR PURPOSE.

HMM... ACTUALLY, I DO HAVE PURPOSE.
WELL, TO PUT IT SIMPLY...

I ENJOY WATCHING MOVING OBJECTS.
IT'S BORING WHEN THINGS STAND STILL, DON'T YOU AGREE...?

A MOTIONLESS PINWHEEL ISN'T WORTH WATCHING...
SHUP

THEN AGAIN, WHEN IT'S STOPPED, IT CAN SOMETIMES BE SENTIMENTAL TOO...
THWSP

EITHER WAY...
I WANT TO MAKE THE PINWHEEL SPIN WITH THE DESTRUCTION OF KONOHA RIGHT NOW...

HUMPH...
YOU HAVEN'T CHANGED A BIT...

READ
THIS
WAY

KA
CHING
TOMP
SAKURA!

FLINCH
!!

I KNEW IT WOULD PAY OFF TO TEACH YOU GENJUTSU DURING THE GENIN SURVIVAL EXERCISES.
YOU REALLY DO HAVE A TALENT FOR GENJUTSU.

HUH...?

UNDO THE GENJUTSU ON NARUTO AND SHIKAMARU AND WAKE THEM UP!

KA
CHINK
I'VE GOT ANOTHER MISSION FOR YOU...

!!

ONE THAT WILL TAKE YOUR FULL FOCUS...
KACHINK
THUD

NARUTO'LL PROBABLY BE HAPPY TO HEAR THAT.
...!

WH-WHAT KIND OF MISSION...?

AN A-RANK ASSIGNMENT...

...THE LIKES YOU HAVEN'T SEEN SINCE THE LAND OF WAVES!!

WHAT...?!

MEET MASASHI KISHIMOTO'S ASSISTANTS
PART 6
ASSISTANT NO. 6: RYO TASAKA

祝
2周年!!!
CELEBRATE THE 2ND ANNIVERSARY !!!
PROFILE
° CAME FROM HIROSHIMA, THE PREFECTURE NEXT TO MINE.
HE'S A TEMPLE BRAT. (BUT HE DOESN'T HAVE A SHAVED HEAD.)
° A PUPPY-EYED, KIND OF GENDER-NEUTRAL, CUTE BOY.
° IF ONE IS BITING, ANYTHING GOES (OTHER THAN DIRTY JOKES).
° QUICK-WITTED (SHARP FELLOW).
° A GAME SHARK.
° JUST LIKE ASSISTANT NO. 4 TAKEMI KAWAHARA (MALE), KNOWS PRACTICALLY ALL THE DIALOGUE AND SCENES FROM *ROKUDENASHI BLUES*, AND THUS, THE TWO ARE ALWAYS GETTING KICKS OUT OF TALKING "*ROKUDENASHI* SPEAK."
R '02
JOBS: BETA [COLORS IN THE BLACK AREAS (HAIR, CLOTHING, ETC.)], TONING, BACKGROUNDS.
PLEASE KEEP STRIVING EVEN HARDER THAN THE MAIN CHARACTER!!
TASAKA RYO

Number 117:
NARUTO
The Imparted Mission...!!

KACHINK
AIEE!

SASUKE IS PURSUING GAARA AND THE OTHER SAND NINJA.

UNDER THESE CONDITIONS, WHAT DO YOU WANT US TO DO...?!!
...MASTER!! AN A-RANK ASSIGNMENT...?!
SPLA

SAKURA... YOU UNDO THE GENJUTSU ON NARUTO AND SHIKAMARU...
...AND CHASE AFTER SASUKE.
SLICE

WHAT?!

IT WORRIES ME... THAT WEIRD CHAKRA...

SHHU

B-BUT, IN THAT CASE...
WHY DON'T WE WAKE UP INO AND CHOJI TOO AND GO EN MASSE...!

FAP
I SUSPECT THERE IS ALREADY A LARGE NUMBER OF SAND AND SOUND NINJA INSIDE OUR VILLAGE.
MOVEMENT BY MORE THAN A BASIC TROOP UNIT OF FOUR WILL DESTROY ANY ADVANTAGE OF SWIFTNESS AND MAKES IT HARDER TO HIDE FROM THE ENEMY...
THEY TAUGHT THAT DURING THE PATROL DRILLS AT THE ACADEMY, DIDN'T THEY?

OH!
RIGHT!

HUH...?!
BUT YOU JUST SAID FOUR...
WHO'S THE FOURTH...?!

KUCHIYOSE NO JUTSU! ART OF SUMMONING!!!

WMP

!!

PAKKUN...
...WILL TRACK SASUKE FOR YOU...!!

D-DON'T TELL ME...! OUR FOURTH...
...IS THIS LITTLE DOGGIE...?!!

READ THIS WAY

!!
HOP
HOP
HOP

HEY, YOU! LITTLE GIRL!!
DON'T YOU DARE CALL ME "A CUTE LITTLE DOGGIE"!

I DIDN'T...
...SAY "CUTE"...

ALL RIGHT! SAKURA...
...UNDO THE GENJUTSU ON NARUTO AND SHIKAMARU!

O-OKAY!
SQUEEZE

PEEK
PEEK

KAI! RELEASE!!

SHWIP
SHWIP

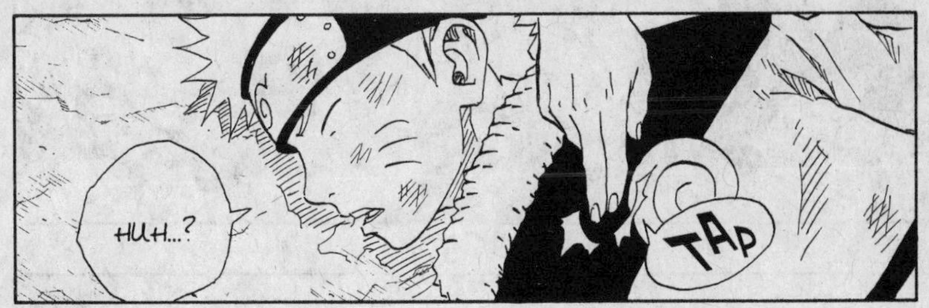
TAP
HUH...?

...EH? WHAT HAPPENED...? SAKURA...
SHUP

I'LL TELL YOU LATER!!
STAY DOWN!
HUH?!!

?
CRAWL CRAWL
POP

...?!

READ THIS WAY

...!

SHIKAMARU, YOU... FROM THE GET-GO...?!

CLAMP

YEOW!!
FWUMP
YOU KNEW HOW TO REVERSE GENJUTSU TOO!
WHY WERE YOU PRETENDING TO BE ASLEEP!!

HUMPH... I DIDN'T WANT TO GET DRAGGED INTO IT!
YOU!!
PINCH
NO THANKS... I DON'T CARE ABOUT SASUKE...

CHOMP

OWW!!

KACHINK

KACHINK

BLUR
WH-WHAT THE HECK? WHAT'S...?!

NARUTO, BEHIND YOU...!

THWAK

UGH!

HUH?

FAST...
I'M NOT JUST FAST...
SHA HAH!!
KA
BOOM

MASTER GUY!!
...?!

OKAY, HERE'S YOUR MISSION!
ONCE YOU'VE HEARD IT... HEAD OUT THROUGH THAT HOLE!

CHASE AFTER SASUKE, CONVERGE ON HIM, AND STOP HIM!
AND THEN WATCH AND WAIT SOMEWHERE SAFE UNTIL YOU RECEIVE NEW ORDERS!

?!

DID SOMETHING HAPPEN TO SASUKE...?
I'LL EXPLAIN ON THE WAY!
SHUP

LET'S GO!
SHOOM
WAAH!
BWUMP

SHEESH, WHY ME...?
MUTTER MUTTER
SHA...

WHOOM

DO YOU THINK JUST THE THREE OF THEM WILL BE ENOUGH?
PAKKUN'S WITH THEM. THEY'LL BE ALL RIGHT FOR NOW...
AS LONG AS THEY DON'T PUSH TOO MUCH...

...

BLUR

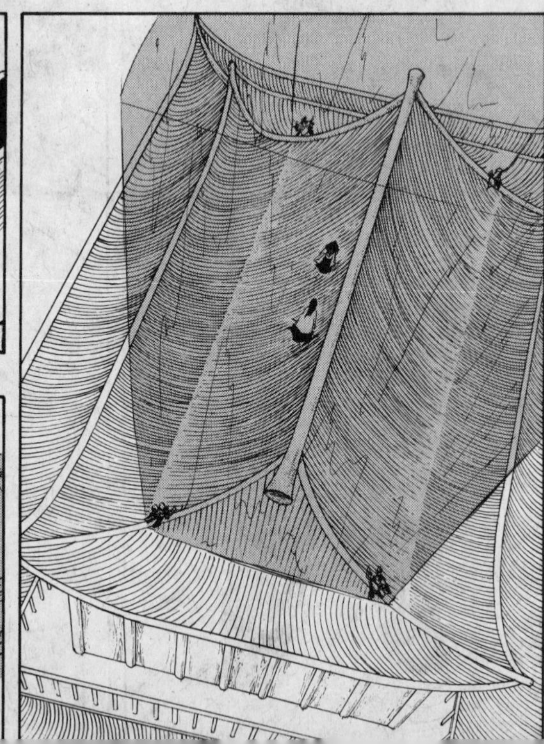

SFF

FWIP

SHU
SFF
HEH HEH HEH... HOW I'VE WISHED TO FIGHT YOU AGAIN...
FWUP
YOU ANTICIPATED YOUR OWN LAST MOMENTS, EH...?

UGH...
IT LOOKS LIKE THIS BARRIER CAN ONLY BE TAKEN DOWN FROM THE INSIDE...

ALTHOUGH IF LORD HOKAGE CAN TAKE OUT EVEN ONE OF THOSE FOUR, WE CAN PROBABLY GO IN TO AID HIM.

HEY, THEY'RE ABOUT TO START!

TIME TO ERECT THE INNER BARRIER, AS WELL.

EXACTLY!

...

KS

SH

HAH!!

HUMPH... IT DOESN'T LOOK EASY TO ESCAPE FROM...

OF COURSE NOT.
BESIDES, YOU WOULDN'T WANT ANYONE TO INTERFERE AND GET IN THE WAY, WOULD YOU?!

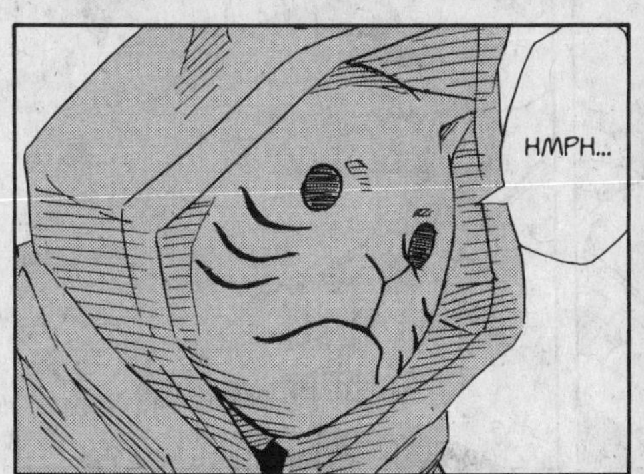
HMPH...

READ THIS WAY

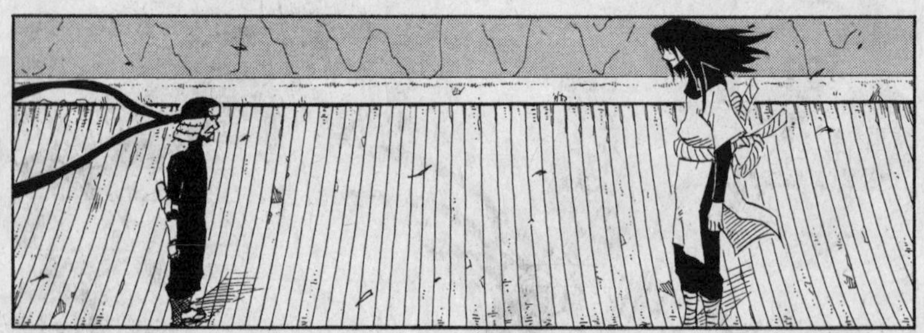

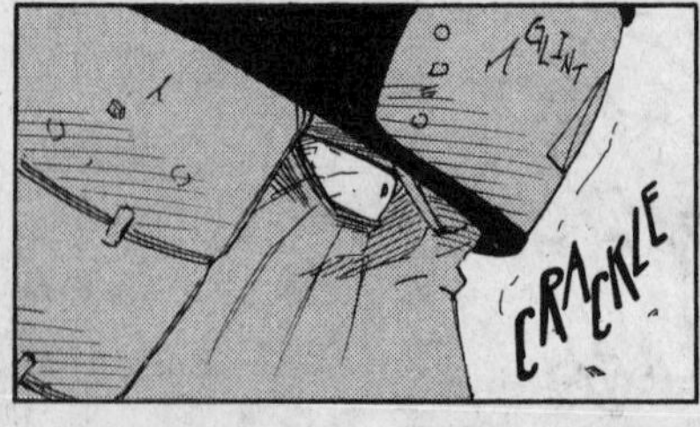

代目火影
CHAK
SHUNK
SHWIP
SHWIP
SHWIP
SHWIP
SHWIP
SHWIP

READ
THIS
WAY

SHURIKEN SHADOW DOPPELGANGER TECHNIQUE!

SPLIT

SHOWER

BRAKE

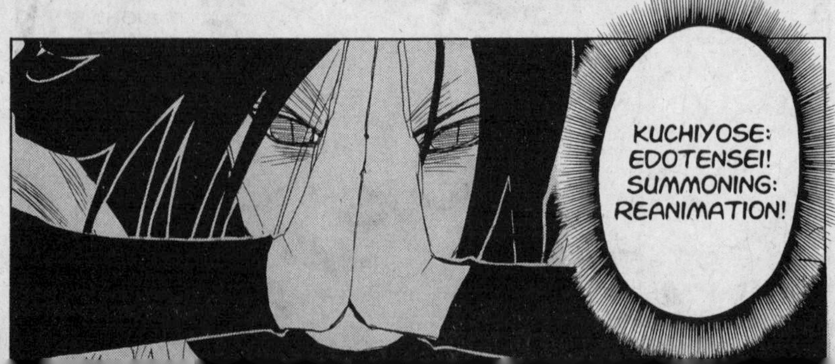
KUCHIYOSE: EDOTENSEI! SUMMONING: REANIMATION!

HE'S USING THEM AS A SHIELD...!
COULD HE REALLY BE RAISING *THOSE* SPIRITS...?!
SHWIP

ONE!!
DOOM

TWO!!
BANG

SHWIP
UGH... I MUST PREVENT HIM FROM RAISING THE THIRD, NO MATTER WHAT...

THOCK THOCK THOCK THOCK THOCK THOCK

THREE!!

CREEEAK...
CLOMP
SO...
HE MANAGED TO BLOCK THE THIRD... AH, WELL, NO MATTER!

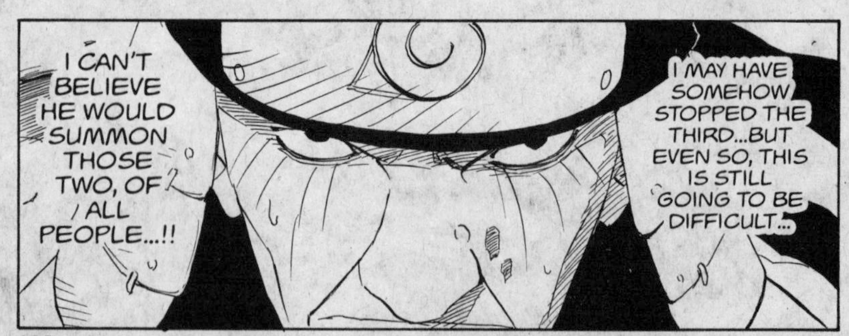

I CAN'T BELIEVE HE WOULD SUMMON THOSE TWO, OF ALL PEOPLE...!!
I MAY HAVE SOMEHOW STOPPED THE THIRD...BUT EVEN SO, THIS IS STILL GOING TO BE DIFFICULT...

NARUTO

岸本斉史

Thanks to everyone's support, *Naruto* has finally become an animated series!

I wrote in the first manga volume, "The first time I won an award...I was so happy." And when my first comic book was published, I was 10 times happier still.

But the anime makes me 100 times happier! So please watch the *Naruto* anime *and* keep reading the manga.

Oh! But I guess I'm happiest knowing that people are still enjoying *Naruto*. Yup, that's it!

—*Masashi Kishimoto*, 2002

NARUTO

SHONEN JUMP MANGA

NARUTO

VOL. 14

HOKAGE VS. HOKAGE!!

STORY AND ART BY

MASASHI KISHIMOTO

SAKURA サクラ

Smart and studious, Sakura is the brightest of Naruto's classmates, but she's constantly distracted by her crush on Sasuke. Her goal: to win Sasuke's heart!

NARUTO ナルト

When Naruto was born, a destructive fox spirit was imprisoned inside his body. Spurned by the older villagers, he's grown into an attention-seeking trouble-maker. His goal: to become the village's next *Hokage*.

SASUKE サスケ

The top student in Naruto's class, Sasuke comes from the prestigious Uchiha clan. His goal: to get revenge on a mysterious person who wronged him in the past.

The Third Hokage 三代目火影

The leader of Konohagakure. He was retired, but stepped back into the position when the fourth Hokage was killed by the Nine-Tailed Fox.

Gaara 我愛羅

Mysterious, bloodthirsty Gaara is one of the scariest – and strangely familiar – ninja Naruto has ever encountered.

Orochimaru 大蛇丸

A nefarious master of disguise with a master plan of total revenge against the Third Hokage – for what exactly we have yet to learn.

Shikamaru シカマル

One of Naruto's classmates. He specializes in the Shadow Possession technique, and is a skilled ninja despite his lazy demeanor.

Pakkun パックン

A talking dog and excellent tracker who's also a loyal companion to Naruto's teacher Kakashi. Pakkun watches over his students whenever Kakashi can't.

Kakashi カカシ

Although he doesn't have an especially warm personality, Kakashi is protective of his students.

THE STORY SO FAR...

Twelve years ago, a destructive nine-tailed fox spirit attacked the ninja village of Konohagakure. The *Hokage*, or village champion, defeated the fox by sealing its soul into the body of a baby boy. Now that boy, Uzumaki Naruto, has grown up to become a ninja-in-training, learning the art of *ninjutsu* with his teammates Sakura and Sasuke.

The Chunin Exams come to a shocking conclusion! As Sasuke and Gaara face off, an invasion commences, halting the exams for good. Sasuke takes off after the fleeing Gaara, and Kakashi sends Naruto, Sakura and Shikamaru after him. As Chaos Spreads, Orochimaru, disguised as Kazekage, takes the Third Hokage hostage. Orochimaru's *Operation Destroy Konoha* is under way, complete with a dastardly – and forbidden – secret weapon...

NARUTO

VOL. 14
HOKAGE VS. HOKAGE!!

CONTENTS

Number 118: Detainment...!!

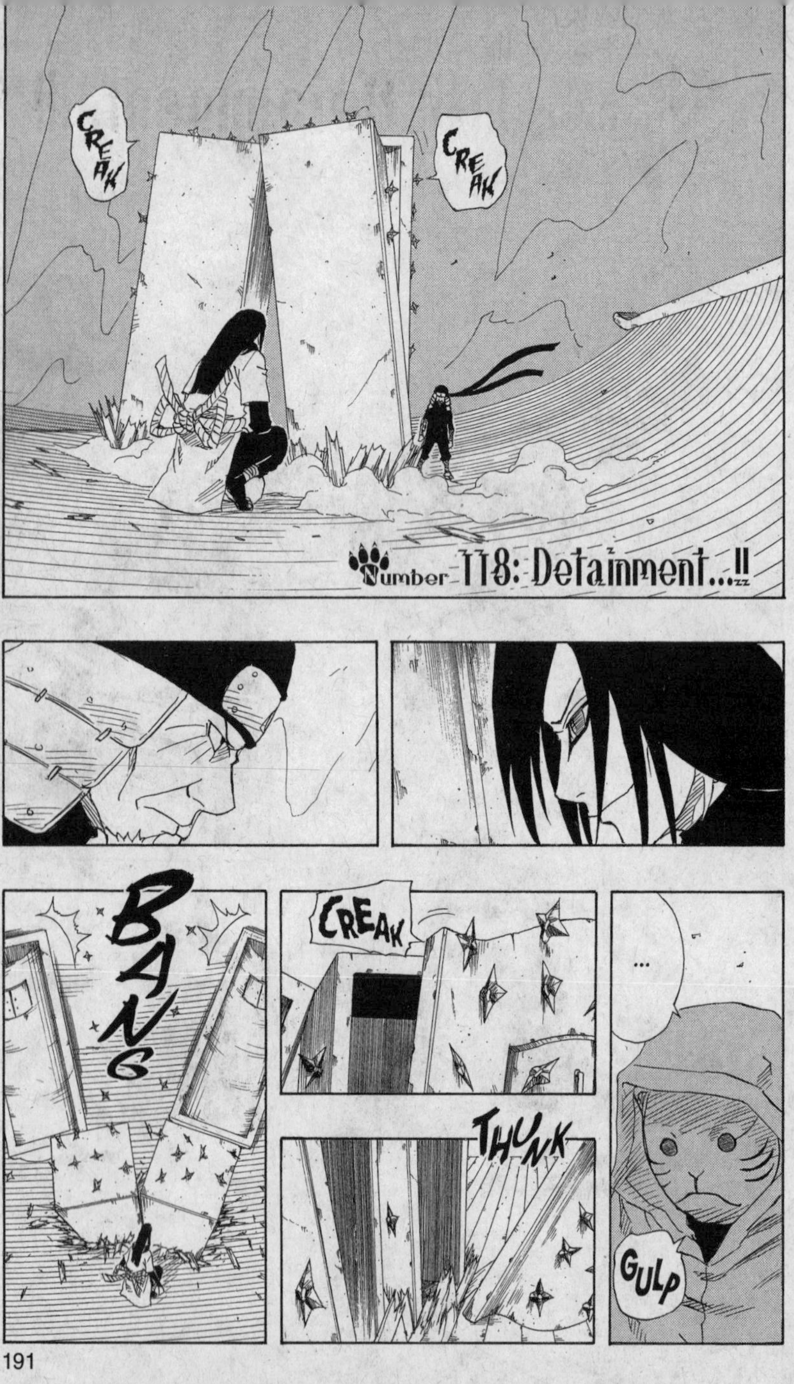

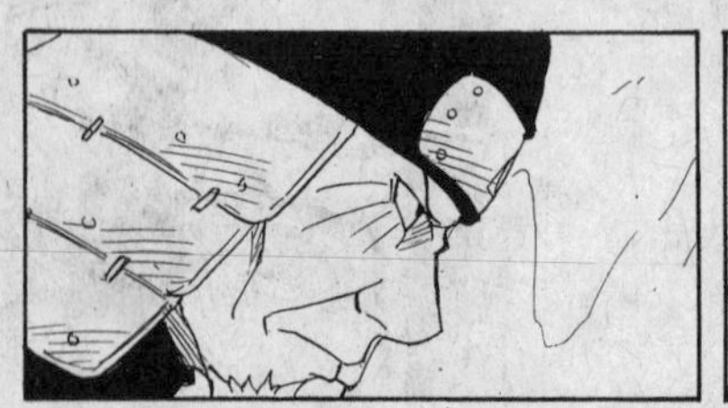

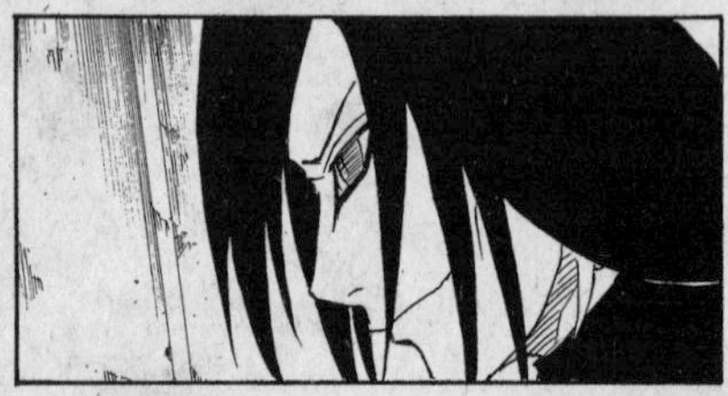

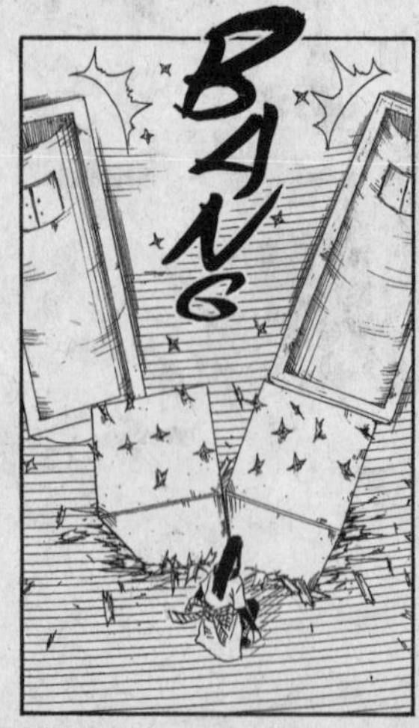
BANG

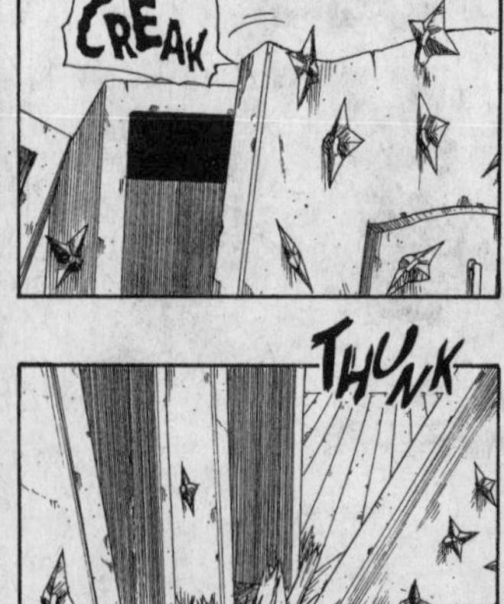
CREAK
THUNK

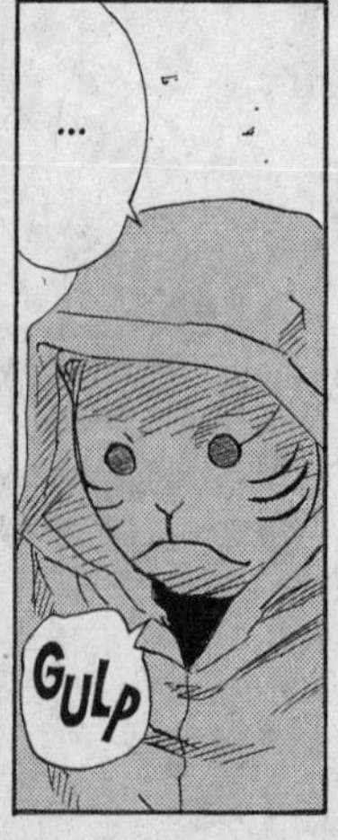
...
GULP

Number 118: Detainment...!!

READ THIS WAY

!!
N-NO! THOSE ARE...?!

...?!
THEY'RE WHAT...?

LONG TIME NO SEE... SARU...
AH... IT'S YOU...
YOU'VE AGED, SARUTOBI...

I NEVER IMAGINED I WOULD SEE YOU TWO AGAIN. AND UNDER SUCH CIRCUM-STANCES...
I AM SO SORRY...

THIS IS... NOT GOOD...
HE SUMMONED THEM... BUT WHO ARE THEY?!

PLEASE PREPARE YOUR-SELVES...

FIRST HOKAGE! SECOND HOKAGE!!

HUH?!..

THAT'S RIGHT!
THE RAVEN-HAIRED ONE IS THE FIRST HOKAGE, AND THE WHITE-HAIRED ONE THE SECOND HOKAGE. BOTH FAMED AS THE ULTIMATE SHINOBI, THEY'RE THE HOKAGE WHO CREATED AND SHAPED KONOHA INTO WHAT IT IS...!

READ
THIS
WAY

REANI-MATION, EH...?
AND THAT STRIPLING OVER THERE IS THE ONE WHO SUMMONED US WITH THE FORBIDDEN JUTSU? IMPRESSIVE ...
KSSH
KSSH

WHICH MEANS, SARUTOBI...
...WE MUST FIGHT YOU...

ENOUGH WITH THE OLD FOLKS' SMALL TALK.
CLUNK
CLUNK
WHY DON'T WE GET STARTED?

WAR... NO MATTER WHAT THE ERA...

MOCKING THE DEAD...
NOTHING GOOD EVER COMES FROM PLAYING WITH TIME.

...HEH HEH HEH, YOU KNOW YOU LIKE IT!

SHOOM

HUH! SO THAT'S WHAT WAS HAPPENING!
THAT SASUKE, HE'S ALWAYS IN SUCH A HURRY!!

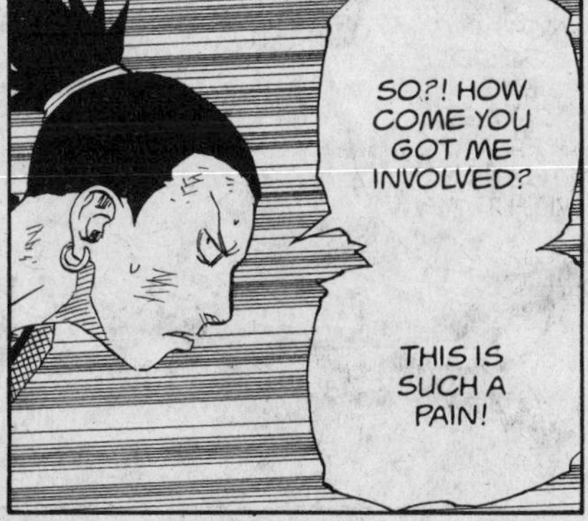
SO?! HOW COME YOU GOT ME INVOLVED?
THIS IS SUCH A PAIN!

I HAD NO CHOICE! IT WAS MASTER KAKASHI'S COMMAND!

READ THIS WAY

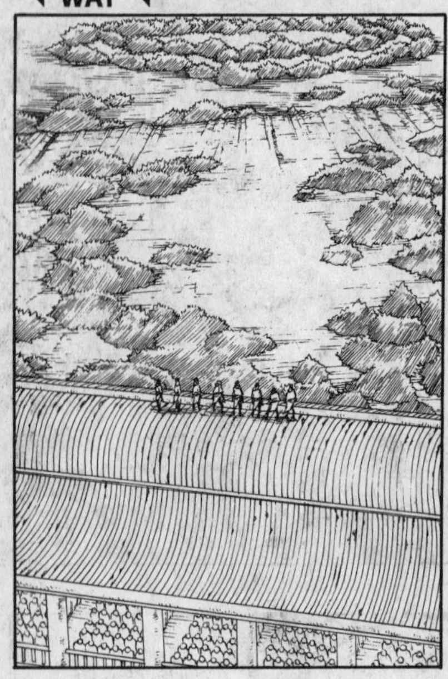

SHOOM
SHOOM
SHOOM

!!
SNIFF
SNIFF

HEY!! ALL OF YOU, HURRY UP!
HUH...? WHY?!

THERE ARE TWO SQUADS, THAT MEANS **EIGHT** SHINOBI! ACTUALLY...
PLUS ONE MORE... **NINE** SHINOBI ON OUR TAILS!

!!
HEY, ALREADY?! YOU'VE GOT TO BE JOKING!!

IT DOESN'T LOOK LIKE THEY KNOW OUR EXACT POSITION YET...
...BUT THEY'RE DEFINITELY GAINING ON US, AND GUARDING AGAINST AMBUSH.
DARN!
THEY'RE PROBABLY ALL CHÛNIN OR ABOVE... IF THEY CATCH UP TO US, WE'RE DEAD!

READ THIS WAY

DEAD...!!

DARN IT! THEN WHY DON'T WE AMBUSH THEM AND GET RID OF 'EM?!

AMBUSH... MIGHT NOT BE A BAD IDEA...

IF WE LIE IN WAIT FOR THEM, WE'LL DEFINITELY HAVE THE UPPER HAND!
EVEN IF THERE ARE TWICE AS MANY OF THEM AS US, AS LONG AS WE SURPRISE THEM...

NOPE, WON'T WORK. THEY'RE ALL MINIONS OF OROCHIMARU, A FORMER KONOHA SHINOBI.

FEH... I THOUGHT WE MIGHT HAVE A CHANCE, BUT I GUESS NOT...

HUH?! WHY NOT? I DON'T KNOW WHAT YOU'RE GETTING AT!
YEAH, WHAT DO YOU MEAN?!

LISTEN UP!
AMBUSHING THE ENEMY IS NORMALLY AN ADVANTAGEOUS BATTLE TACTIC, BUT ONLY IF THESE TWO ESSENTIAL CONDITIONS ARE MET...

YOU ARE BOTH SO CLUELESS!

FIRST, THE PURSUED MUST BE ABLE TO MOVE ABOUT SILENTLY AND LOCATE THE ENEMY FIRST!
TOMP
SECOND, THE PURSUED MUST BE ABLE TO SWIFTLY FIND, SECURE, AND CONCEAL THEMSELVES IN A POSITION WHERE THEY CAN INFLICT THE MOST SURPRISE AND DAMAGE TO THE CHASERS!

AN AMBUSH IS EFFECTIVE ONLY IF BOTH CONDITIONS CAN BE ACHIEVED.
IN OUR CASE...WELL, SINCE WE HAVE A NINJA DOG'S NOSE, THE FIRST WON'T BE TOO DIFFICULT.

BUT THE SECOND... THE SECOND NORMALLY WOULDN'T BE IMPOSSIBLE, SINCE WE KNOW OUR OWN VILLAGE BETTER...
...AND CAN PINPOINT THE BEST POSITIONS FOR MAXIMUM SURPRISE.
BUT THAT WON'T FLY AGAINST MINIONS OF A FORMER FELLOW KONOHA SHINOBI!

?
OUR PURSUERS HAVE STUDIED OUR GEOGRAPHY AND PRACTICED IN PREPARATION FOR THIS ATTACK WITH MOCK BATTLES.
AND THEY'RE PROBABLY ALL MASTERS OF PURSUIT JUTSU.

EVEN SO, AN AMBUSH MIGHT STILL BE TO OUR ADVANTAGE...
...EXCEPT THAT THERE ARE TOO MANY UNCERTAINTIES!
BESIDES, OUR "FRIENDS" WERE ASSEMBLED SPECIFICALLY FOR THIS PLOT, WHILE OUR GROUP IS COMPOSED OF...

IRK
...A DUNCE...

IRK
...A KUNOICHI WITHOUT ANY PARTICULAR TALENT...

...A DOG...

...AND THE NUMBER ONE SLACKER, ME!

YOU SEE, BATTLE STRATEGY ...
...COMES FROM COMPREHENDING YOUR OWN EXISTING FIGHTING STRENGTH AND FORMULATING THE BEST POSSIBLE PLAN BASED ON THAT!!
AND SO, WHAT'S WITHIN THE REALM OF POSSIBILITY FOR US RIGHT NOW IS JUST ONE THING...
SHOOM

ONE THING...?!

A DIVERSIONARY TACTIC DISGUISED AS AN AMBUSH!

ONE OF US STAYS BEHIND...
...AND DELAYS THEM BY MAKING IT LOOK LIKE WE'RE LYING IN WAIT.

IN OTHER WORDS...
...A DECOY...

THAT'S RIGHT. IF THAT PERSON CAN DETAIN THEM, THE ENEMY WILL LOSE TRACK OF THE OTHER THREE...
...AND WE'LL BE ABLE TO SHAKE THE PURSUIT.
HOWEVER, THE ONE WHO GETS TO BE THE DECOY WILL MOST LIKELY...

...DIE.

SO... ANY VOLUNTEERS?
WE NEED OUR DOGGIE GUIDE IN ORDER TO FIND SASUKE, WHICH MEANS...

...!

...!

...

I'M THE ONLY CHOICE...

GLARE
ALL RIGHT, I'LL...

READ THIS WAY

YOU?!
!!

WHY YOU?!

IT'S BETTER THAN ALL OF US GOING DOWN TOGETHER.
BESIDES, THE ONLY ONE OF US WHO HAS ANY CHANCE OF PULLING OFF THE DECOY ACT AND EVEN POSSIBLY SURVIVING...
SNAG!

...IS ME.
TAP

!
!
THUMP
THUMP
THUMP

THE SHADOW POSSESSION TECHNIQUE IS FUNDA-MENTALLY A DETAINMENT JUTSU, ANYWAYS...

WELL! I'LL CATCH UP WITH YOU ALL LATER... SO HURRY UP AND GO!!

SHA
I'M COUNTING ON YOU!!

GLARE
SHIKAMARU...

SHOOM
...
SHOOM
I NEVER SAW SHIKAMARU AS THE RELIABLE TYPE...

SHOOOM

!

READ THIS WAY

HEH HEH... THEY'RE SO GREEN ...

HEY, THE ENEMY'S STILL GAINING ON US!
IS HE REALLY TRYING TO DELAY THEM?!

!!
D-DON'T TELL ME...

MAYBE HE'S RUN OFF!

SHIKAMARU MAY BE A SLACKER...
...BUT HE'S **NOT** A TRAITOR!

PHEW... WE'VE MANAGED TO SHAKE THEM...

TMP
HEH

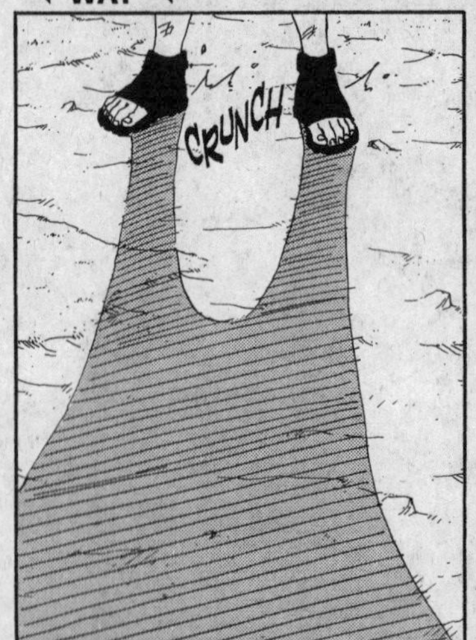

JUST KIDDING. THAT'S HOW I AM, YOU KNOW...

OH! AND BY THE WAY... **THIS** IS THE WAY I MADE THE PAW PRINTS.

HUF

HUF

SNIFF
SNIFF

WHAT THE...? HE'S STILL JUST A KID! I CAN'T BELIEVE WE FELL FOR SUCH A SIMPLE TRICK...!
SO **THIS** IS KONOHA'S FAMED SHADOW PARALYSIS TECHNIQUE, HUH...?

Number 119: The Life I Wanted...!!

YOU GUYS ARE OUT OF DATE!

HUF
TIMES HAVE CHANGED...
WE CALL IT **THE KAGEMANE SHADOW POSSESSION TECHNIQUE** NOW, MISTER!
HUF

DARN... IT WAS FOOLISH TO ENGAGE THEM LIKE THIS...
I'VE USED UP TOO MUCH CHAKRA... I'M NOT GOING TO LAST TOO MUCH LONGER...
HUF

Number 119: The Life I Wanted...!!

THERE ARE TWO SQUADS, THAT'S EIGHT SHINOBI... ACTUALLY, PLUS ONE MORE... 9 SHINOBI TOTAL ON OUR TAILS.

SHK
JUST AS I THOUGHT, THE NINTH SHINOBI'S ROLE IS AIDING AND DEFENDING THE OTHER EIGHT FROM A HIDDEN POSITION...
STAYING A FIXED DISTANCE AWAY, MOVING FROM THE REAR, MATCHING THE ENEMY'S ASSAULTS...
SHUP

WELL, IN ANY CASE...
...LET'S SEE WHERE YOU'RE HIDING.

THIS SHOULD...
STRETCH

SHUK
...CLARIFY THINGS!!

KA CHINK
KA CHINK
KA CHINK

!!

SHUKK
KLINK

HEH HEH...

HUF
HUF

...!
OVER THERE!
HUF
HUF
HUF

GYOOON

DARN IT... I CAN'T MAKE MY SHADOW MOVE ANY FASTER...
WHICH MEANS I HAVE NO ENERGY LEFT TO DIVERT TO MY CHAKRA...
HUF
HUF

IT'S USELESS ...
WE KNOW HOW YOUR TECHNIQUE WORKS.

FEH...
HUF

HUF
...SO THIS IS IT, HUH...
HUF

IT SEEMS YOU'VE REACHED YOUR LIMIT.
YOUR SHADOW POSSESSION, OR WHATEVER YOU CALL IT, WILL FAIL SOON... SO PREPARE YOURSELF!

SIGH... I USED TO REALLY WANT TO BE JUST AN AVERAGE NINJA MAKING AN AVERAGE LIVING...
...MARRY A REGULAR GIRL WHO'S NOT SUPER PRETTY OR SUPER UGLY, HAVE TWO KIDS, A GIRL AND THEN A BOY...

RETIRE WHEN MY DAUGHTER GOT MARRIED AND MY SON SUCCESSFULLY BECAME A NINJA...
...AND THEN JUST SPEND THE REST OF MY DAYS PLAYING SHOGI OR GO, A CAREFREE AND LEISURELY RETIREMENT...

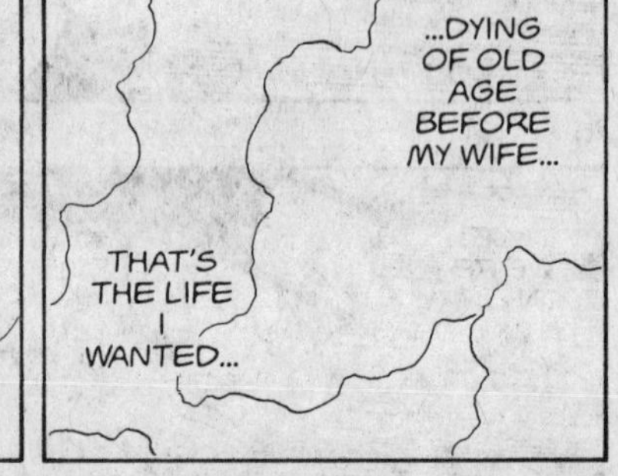
...DYING OF OLD AGE BEFORE MY WIFE...
THAT'S THE LIFE I WANTED...

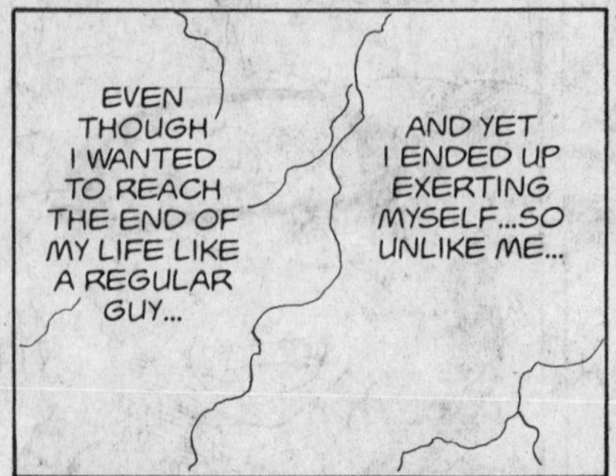
EVEN THOUGH I WANTED TO REACH THE END OF MY LIFE LIKE A REGULAR GUY...
AND YET I ENDED UP EXERTING MYSELF...SO UNLIKE ME...

...I HAD TO GO AND GET MYSELF INTO THIS TIRESOME SITUATION...

HMM?!
OUR PURSUERS HAVE STOPPED!!

HIS TACTICS MUST HAVE WORKED!!
YES!

YOU MEAN SHIKAMARU...?!

NICE! WE'RE ON OUR WAY, SASUKE!

AND SHIKAMARU...

...YOU BETTER SURVIVE AND COME CATCH UP TO US!!

HUF
LIKE YOU WERE SAYING... IT SEEMS I'M AT THE END OF MY ROPE...
HUF

SNIP

SHHH
HEY... IT'S ABOUT TIME FOR YOU TO COME OUT.

AND TAKE THIS KID'S HEAD OFF WHILE YOU'RE AT IT.

SHUDDER
!!

URK
SHOOM

FINALLY CAUGHT UP TO YOU ...
...ASUMA... WHAT'RE YOU...?

!!

FWUMP
DASH
THUD!!
FWAK

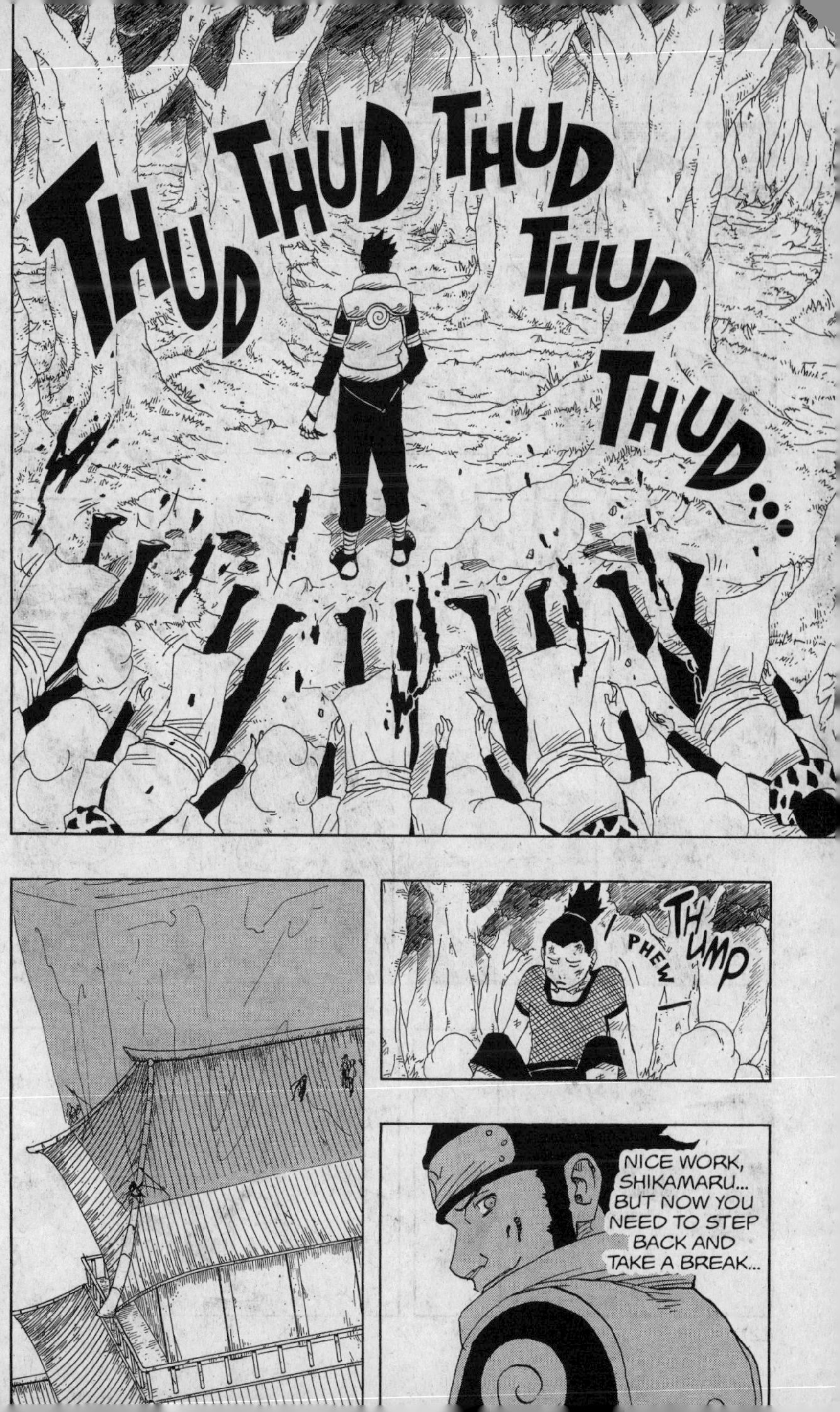

THUD THUD THUD THUD THUD THUD...

THUMP
PHEW

NICE WORK, SHIKAMARU... BUT NOW YOU NEED TO STEP BACK AND TAKE A BREAK...

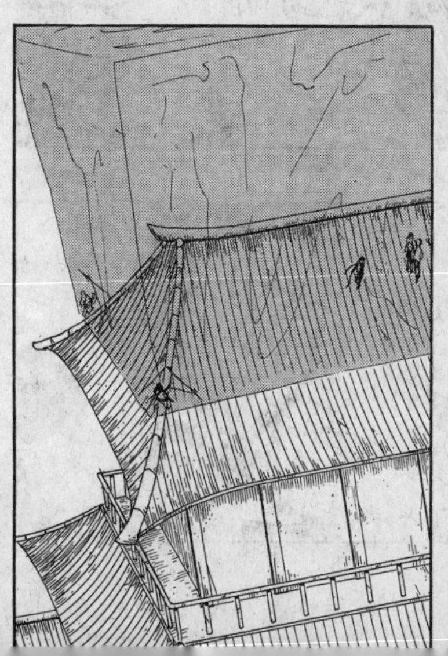

WELL THEN, SHALL WE BEGIN?

...

SHNK

SHOVE
SQUELCH

BUT FIRST, I NEED YOU RESTORED TO YOUR ORIGINAL FORMS...

SQUICH

FIZZ

FIZZ

FIZZ

WHUMP

READ THIS WAY

THEY LOOK MORE AND MORE LIKE THEIR OLD SELVES...

THEY'RE INFUSED WITH MORE LIFE FORCE...
WHAT IS THAT JUTSU...?!

EDO TENSEI ...
IT'S A FORBIDDEN SUMMONING TECHNIQUE THAT RECALLS AND REVIVES THE DEAD INTO THIS WORLD...

NORMALLY, SUMMONING REQUIRES A SMALL AMOUNT OF BLOOD AS PAYMENT...
...BUT I'VE HEARD THAT THIS JUTSU, BECAUSE IT INVOLVES CALLING FORTH AND KEEPING A SOUL OF THE DEAD IN THIS PLANE...
...REQUIRES THE SACRIFICIAL USE OF A LIVING BODY AS A VESSEL FOR THAT SOUL.

YOU MEAN THOSE BODIES WERE FROM OTHER **PEOPLE**...?!!

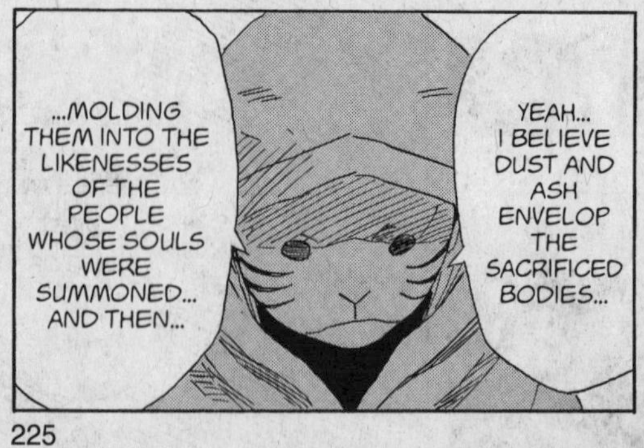

YEAH... I BELIEVE DUST AND ASH ENVELOP THE SACRIFICED BODIES...
...MOLDING THEM INTO THE LIKENESSES OF THE PEOPLE WHOSE SOULS WERE SUMMONED... AND THEN...

...THROUGH THE SPELL NOTES EMBEDDED INSIDE THE HEADS, THOSE SOULS' PERSONALITIES ARE SUPPRESSED, TRANSFORMING THEM INTO MERE KILLING MACHINES!!

HEH HEH HEH...
PERFECT...

...

HEH HEH HEH... DO YOU GET IT NOW?
THERE'S AN INCREDIBLE JOY AND SENSE OF ACCOMPLISH-MENT FROM...
...WOUNDING THOSE YOU ONCE CALLED YOUR TEACHERS!

I PREPARED THIS LITTLE SCENARIO PRECISELY SO THAT YOU COULD EXPERIENCE THAT JOY...

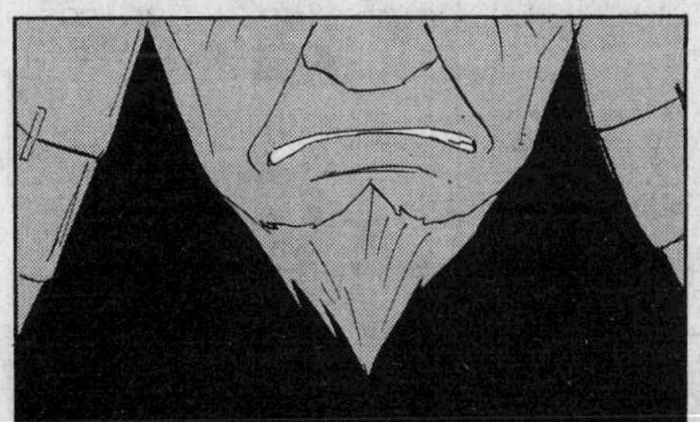

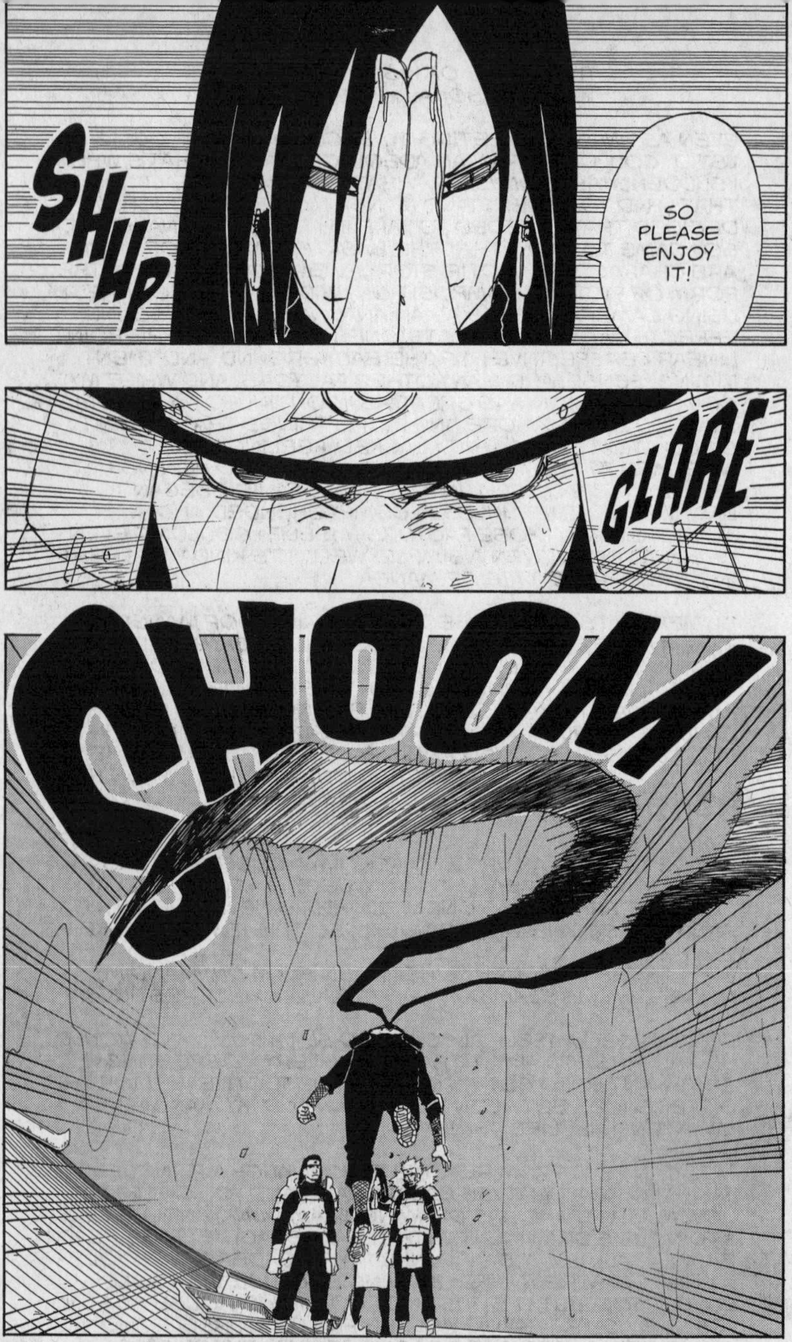

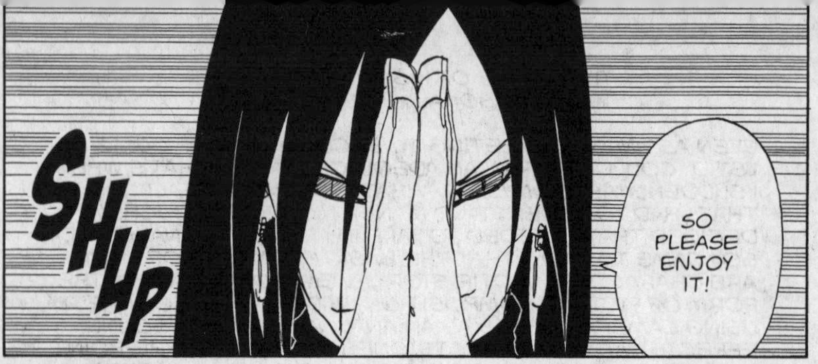
SO PLEASE ENJOY IT!
SHUP

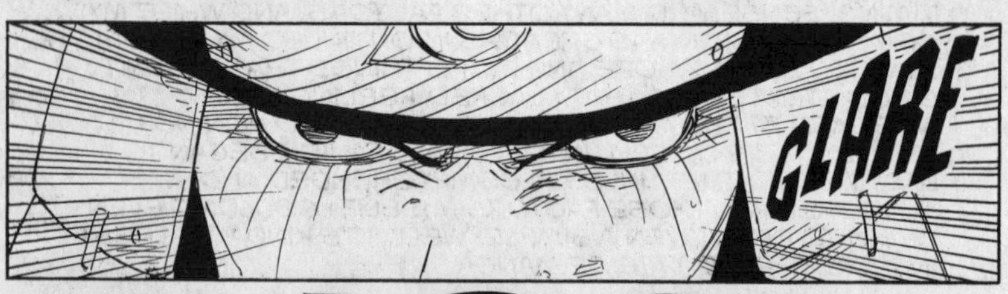
GLARE

SHOOM

THE WORLD OF KISHIMOTO MASASHI
MY PERSONAL HISTORY, PART 19

EVEN AS I WAS COMPLETING MY SECOND YEAR OF COLLEGE, I STILL COULDN'T DRAW AN ADEQUATE MANGA. THAT'S WHEN I SUDDENLY ASKED MYSELF, "WHAT IS MANGA?" REALIZING THAT I HAD TO UNDERSTAND MANGA MORE THOROUGHLY, I DECIDED THAT I NEEDED TO TAKE IT APART AND ANALYZE IT. SO I CAME TO KNOW THAT THE BASIC ELEMENTS OF MANGA ARE CHARACTERS, MOTIF, STORY, THEME, DIRECTION IN THE FORM OF PICTURE COMPOSITION (WIDE ANGLE, ZOOM IF USING CAMERA ANGLES AS AN ANALOGY), SOUND (SOUND EFFECTS), ACTION, EFFECTS, ONE-, TWO- AND THREE-POINT LINEAR PERSPECTIVE FOR THE BACKGROUND, AND THEN TIMING, SENSE, AND MANY OTHER FACTORS. AND WHILE MY COMPREHENSION WAS GREAT, AS I CONTINUED MY ANALYSIS I STARTED SEEING MORE AND MORE THINGS THAT I WASN'T GOOD AT OR SKILLS THAT I LACKED. FEELING OVERWHELMED BY THE AMOUNT OF LEARNING AND HONING I STILL HAD TO DO, I FELL INTO A SMALL PANIC. I BEGAN TO UNDERSTAND THAT UNLESS I COMPREHENDED AND MASTERED ALL THOSE FACTORS MYSELF, I COULDN'T EVEN BEGIN TO DRAW EVEN A SIMPLE "WELL, IT'S KINDA INTERESTING" LIGHT-READ TYPE OF MANGA.

SOMEHOW, I SUDDENLY BECAME TERRIFIED OF MANGA, THINKING OF THEM AS MONSTERS, AND BECAME AFRAID OF DRAWING MANGA. THAT PAINFUL PERIOD LASTED FOR SEVERAL MONTHS, AND JUST AS I WAS SLIDING INTO AN EMOTIONALLY DRAINED STATE, A FRIEND OF MINE BOUGHT AN ISSUE OF JUMP AND STARTED READING *SLAM DUNK* IN MY ROOM... WHEN I LOOKED AT HIS FACE, I NOTICED THAT HE HAD AN AVID AND HAPPY EXPRESSION. AND THEN, WHEN HE FINISHED THE CHAPTER, HE EXCLAIMED, "WOW! *SLAM DUNK* IS SO COOL!!"

SUDDENLY, I HAD AN URGE TO ASK HIM A QUESTION. THIS QUESTION WAS A REALLY SCARY QUESTION FOR ME TO ASK. FOR THAT FRIEND WAS ONE WHO WOULD NEVER LIE TO ME, AND HE ALSO KNEW MANGA WELL. SO THIS IS WHAT I ASKED:

"WHAT'S THE DIFFERENCE BETWEEN *SLAM DUNK* AND MY MANGA? WHY IS *SLAM DUNK* SO COOL AND INTERESTING?"

OF COURSE, I MYSELF ALSO LOVED *SLAM DUNK*, AND WOULD BE THE FIRST TO ADMIT THAT IT WAS VERY INTERESTING! I JUST WANTED TO GET AN OUTSIDE, OBJECTIVE VIEW OF THE DIFFERENCES BETWEEN *SLAM DUNK* AND MY MANGA.
MY FRIEND REPLIED THUS:

"YOU CAN TELL FROM READING IT HOW MUCH MR. INOUE TAKEHIKO REALLY LOVES BASKETBALL. AND YOU CAN FEEL HOW MUCH FUN HE HAS DRAWING *SLAM DUNK*, AND IT'S LIKE MR. INOUE'S DRAWING IT WITH THE MESSAGE 'PLEASE READ IT, BASKETBALL IS LOTS OF FUN' TO THE READERS. WITH YOUR MANGA, I'M SURE YOU'RE DRAWING BECAUSE YOU REALLY LOVE IT TOO, BUT IT'S JUST NOT COMING THROUGH AS FUN... IT'S LIKE, YOU'RE HAVING ALL THE FUN BY YOURSELF AND WE'RE BEING LEFT OUT OR LEFT BEHIND. THERE'S NO SENSE OF 'PLEASE READ IT'..."

Number 120: Hokage vs. Hokage!!

SHUP
SHUP

GLINT
GLINT

SHAA
FIRE STYLE! KARYU-ENDAN!
DRAGON'S FLAME!!

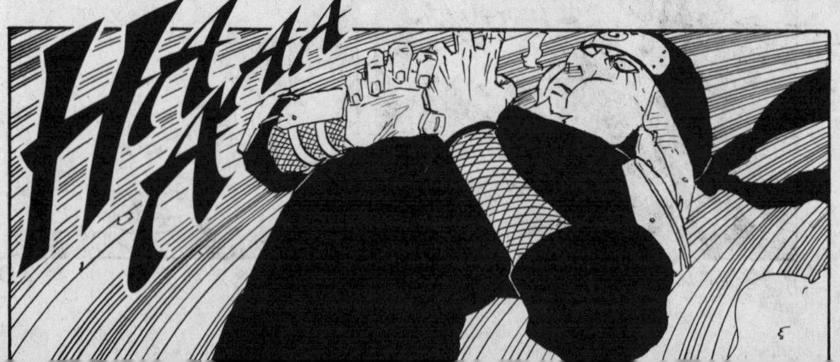
HYAAA

WATER STYLE!
SUIJINHEKI! WALL OF WATER!!

WHOOO
Number 120:
Hokage vs. Hokage!!
UGH!
GOOSH

HE INVOKED SUCH A TREMENDOUS WATER TECHNIQUE ON DRY LAND!
UNBELIEV-ABLE!!

IT SHOWS WHY HE WAS NAMED HOKAGE...

SHUP
WATER STYLE: SUIRYUDAN! WATER DRAGON ATTACK!!

VOOM

SHHUP
EARTH STYLE: DORYUHEKI! MUD WALL!
SHUP
UGAAH
KA BOOM
SPLOOSH
ZKKSH

SHUP
SECRET JUTSU...
WOOD STYLE!
SHUP

JUKAIKOTAN! DEEP FOREST EMERGENCE!

THIS IS THE FIRST HOKAGE'S SECRET JUTSU... NOT GOOD!!
!!
SNIK

SHUP
SHUP

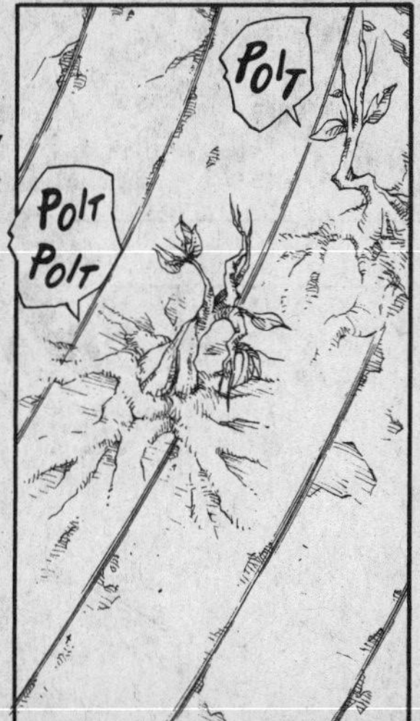
POIT
POIT POIT

DASH

TAP

KA-BOOF

HE USED HIS CHAKRA AS A LIFE SOURCE...!! SO THIS IS THE FIRST HOKAGE'S LEGENDARY WOOD STYLE NINJUTSU THAT QUELLED TURBULENT TIMES AND CARVED OUT KONOHA...!!

HO HO... YOU'VE BEEN TRAPPED, MASTER SARUTOBI...

AARGH...
GGGH

NGGGH

NINJA ART: KUCHIYOSE! SUMMONING!!
I CALL THEE...!!

BOOF
MONKEY KING ENMA!!
HUMPH... A GERIATRIC MONKEY KING, EH...?
'TIS SAD, SARUTOBI...
AND ALL BECAUSE YOU FAILED TO KILL HIM THAT DAY!!
OROCHIMARU...
SO IT HAS COME TO THIS, AFTER ALL...!

ENMA!!
INDESTRUC-TIBLE NYOI STAFF!!
I'M GETTING TO IT RIGHT NOW...
TSK! TOO LATE!!
WHOOSH
ALL RIGHT...
TRANSFORM!!
BOOF
FWIK
YES!

WHAT A HIGH-LEVEL NINJUTSU CONTEST...!
THIS IS WHAT IT TAKES TO BE HOKAGE...

TAK
GSSH
TMP

HO HO... IT'S FINALLY GETTING INTERESTING ...

ZWOO

WITH ONE SWING OF KUSANAGI...

ZYUU

CHAK
GO, ENMA!!
EVEN IN THIS SOLID METAL FORM, THE KUSANAGI BLADE WILL INFLICT PAIN...!
SHOOM
SWOOP
SWISH

BYOO
KSSH
!!
BOFSH
!!
?!
URK

I CAN'T BELIEVE YOU LEAPT RIGHT IN WITHOUT EVEN USING SHADOW CLONES...

WHAM
SPLASH
SPLASH

AGE HAS CAUGHT UP WITH HIM...

A JUTSU LIKE THE SHADOW DOPPELGANGER TECHNIQUE, WHICH SPLITS ONE'S CHAKRA INTO EQUAL PIECES... IF THINGS GO WRONG, IT'S LIKE THROWING AWAY CHUNKS OF CHAKRA...
THE AMOUNT OF CHAKRA LORD HOKAGE POSSESSES HAS DECLINED SINCE HIS YOUTH...
NO... IT ISN'T THAT HE'S NOT USING THEM, BUT RATHER THAT HE **CANNOT**...

IT'S NOT LIKE YOU... WHAT'S THE MATTER?
HUF
HUF

READ THIS WAY

UGH...
HUF
THE NYOI STAFF IS STARTING TO FEEL SO HEAVY...
HUF
HUF

HO HO HO... YOU'RE THE ONE NICKNAMED "PROFESSOR" BECAUSE YOU KNEW AND COULD PERFORM ALL EXISTING KONOHA JUTSU...
...PLEASE DON'T DISAPPOINT ME.

SHU
SHU

BOOM

HUF
HUF

I SEE... AS HE WAS BEING KICKED, HE PLANTED SMOKE BOMBS.
HO HO... TOO BAD IT'S FUTILE...

SUUSH

SUUSH

SUSH

JUST AS I FEARED... UNLESS I DO SOMETHING ABOUT THE BOUND SOULS THEMSELVES...
...NOTHING I DO WILL MATTER...
HUF
HUF

YOUR BREATH...
...IS GETTING RAGGED.

READ THIS WAY

HUF
IN WHICH CASE, I HAVE NO CHOICE BUT TO USE ...
...THE FOURTH HOKAGE'S JUTSU AFTER ALL...
HUF

WELL, WHAT ARE YOU GOING TO DO?

ENOUGH WITH COMPARING JUTSU!
SPLISH
THIS MOMENT MARKS THE BEGINNING OF A REPULSIVE BLOOD-DRENCHED BATTLE...

HUF
HUF
HUF
...MOST APPROPRIATE FOR SHINOBI!

THE WORLD OF KISHIMOTO MASASHI
MY PERSONAL HISTORY, PART 19 (CONTINUED)

WHEN I HEARD THE TRUTH, IT DID DEFLATE ME, BUT I CONTINUED TO POSE THE SAME QUESTION TO OTHER FRIENDS OF MINE. AND YET I KEPT GETTING SIMILAR RESPONSES FROM THEM AS WELL.

AND THEN, IT CAME TO ME. THERE ARE MANY DIFFERENT ELEMENTS TO DRAWING MANGA, BUT THE MOST IMPORTANT PRINCIPLE IS...

"ONE MUST HAVE FUN DRAWING ONE'S OWN MANGA. AND THEN, WHAT'S EVEN MORE CRITICAL IS TO BE AWARE OF ONE'S AUDIENCE AND DRAW FOR THE READERS' ENJOYMENT. EVERYTHING MUST BE FOR THE READERS. ONE MUST BE ABLE TO CHANGE THE EXPRESSIONS ON THEIR FACES AND MAKE THEM SAY 'WOW! THAT IS SO COOL!' WHEN THEY'VE FINISHED READING IT!!"

AND AFTER A LITTLE WHILE, I REALIZED THAT THIS IS WHAT IS MEANT BY "ENTERTAINMENT." IT'S IMPORTANT TO GRASP THE PRACTICAL ASPECTS OF DRAWING MANGA, BUT AS LONG AS ONE DRAWS THINKING "I'M GOING TO BE AN ENTERTAINER!!" I FEEL THAT THE OTHER THINGS WILL QUIETLY AND NATURALLY FALL INTO PLACE.

I AM STILL LEARNING NEW THINGS EVERY DAY.

Number 121:
The Terrible Experiment...!!

HUF
三代目火影
HUF

EDO TENSEI... REANIMATION...
WHICH MEANS THE JUTSU WON'T UNRAVEL EVEN IF I KILL OROCHIMARU...
HUF

IN WHICH CASE... FIRST LORD, SECOND LORD, PLEASE FORGIVE ME...

SHA
...I HAVE NO CHOICE BUT TO CAST THIS JUTSU.

HUF
HUF
SHHHH
HUF
SHHHH
HUF

READ THIS WAY

MY, MY, HOW WE'VE AGED.
I'VE NEVER SEEN YOU STRUGGLING LIKE THIS...

HEH HEH HEH HEH...

HUF
HUF
HUF
WHAT'S... SO FUNNY...?

IT'S SO PITIFUL...
...THAT EVEN YOU, WHO HAS BEEN HAILED AS A SHINOBI GOD, ARE VULNERABLE TO THE PASSAGE OF TIME...
SHK

...!

!!
!
HUF
HUF

RRIP RRIP

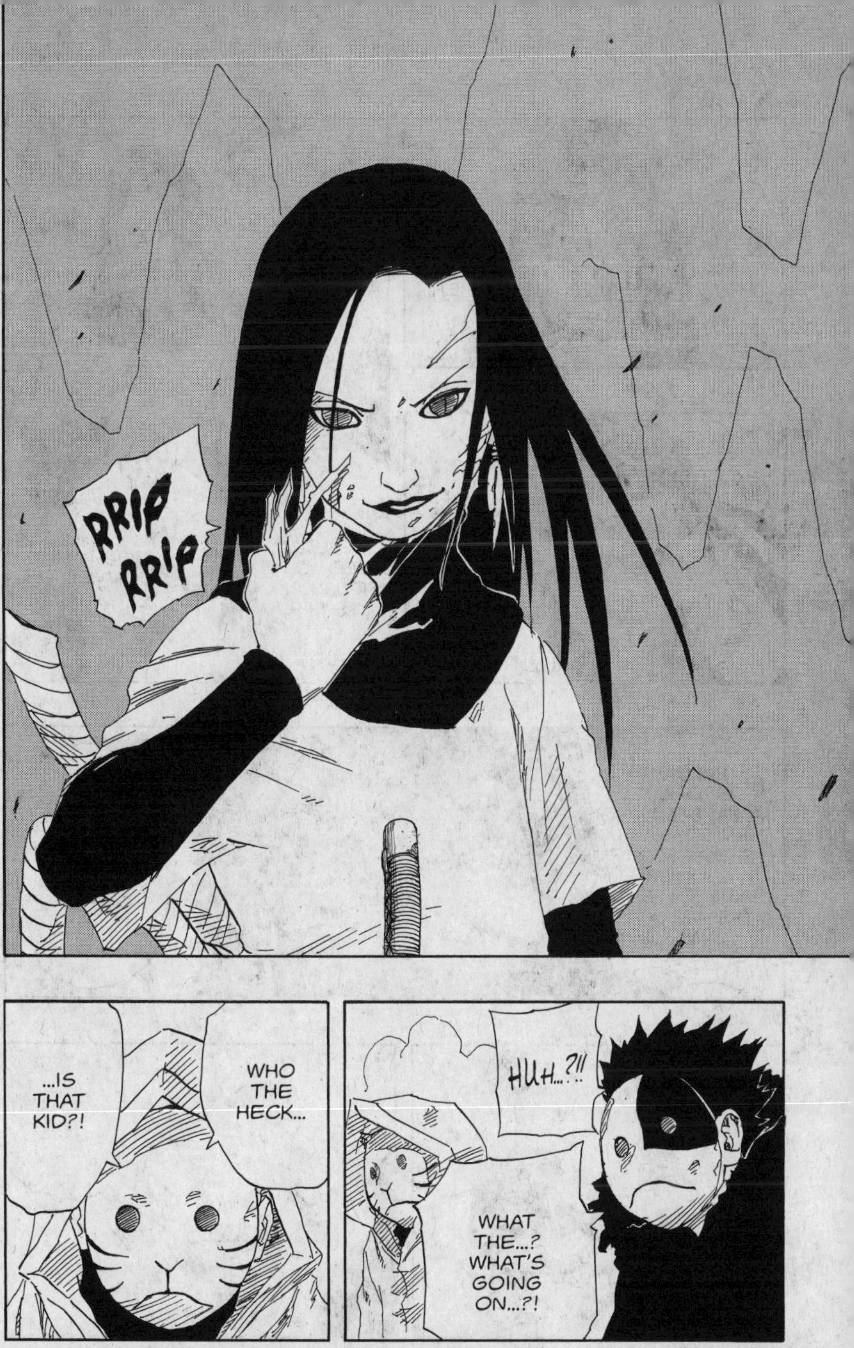

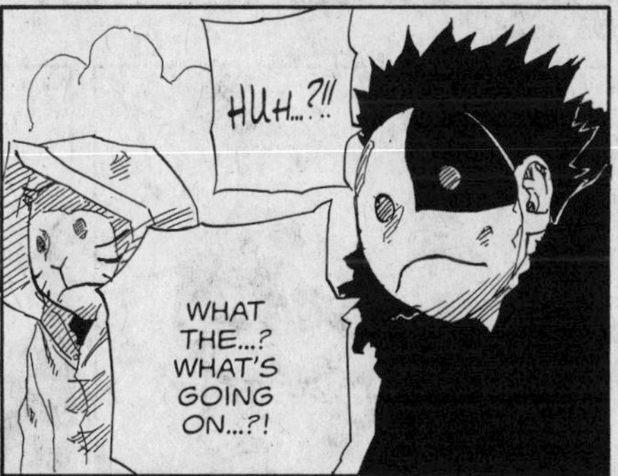

HUH...?!!
WHAT THE...? WHAT'S GOING ON...?!

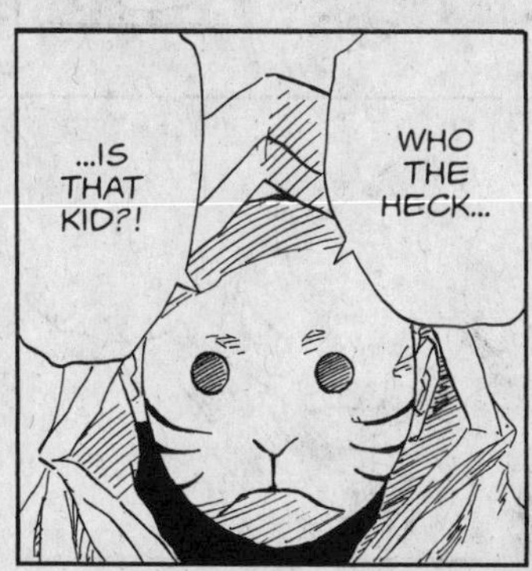

WHO THE HECK...
...IS THAT KID?!

READ THIS WAY

...?!!
WHO IN THE WORLD ARE YOU?!

HEH HEH HEH...
WAS IT TOO SUDDEN FOR YOU TO COMPRE-HEND?

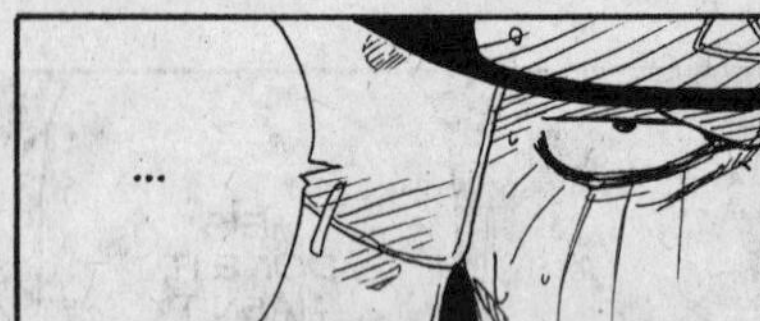
...

IT IS STILL I, OROCHIMARU.

...!!

!!

WHAT IS GOING ON...? AS ONE OF THE LEGEND-ARY THREE SHINOBI, HE'S GOT TO BE WAY PAST 50 YEARS OLD...
THIS GUY'S TOO YOUNG...
...PLUS, THAT IS NOT THE OROCHI-MARU FACE WE KNOW!!

HE'S DONE IT, HASN'T HE...?

D-DON'T TELL ME YOU'VE PERFECTED *THAT* FORBIDDEN JUTSU...

HEH HEH HEH...
IN THE DECADE SINCE I LEFT THE VILLAGE, I'VE STRUGGLED...

YOU TERRIBLE, INHUMAN FELLOW...

READ
THIS
WAY

THE MAIN REASON I COULD NOT SELECT YOU AS THE FOURTH HOKAGE...
...IS YOUR WARPED THINKING...

SPLASH
SPLASH

SPLASH
SPLASH

SHUP

SPLASH
SPLASH

SQUELCH
SQUISH
SHA
SHUD
SHA
SQUISH
SQUICH
SLAM
SHUP

SQUELCH
SQUISH...
SHFF

HO HO HO... I'VE FINALLY BEEN FOUND OUT...

WHAT A SHAME.

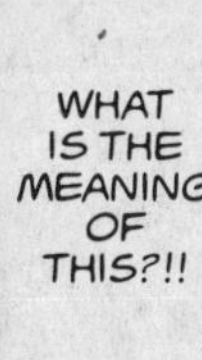

WHAT IS THE MEANING OF THIS?!!

THERE HAVE BEEN A SPATE OF DISAPPEARANCES RECENTLY, ONE AFTER ANOTHER, OF NOT JUST GENIN AND CHÛNIN, BUT EVEN SEVERAL BLACK OPS AGENTS...
AND WE RECEIVED A REPORT THAT **YOU'VE** BEEN ACTING IN A SUSPICIOUS MANNER...

AND I THOUGHT I HAD RIGGED ENOUGH BOOBY TRAPS...

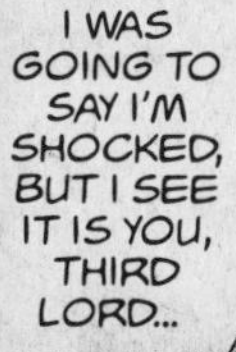

I WAS GOING TO SAY I'M SHOCKED, BUT I SEE IT IS YOU, THIRD LORD...

LORD OROCHIMARU... WHY WOULD A SHINOBI OF YOUR CALIBER ENGAGE IN SUCH THINGS...?!!
HEH HEH HEH... WOULD YOU LIKE ME TO KILL YOU TOO?
!

OROCHIMARU!! SO IT HAS BEEN YOU...
TELL ME!! WHAT HAVE YOU BEEN DOING HERE?!
AH WELL! NOW THAT THE CAT'S OUT OF THE BAG...
I GUESS THERE'S NO USE HIDING IT ANYMORE...
I'M EXPLORING JUTSU DEVELOPMENT!
OROCHI... YOU...
YOU'VE BEEN CONDUCTING LIVE HUMAN EXPERI-MENTS...
FORBIDDEN JUTSU, EH...
WHAT IS IT THAT YOU SEEK?

EVERYTHING!
...EVERYTHING?!
I WANT TO ACQUIRE ALL JUTSU AND GRASP ALL OF THIS WORLD'S PRINCIPLES...
AND THUS DID THE FELLOW WHO FIRST MIXED BLUE AND YELLOW...
...NAME THE NEWLY CREATED COLOR GREEN.
I WISH TO DO THE SAME...
SAY BLUE IS CHAKRA, THEN YELLOW IS SIGNS AND GREEN IS JUTSU...
JUST AS THERE ARE AN INFINITE NUMBER OF COLORS, SO ARE THERE THOUSANDS IF NOT TENS OF THOUSANDS OF JUTSU OUT IN THE WORLD...
HOWEVER, IN ORDER TO OBTAIN EACH AND EVERY JUTSU THAT EXISTS, AND THE PRINCIPLES BEHIND THEM, I NEED A LONG, LONG TIME...
AND HE WHO MASTERS ALL IS TRULY WORTHY OF THE TITLE "THE ULTIMATE BEING"...

READ THIS WAY
FOR ME, THE LIFESPAN OF THE FLESH IS MUCH TOO SHORT...
...EVEN IF I HAD BECOME HOKAGE. FOR ONCE ONE IS DEAD, IT'S ALL OVER...
OROCHI-MARU...
DON'T TELL ME THE JUTSU YOU WERE EXPERI-MENTING WITH HERE WAS...
YES... IT'S THAT WHICH YOU FEAR...
...
...
FURÔFUSHI NO JUTSU... THE ART OF IMMORTALITY!

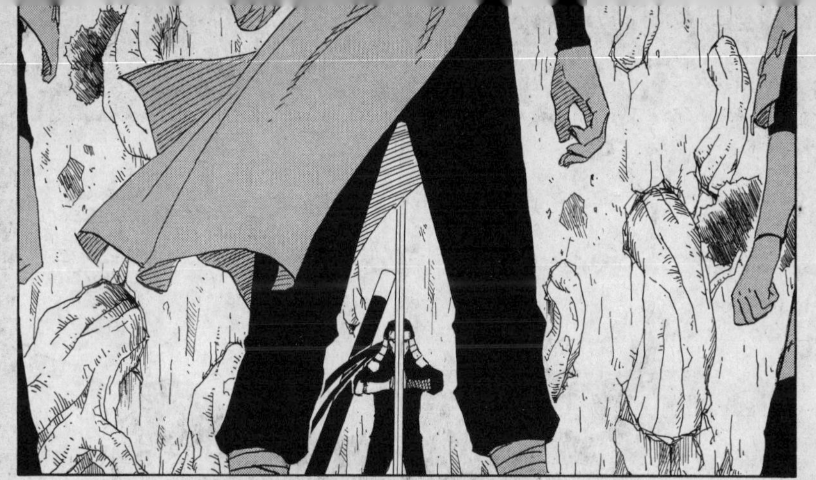

...

THE ART OF IMMORTALITY IS A METHOD OF KEEPING ONE'S MIND AND SOUL ANCHORED IN THIS WORLD FOR ETERNITY...
IT'S A TENSEI JUTSU, A TRANSFERENCE TECHNIQUE WHERE I FIND A NEW BODY TO INHABIT, THEN INSERT MY MIND AND SOUL INTO IT AND TAKE IT OVER...

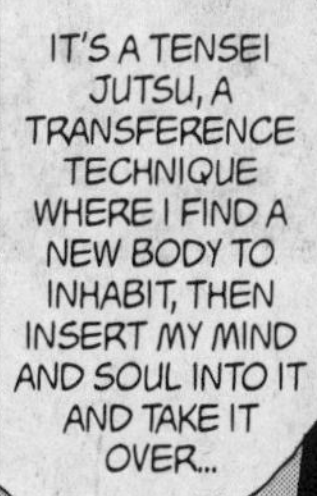

HEH HEH HEH... THE REASON I WAS ASSUMING MY OLD APPEARANCE UNTIL NOW...
...WAS THAT I WANTED YOU TO FEEL NOSTALGIC ABOUT OUR REUNION, MASTER....

FEH..!
(HUF)

AGING IMPARTS A SENSE OF FUTILITY, DOES IT NOT?
I FEEL IT DEEPLY SEEING YOU LIKE THIS...

YOU WILL DIE HERE AND I SHALL OBTAIN A BODY THAT IS EVEN YOUNGER, STRONGER, AND MORE BEAUTIFUL THAN THIS ONE.
KONOHA SHALL TRULY PROVIDE ME WITH MUCH ENJOYMENT...

...

HEH

I SEE...
YOU MEAN UCHIHA SASUKE!

Number 122: The Bestowed Will!!

YESSS... THAT'S RIGHT...
DEAR LITTLE SASUKE...

(HUF)
(HUF)
...

A TRANSFERENCE TECHNIQUE WHICH GIVES YOUR MIND AND SOUL IMMORTALITY THROUGH STEALING OTHERS' BODIES...
THAT FACE... THAT BODY... HOW MANY OTHERS HAVE THERE BEEN?

THIS IS ONLY MY SECOND ONE, I THINK...
AND I PLAN ON GROOMING SASUKE A BIT MORE TO MY TASTE BEFORE POSSESSING HIM... HEH HEH...

UGH...

HO HO HO... BUT IN ORDER TO HAVE YOU DIE RUING YOUR LIFE AND CURSING YOUR FATE...
SHA

...I SUPPOSE THIS FACE IS BETTER, AFTER ALL...
SHA
DAA

...

SHUP

MONSTER!

!!
LORD HOKAGE!!!
KSSSH

READ
THIS
WAY

HEH HEH
HEH...
YOU REALLY
SHOULDN'T
RELAX
YOUR
GUARD,
MASTER!
YOU'VE
ALWAYS
BEEN
SO
NAÏVE.

DRIP
DRIP...

WHAT'S
THE
MATTER?
IT'S
NOT LIKE
YOU...
...SORRY...
HUF
HUF
HUF

...

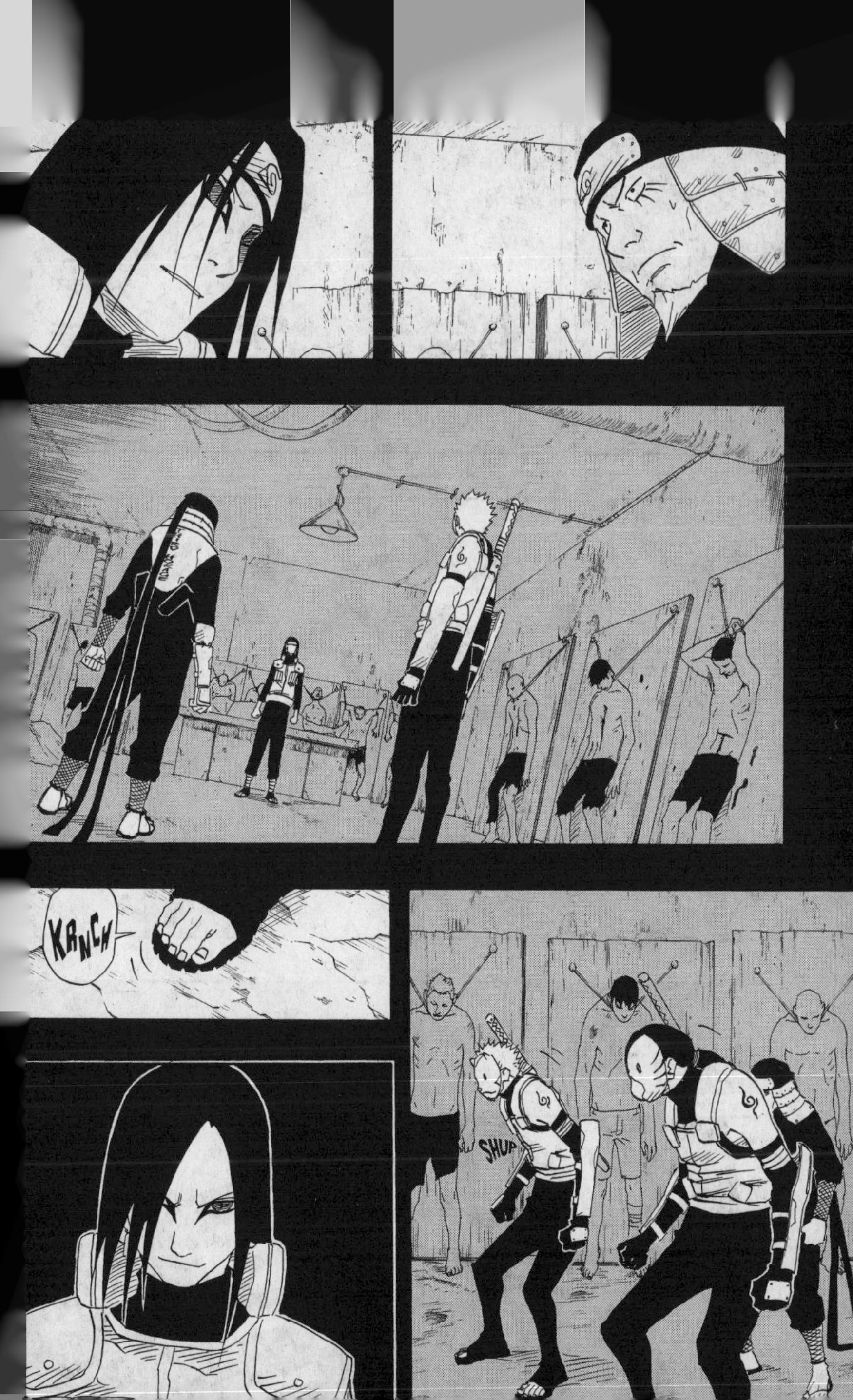
KRNCH
SHUP

PUPILS WHO CONCEALED MALICE AND AMBITION...
I HAD PICKED UP...
...THAT YOU HAD SUCH FOUNDATIONS WITHIN YOU...
I KNEW, AND YET PRE-TENDED I HADN'T NOTICED...
...BECAUSE IT WAS STILL AN ERA OF CONFLICT, AND YOU WERE A POWERFULLY TALENTED GENIUS, THE LIKES OF WHICH IS SEEN ONLY ONCE EVERY FEW DECADES...
I HAD HOPED YOU WOULD INHERIT MY WILL AND STRENGTH... THAT'S WHAT I WISHED.
AND THUS MY INDULGENCES HAVE BROUGHT ABOUT THESE CIRCUM-STANCES... BOTH THEN AND NOW...

YOU'RE GOING TO KILL ME? ME...?
POOF
CAN YOU REALLY DO IT...
SHA
... MASTER SARUTOBI ?
THUNK
THUD

!!
!!
...
...
SARUTOBI... YOU...
YOU WERE RIGHT... I COULDN'T KILL YOU...
DASH

GRAB
HERE I COME!
TWITCH
!
BUT I SHALL KILL YOU AND RECTIFY THE ERRORS OF THE PAST RIGHT NOW!!
POOF
POOF
POOF
FOOSH
FOOSH
IT'S ALREADY TOO LATE!!

POOF
KAGE-BUNSHIN NO JUTSU! ART OF THE SHADOW DOPPELGANGER!
!!
POOF

!
NO...! WHY SHADOW DOPPELGANGERS...?!!

HEH... YOU REALLY HAVE LOST YOUR MIND...
TO PURPOSELY SHORTEN YOUR LIFE IN YOUR HASTE...

!!
D-DON'T TELL ME YOU'RE...?!

SHEEP
未

BOAR
亥

SNAKE
巳

RAT
子

DOG
戌

RABBIT
卯

SNAKE
巳

HORSE
午

BIRD
酉

KO OM
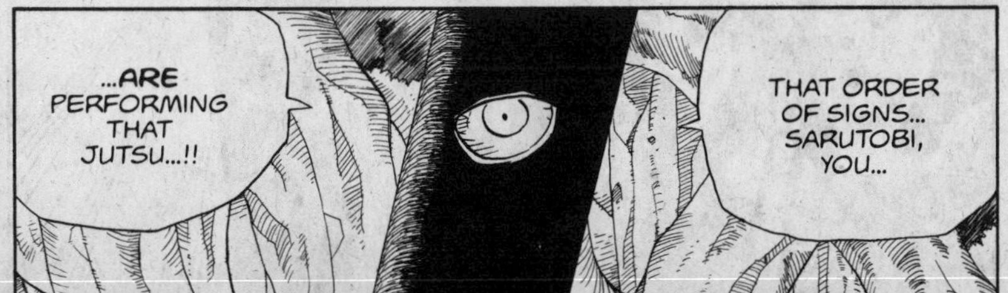
THAT ORDER OF SIGNS... SARUTOBI, YOU...
...ARE PERFORMING THAT JUTSU...!!

BOOM

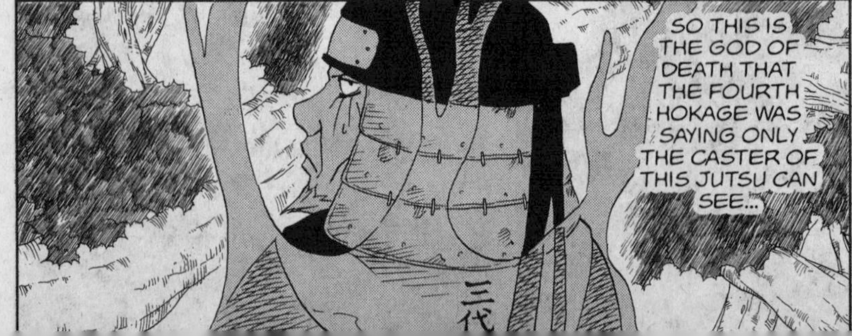
SO THIS IS THE GOD OF DEATH THAT THE FOURTH HOKAGE WAS SAYING ONLY THE CASTER OF THIS JUTSU CAN SEE...
三代

NO MATTER WHAT YOU TRY, IT'S TOO LATE... I HAVE WON.
KONOHA WILL FALL!

THE VILLAGE OF KONOHA IS MY HOME!
AS HOKAGE, THE CENTRAL PILLAR OF KONOHA, I AM SOLELY RESPONSIBLE FOR THE DEFENSE OF THIS VILLAGE.
AS THE ONE WHO INHERITS AND IS ENTRUSTED WITH KONOHA'S WILL... I WILL NOT GO DOWN SO EASILY!

GENJUTSU!
KOKUANGYÔ NO JUTSU! THE ART OF INFINITE DARKNESS!

SHOOM
!

EVEN YOUR MOUNTAINSIDE IMAGE WILL EVENTUALLY WEAR AWAY AND BE OBLITERATED.

!!

THOOM

UGH!

YOU SPOUT NONSENSE. YOU'RE MERELY ONE LEADER IN A LONG LINE OF MANY FOR ONE LOWLY ORGANIZATION.

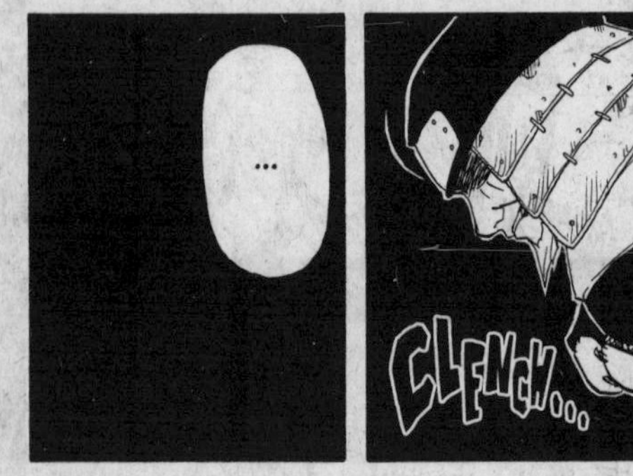

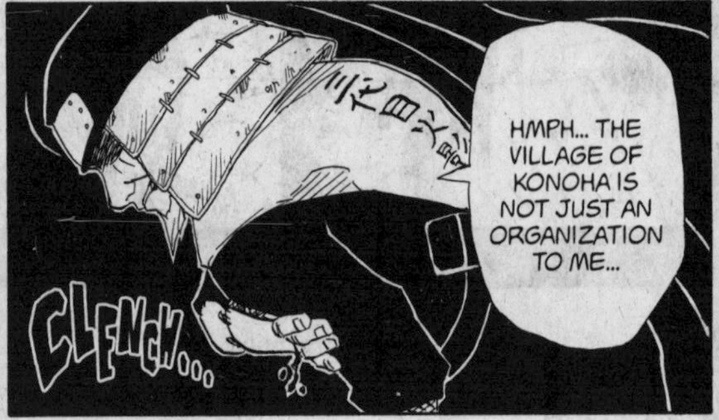

HMPH... THE VILLAGE OF KONOHA IS NOT JUST AN ORGANIZATION TO ME...
CLENCH...

IN KONOHA EVERY YEAR NEW SHINOBI ARE BORN AND RAISED...

THEY LIVE... FIGHT... AND DIE IN ORDER TO PROTECT THE VILLAGE... AND THOSE WITHIN ITS WALLS...

EVERYONE IN THE VILLAGE, EVEN THOUGH WE ARE NOT CONNECTED BY BLOOD...

READ THIS WAY
...IS PRECIOUS TO ME... THEY ARE MY...
...FAMILY!

HEH HEH HEH... THEN I SHALL KNOCK DOWN AND BREAK YOU, THEIR PILLAR...
...AND DESTROY THE HOUSE OF KONOHA.

HMPH! EVEN IF YOU KILL ME, THAT PILLAR SHALL NOT BREAK!!

I INHERITED THE WILL OF THE FIRST LORD, THE SECOND LORD, AND OF KONOHA—

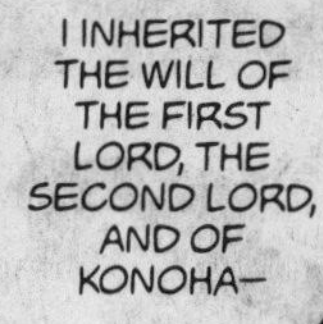

NO MATTER HOW HARD YOU TRY TO DESTROY KONOHA-GAKURE...

I AM THE THIRD HOKAGE!!!

READ THIS WAY

A NEW HOKAGE WHO INHERITS MY WILL SHALL EMERGE AS ITS PILLAR...
...AND DEFEND THE HOUSE OF KONOHA!!

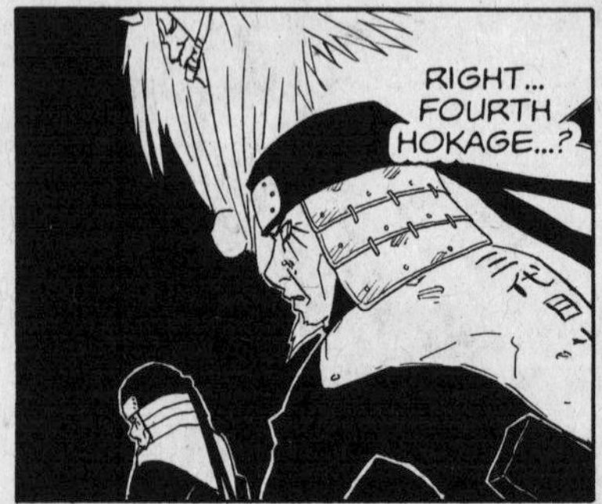
RIGHT... FOURTH HOKAGE...?

OROCHIMARU!! LET ME REVEAL FOR YOU MY TRUMP JUTSU, ONE EVEN YOU DON'T KNOW!
SEALING JUTSU! SHIKIFÛJIN! REAPER DEATH SEAL!!

HEH

Number 123: The Final Seal

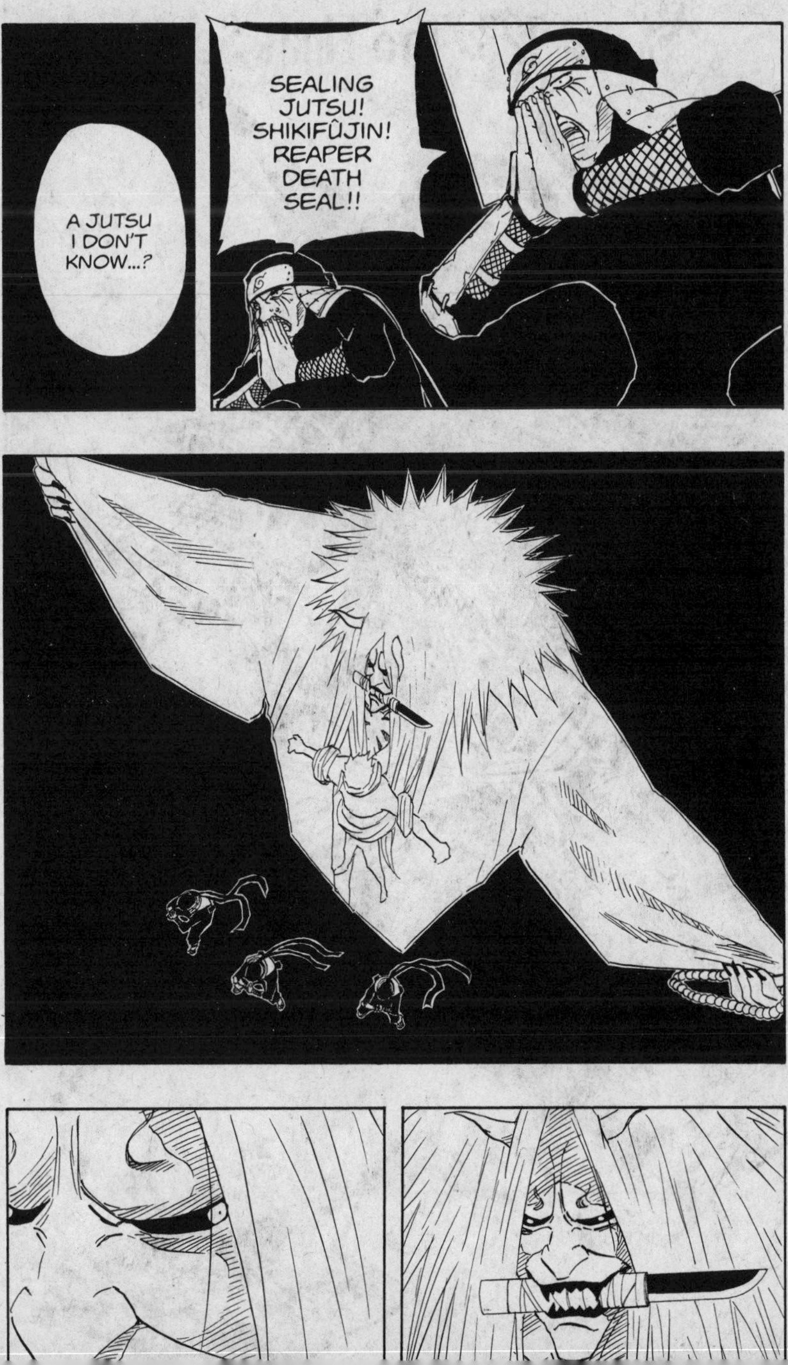

SEALING JUTSU! SHIKIFÛJIN! REAPER DEATH SEAL!!

A JUTSU I DON'T KNOW...?

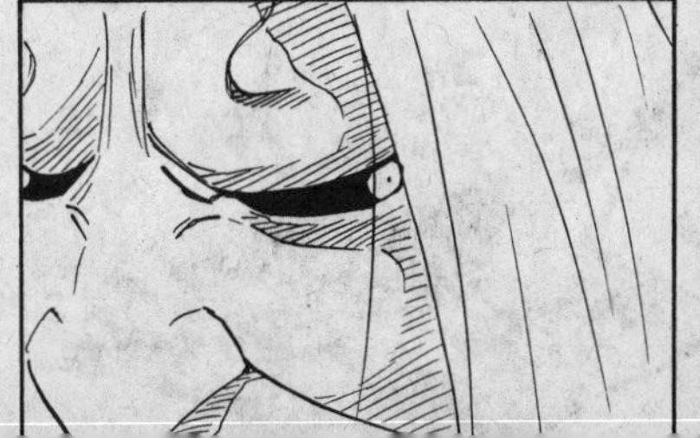

CLACK
I'VE GOT TO HURRY... THIS DARKNESS IS DANGEROUS...
THEN SHOW ME...
...THIS SUPPOSED JUTSU...!
!!
UGH...
KSSH
KSSH
KSH
KSSH
UGH!!
KOOM

BOOSH
!!

WHAT'S THE MATTER? ARE YOU PLANNING TO JUST LET YOUR PREDE-CESSORS PUMMEL YOU TO DEATH?
UGH...
PLEASE HURRY UP AND SHOW ME THIS JUTSU.

HUF
HUF
CLAMP

NOT READY YET ...

READ THIS WAY

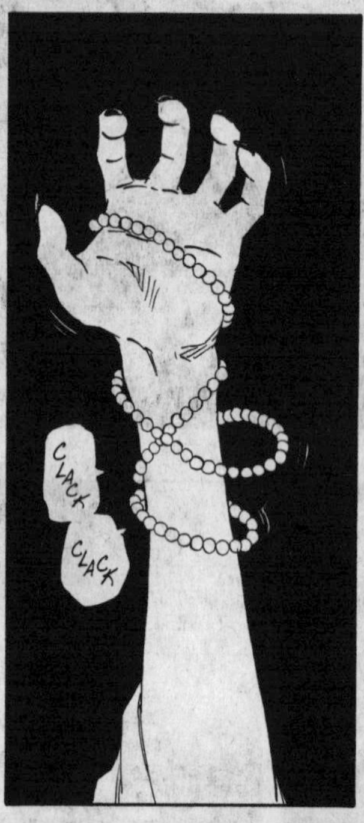
CLACK
CLACK

CLACK

SHNK

GYUUU

URK!
UGH!!

...I MADE IT JUST IN TIME...
HUF
HUF
PLIP
HUF

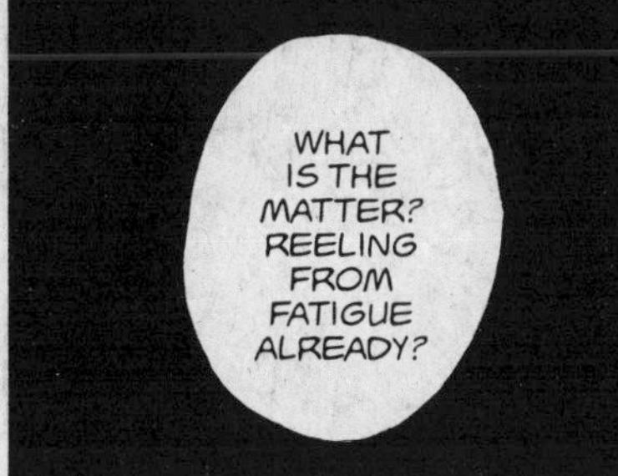
WHAT IS THE MATTER? REELING FROM FATIGUE ALREADY?

UNH... WHAT IS GOING ON IN THERE...?!

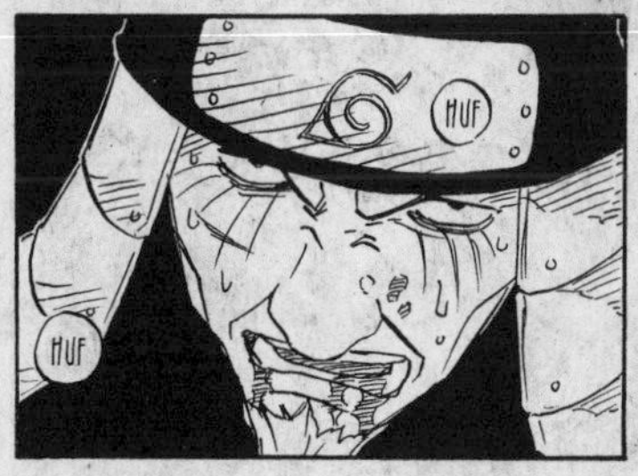
HUF
HUF

DASH

ALL THAT'S LEFT IS TO CAPTURE THEM...!!

TMP

!
SNIFF SNIFF

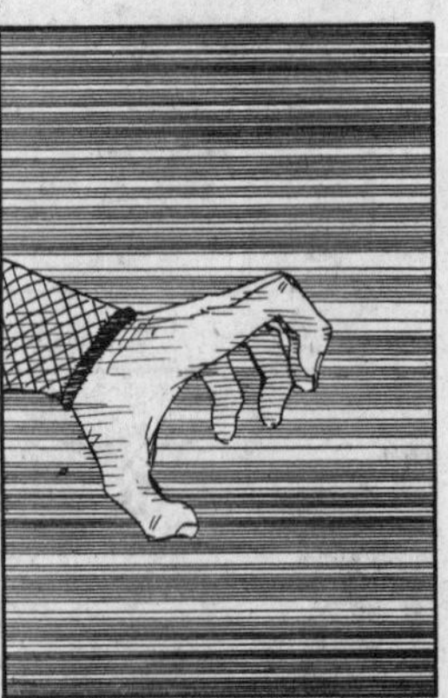

GRAB

GOTCHA!!

HURK

UGH...
...

GRRRMM
I WILL NOT LET GO OF YOU...!!

I SUMMON THEE!

READ THIS WAY

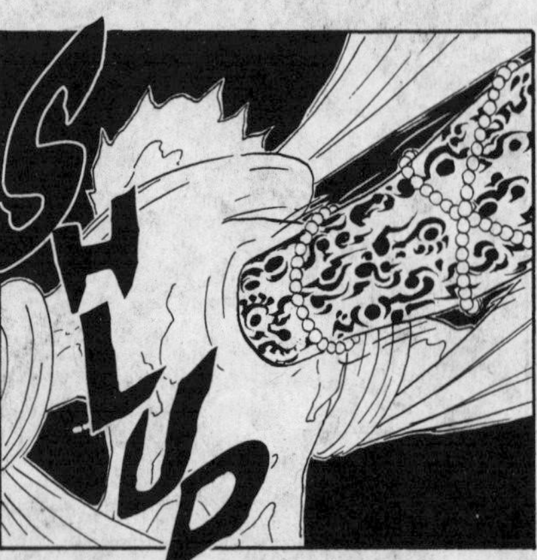
SHLUP

FOOSH
UGH!!

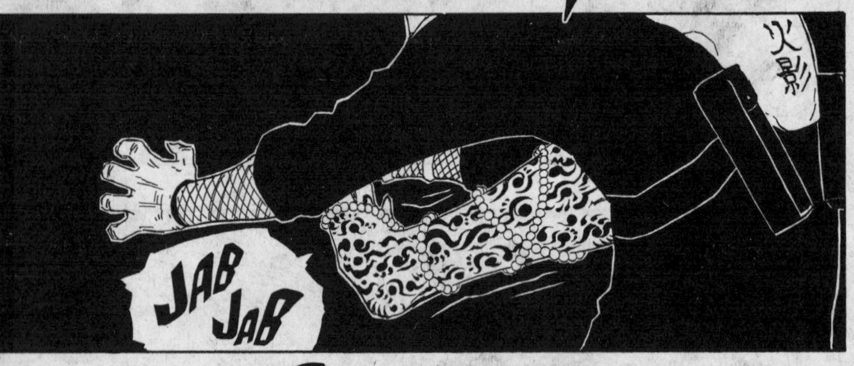
火影
JAB JAB

HUF
HUF
HUF

SLITHER

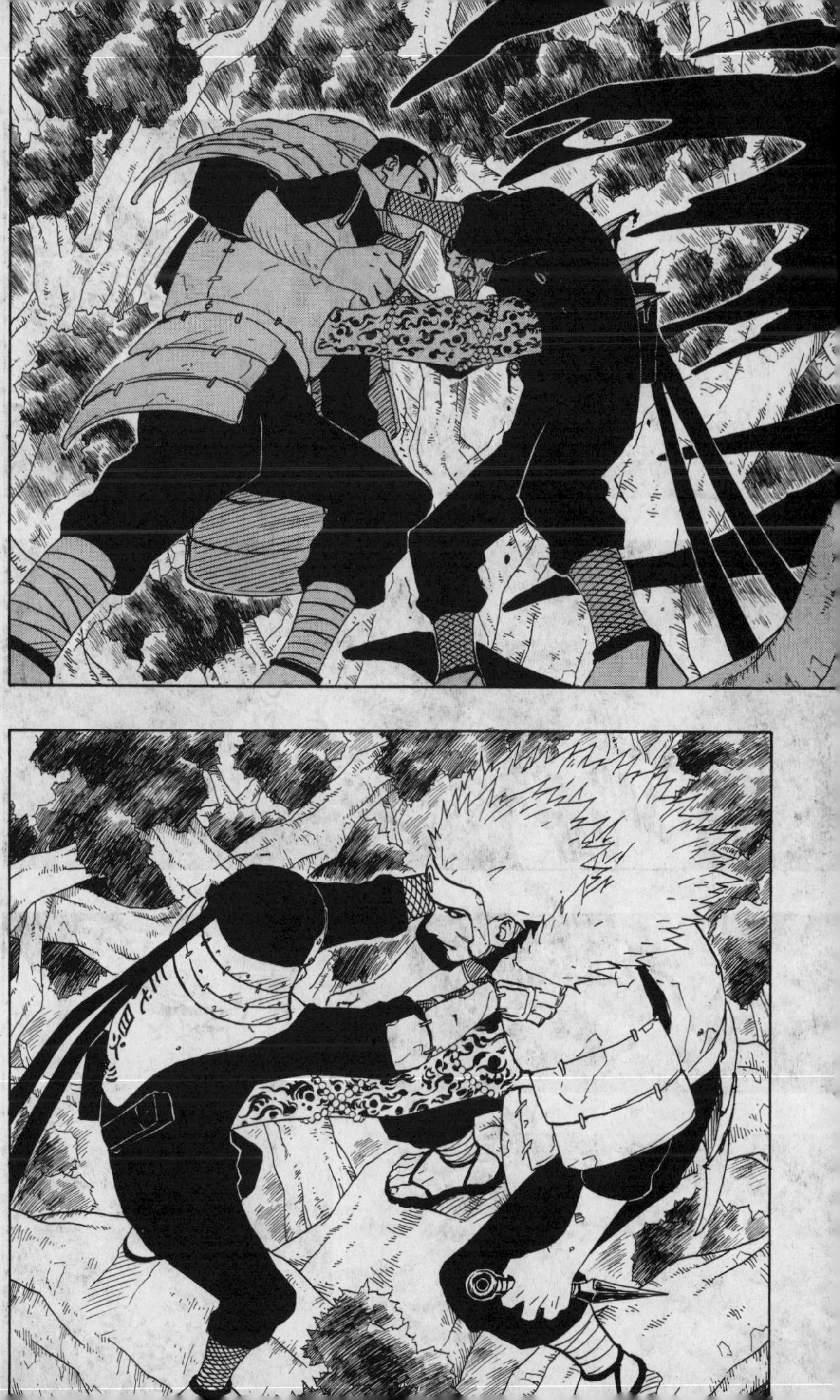

...!!
THE DARKNESS VANISHED. WHAT IS THIS JUTSU?!

SARUTOBI!!

YANK
SO SORRY... SARUTOBI...

FORGIVE US FOR TROUBLING YOU...

PLEASE FORGIVE ME...
FIRST LORD!
SECOND LORD!

SEAL!!
UGH!!
UNH!!

HUF
HUF
HUF
HUF
HUF
HUF

FSSSSH

SKSSSH

WILLFULLY TAKING EVEN YOUR OWN SUBORDINATES' LIVES... MAKING A MOCKERY...

...

EACH AND EVERY KONOHA COMRADE IS A PART OF MY OWN BODY...

THE VILLAGERS BELIEVE IN ME, AND I BELIEVE IN ALL OF THEM... THAT IS WHAT BEING HOKAGE MEANS...!

SARU... YOU MUST LOVE THE VILLAGE AND PROTECT THOSE WHO TRUST IN YOU. AND THEN, YOU MUST NURTURE THEM, THOSE TO WHOM YOU CAN ENTRUST THE FUTURE...
FOR, STARTING TOMORROW, YOU...

...ARE HOKAGE...!!
...MY SUBORDINATES' LIVES? HOW LONG ARE YOU GOING TO KEEP SPOUTING SUCH NONSENSE...?!

READ
THIS
WAY

HUF
HUF
HUF
HUF
HUF
HUF

POOF
POOF
HUF
HUF
HUF

COME!
ENMA!!

SNATCH

FLASH
KACHUNK
BASH
BASH
BASH
BASH

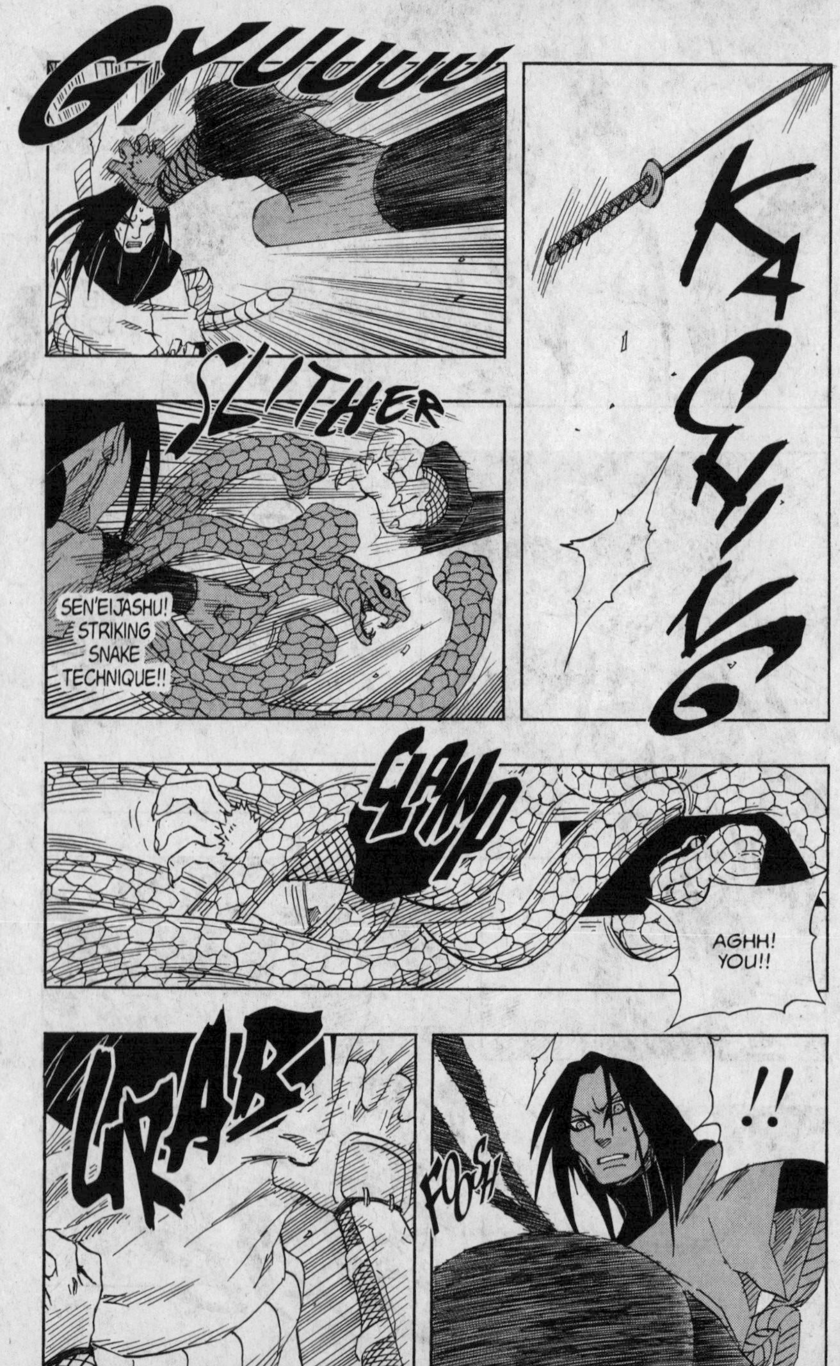
KACHING
GYUUUUU
SLITHER
SEN'EIJASHU! STRIKING SNAKE TECHNIQUE!!
AGHH! YOU!!
CLAMP
!!
FOOSH
GRAB

YANK
THIS IS IT, THE END!!
UNH!

SHUNK

KOSH

!!
JAB

SHUDDER
UGH...
WHAT... IS HAPPENING TO ME...?

UNH... NO...

READ
THIS
WAY

SHA
HYUU
DIE!!
SHOOM
FWASH

THE WORLD OF KISHIMOTO MASASHI
MY PERSONAL HISTORY, PART 20

AROUND THE TIME OF MY THIRD YEAR IN COLLEGE, I STARTED WATCHING MOVIES A LOT. THERE ARE VARIOUS FILM CONCEPTS THAT APPLY TO MANGA, SO THEY ARE GOOD REFERENCES.

PERHAPS BECAUSE OF THAT, I STARTED RENTING VIDEOS MORE AND MORE, UNTIL I WAS WATCHING AT LEAST ONE MOVIE A DAY. EVENTUALLY, EVEN RENTALS WEREN'T ENOUGH, SO I STARTED GOING TO THE THEATER TO WATCH NEW RELEASES. ONE SUCH DAY, I STARTED HEARING RUMORS ABOUT THE BRAD PITT/MORGAN FREEMAN MOVIE "SEVEN." IT WAS A BLOCKBUSTER HIT THAT WAS SECOND IN BOX OFFICE TICKET SALES IN 1996. A PSYCHOLOGICAL THRILLER WHOSE TITULAR THEME REFERS TO THE SEVEN DEADLY SINS, IT RAISED MY EXPECTATIONS QUITE A BIT. "THIS IS A MUST! I'VE GOT TO GET TO THE THEATER!" MY DETERMINATION AND ZEAL KEPT ON CLIMBING! I EVEN DECIDED TO GO TO THE SALON FOR A CUT BECAUSE MY BANGS HAD GROWN SO LONG I WAS AFRAID IT WOULD MAKE IT HARDER TO SEE THE MOVIE SCREEN.

...HOWEVER!! KISHIMOTO WAS NOT YET AWARE AT THIS TIME THAT A FRIGHTFUL INCIDENT WOULD TAKE PLACE AT THAT SALON!!

DUN-DA-DUN-DUN~~~DUN!!!

(I'M GOING TO STRETCH THIS OUT IN TYPICAL MYSTERY/SUSPENSE GENRE FASHION... HURRY ON TO PAGE 138!)

Number 124: The Eternal Battle...!!

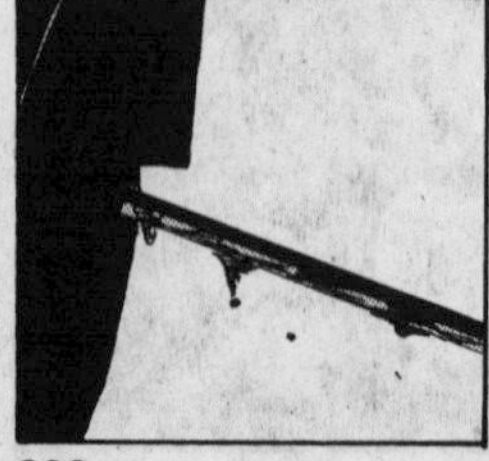

Number 124: The Eternal Battle...!!

READ THIS WAY

UGH...
WHY... DIDN'T YOU EVADE...?!

SSH

NO...!!
DRIP

SSRR

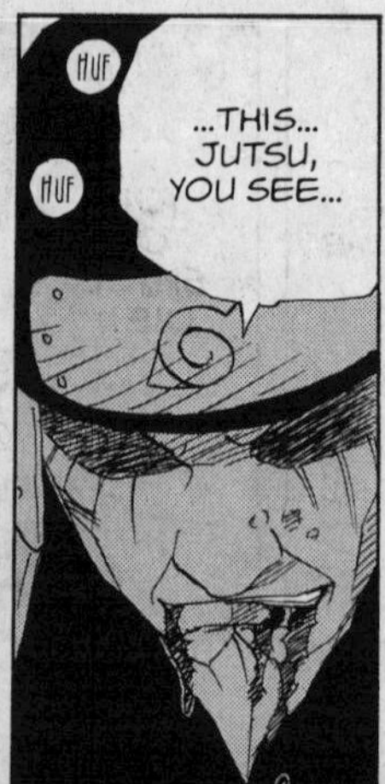
HUF
HUF
...THIS... JUTSU, YOU SEE...

!
UGH... I CAN'T INITIATE... ANY JUTSU...

HUF
HUF
THE CASTER MUST HAND OVER THEIR SOUL TO THE GOD OF DEATH FOR THE JUTSU TO WORK...
IT'S A SEALING JUTSU. IT REQUIRES THE COMPLETE SACRIFICE OF ONE'S LIFE.
HUF
THAT'S WHY I DIDN'T EVADE YOUR BLADE...
I'M GOING TO DIE ANYWAY!!

UNH...
AS SOON AS THE SEAL IS COMPLETED, MY SOUL WILL BE DEVOURED.

...THIS JUTSU BELONGED TO THE HERO WHO ONCE SAVED THIS VILLAGE.
...AND THROUGH THIS JUTSU...

YOU TOO SHALL DIE!!

SO THIS IS WHAT WAS USED...
...TO SEAL THE NINE-TAILED FOX, EH...!!

READ THIS WAY

I CAN'T MOVE...
...!!

INDEED... I SHALL PULL YOUR SOUL OUT OF YOUR BODY...
AND BIND IT...!

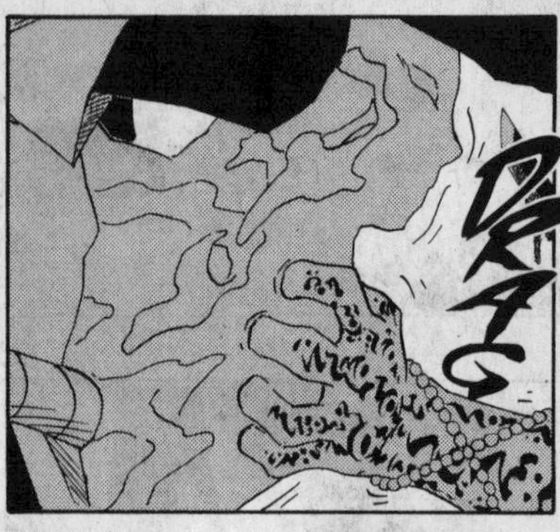
DRAG

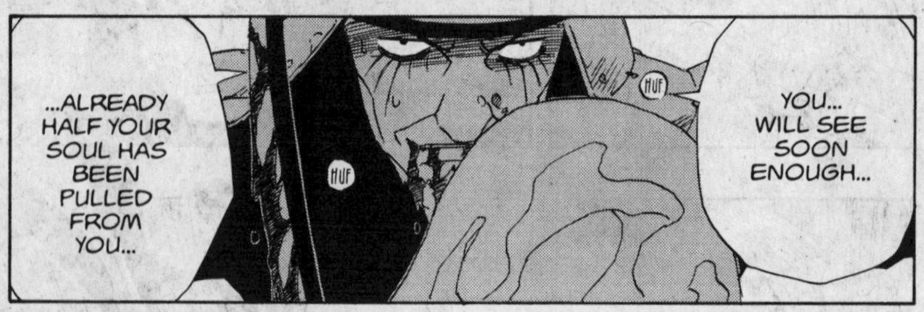
YOU... WILL SEE SOON ENOUGH...
HUF
HUF
...ALREADY HALF YOUR SOUL HAS BEEN PULLED FROM YOU...

THOSE SOULS BOUND... USING THIS JUTSU... WILL NEVER REST IN PEACE...
BUT SUFFER FOR ETERNITY INSIDE THE BELLY OF THE GOD OF DEATH...
BOTH THE CASTER AND THE SEALED...
...THEIR SOULS SHALL TANGLE AND BATTLE EACH OTHER WITH DEEP HATRED FOREVER...

TAK
WHAT...?!!
HOWL

HOWL
SKRCH
RAAAH!!!
CHOMP
THAT'S... THE GOD OF DEATH...?!
ROAR
GNAW GNAW
NO!!
YOU DO NOT GET YOUR WAY... OLD MAN!

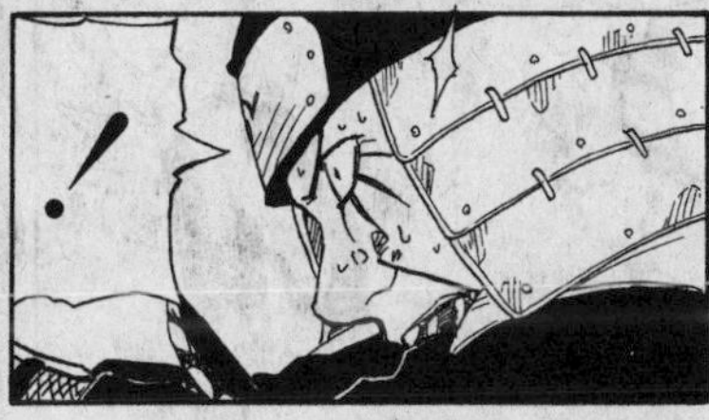
!

FWIP

DRAG

HUF
NOW...
DIE...
HUF

HUF
HUF
HACK

BOOM
いさお屋
佐々木屋
佐

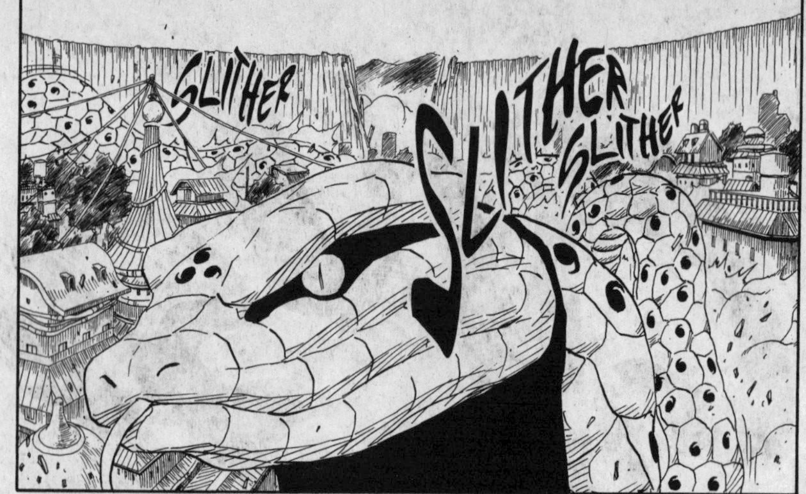
SLITHER
SLITHER
SLITHER

ZOOM

HISS

!!

NINJA ART: KUCHIYOSE! SUMMONING!! YATAIKUZUSHI NO JUTSU! MAYHEM TECHNIQUE!!

GRRR.. THIS IS OUT OF CONTROL !!

READ THIS WAY

HACK

SLAM

VOOSH
THIS... JUTSU...!!

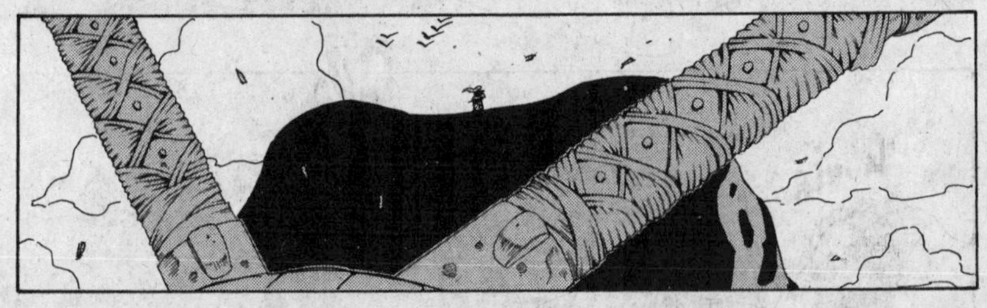

IBIKI... LONG TIME NO SEE...!
SHEESH! IS THAT HULKING BULK OF YOURS THE ONLY THING THAT'S MATURED?! I COULDN'T JUST KEEP WATCHING!

...LORD JIRAIYA...!
"LORD JIRAIYA"...?! YOU MEAN HE OF THE THREE GREAT SHINOBI!?

YOU BABY CHICKS!! OPEN WIDE THOSE BEADY LITTLE EYES OF YOURS AND WATCH CLOSELY!!

THANK THE HEAVENS!!

HERE COMES THE UNORTHODOX NINJA SAGE JIRAIYA! HERE TO RUN AMOK AMONG ALL THE OTHER-WORLDLY CREATURES!!

QUIVER

QUIVER

READ
THIS
WAY

SO IT HAS BEGUN, EH... OROCHIMARU...

SHWF

WHERE'S THE THIRD LORD?

THE EXAMINATION ARENA, SIR!

...I SEE.

...DON'T YOU DARE DIE...!
...OLD MAN.

!

RACE

!!
TAP

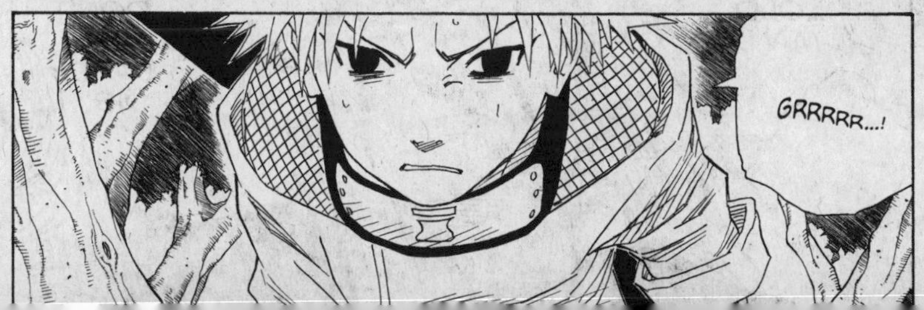
GRRRRR...!

HUF
YOU'RE NOT GETTING AWAY!
HUF

!!
SASUKE'S STOPPED MOVING...
HE'S STILL TOO FAR AWAY...!

!
!

ALL RIGHT!!

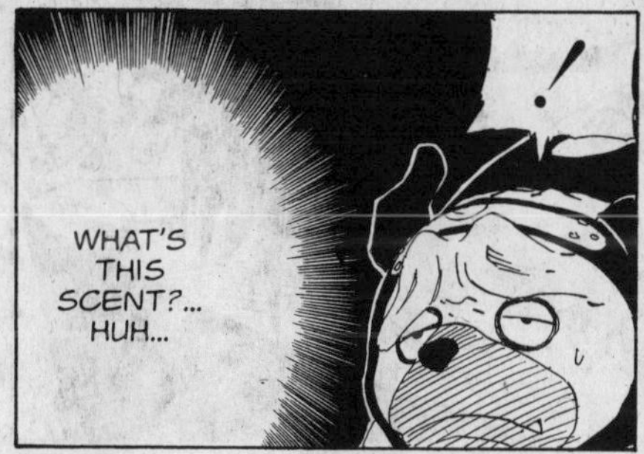
!
WHAT'S THIS SCENT?... HUH...

COMRADES, THERE ARE OTHERS PURSUING SASUKE ALSO!

WHAT?!
ARE THEY FRIENDS?! FOES?!

...I CAN'T TELL...
JUST THAT...

THEY'RE NOT HUMAN!

?!

!

SHF
TEMARI, TAKE GAARA AND GO ON AHEAD!

ALL RIGHT...

...

BOING
I SUPPOSE WE HAVE NO CHOICE... I'LL TAKE YOU ON!

NO...! I WILL BE YOUR OPPONENT...!
!

FOOSH

YOU'RE...

SHINO
...
WHAT ARE YOU DOING HERE?!

JAB

READ THIS WAY

BEFORE YOU LEFT THE ARENA, I HAD MY BEETLES MARK YOU WITH A FEMALE SCENT.
SCUTTLE SCUTTLE
SCUTTLE
EVEN THOUGH IT IS ALMOST ODORLESS...
...THE MALE OF THE SAME SPECIES CAN STILL DETECT IT...
SCUTTLE
SCUTTLE

...UGH...!

UCHIHA SASUKE... CHASE AFTER GAARA...
YOU HAVEN'T COMPLETED YOUR MATCH AGAINST HIM YET.
I'LL FIGHT THIS ONE...
...ESPECIALLY SINCE I WAS SUPPOSED TO HAVE BEEN HIS OPPONENT IN THE FIRST PLACE.

HUMPH...

THE WORLD OF KISHIMOTO MASASHI
MY PERSONAL HISTORY, PART 20 (CONTINUED)

I WENT TO THE SALON TO GET MY BANGS TRIMMED, SO I SAT IN THE HAIRCUT SEAT. MY HEAD WAS FULL OF... "I'M GOING TO GO SEE *SEVEN* TOMORROW--! I WONDER WHAT THE SEVEN DEADLY SINS ARE--?! THE DIRECTOR IS DAVID FINCHER, SO I BET THE FRIGHT SCENES ARE GOING TO BE PRETTY AMAZING! WITH MORGAN FREEMAN AS THE VETERAN DETECTIVE AND BRAD PITT AS THE GREEN YOUNG DETECTIVE, WHAT A FANTASTIC TEAM! I HEARD IT HAS AN UNEXPECTED ENDING, A SUDDEN REVERSAL, BUT I WONDER WHAT IT IS..." I WAS ALL EXCITED. AND JUST AS THEY STARTED CUTTING MY HAIR, SOME WOMAN CAME IN FOR A HAIRCUT AND SAT DOWN IN THE NEXT CHAIR OVER. THIS WOMAN STARTED UP A FRIENDLY CHAT WITH HER STYLIST, BRAGGING, "I WENT ON A DATE YESTERDAY." I HAD NOTHING TO TALK ABOUT WITH MY STYLIST, SO I WAS SILENT AND PRETENDED TO BE ASLEEP. TO MY DISGUST, THE LOUDMOUTHED WOMAN NEXT TO ME STARTED GOING INTO DETAILS ABOUT HER DATE. "GRODY~" I THOUGHT TO MYSELF, BUT... BECAUSE HER VOICE WAS SO LOUD, I ENDED UP HEARING HER BRAGGING TALE WHETHER I WANTED TO OR NOT. SUDDENLY, SHE STARTED SAYING SHE HAD GONE TO THE MOVIES WITH THIS GUY, AND THAT THE FILM THEY HAD SEEN WAS THE CURRENTLY POPULAR *SEVEN*.

JUST AS I WAS THINKING TO MYSELF "I'M GOING TO GO SEE IT TOO, TOMORROW...", OH NO! THAT CHATTERBOX GIRL STARTED DESCRIBING THE PLOT OF *SEVEN*!! NEEDLESS TO SAY, SHE WAS LOUD!! I WANTED TO COVER MY EARS, BUT MY HANDS WERE UNDER THE CAPE BECAUSE I WAS GETTING MY HAIR CUT...!! AND SO, IN THAT MOMENT, I BEGGED THAT WOMAN...

"PLEASE! THE CLINCHER... JUST DON'T SPILL THE CLINCHER, PLEASE~~~~~!!!"

"AND WHAT WAS INSIDE THAT BOX. CAN YOU BELIEVE IT... IT WAS THE HEAD OF BRAD PITT'S WIFE--! AND THEN--!"

...SHE HAD SPILLED IT...

THE NEXT DAY, I DECIDED NOT TO GO SEE *SEVEN*... (I CAN JUST RENT THE VIDEO... ESPECIALLY NOW THAT I KNOW THE WHOLE STORY...) FURTHERMORE, THEY HAD CUT MY BANGS TOO MUCH AND I ENDED UP LOOKING LIKE A BUSINESSMAN.

Number 125:
The Time of Awakening...!!

LEAVE HIM TO ME.
GO!

UNH...

...YOU SOUND PRETTY CONFIDENT, BUT...
ARE YOU SURE ABOUT THIS?

I DON'T NEED YOUR CONCERN...
GIVE ME 10 MINUTES, AND I'LL COME HELP YOU.

READ THIS WAY

HUMPH... I'LL BE DONE BY THEN TOO.
TURN

YOU'RE ALL IGNORANT FOOLS!

YOU ALL... HAVE NO CLUE WHAT TRUE TERROR IS...
EH...

YOU'RE GOING TO TEACH ME WHAT THAT TERROR IS?
AND YOU...
ZZF
ZZF

READ THIS WAY

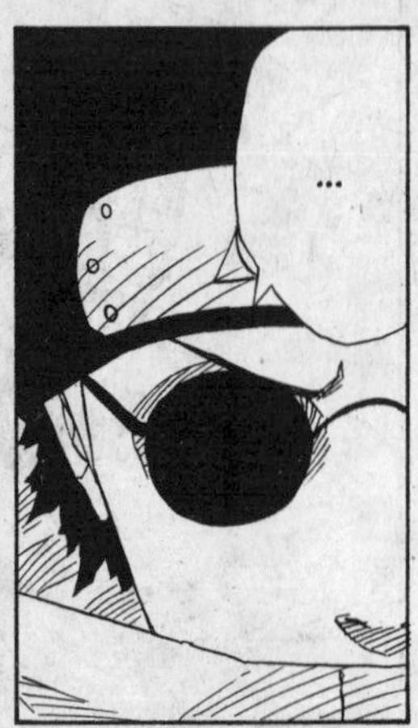

SWARM

RUSTLE

SCUTTLE SCUTTLE...

SWARM
CLIK CLIK CLIK
CREAK CRIK CRIK CRIK

READ THIS WAY

I AM A MEMBER OF KONOHA'S ABURAME CLAN...
WHEN WE FIGHT, NO MATTER HOW PUNY A BUG OUR OPPONENT IS, WE DON'T MOCK THEM... WE FACE THEM FULL STRENGTH!
HEH... THEN COME ON!

...LET ME DOWN... TEMARI...
YOU'VE COME TO, GAARA!?

TAP
TAP

UGH!
JERK

...
IT'S... BEEN AWAKE INSIDE GAARA SINCE EARLIER...!
I DON'T KNOW WHEN IT'S GOING TO EMERGE...

THIS IS BAD... IT'S JUST ME RIGHT NOW...
I CAN'T HANDLE IT BY MYSELF...

!

JUST HURRY UP AND GET OUT OF HERE!

YOU'RE IN THE WAY!

SWAP

GRUNT!

HUF
HUF
HUF

READ THIS WAY

THROB
UNH...

...I DON'T KNOW WHAT YOU SAND FELLAS ARE PLOTTING, BUT...
YOU, I'M GOING TO STOP!

UGH...

WEAVE...
!
THAT'S... UCHIHA SASUKE... WHAT'S GOING ON?!

WHERE'S KANKURO...?!

BESIDES...

I WANT TO SEE WHAT YOU REALLY ARE...

GRRRR

WHAT IS YOUR MOTIVE?

WHY DO YOU SEEK STRENGTH?

READ THIS WAY
...
...
...
...
NONE OF YOUR BUSINESS...
GET LOST... YOU'RE IN THE WAY OF MY TRAINING!!
SHUMP

YOU'VE GOT EYES JUST LIKE MINE...

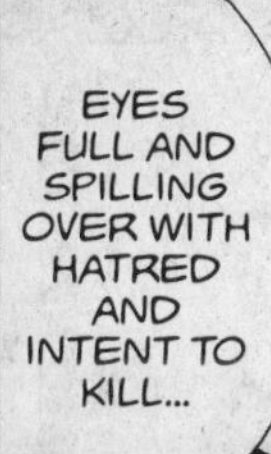
EYES FULL AND SPILLING OVER WITH HATRED AND INTENT TO KILL...

YOU'RE LIKE ME...

DO NOT FORGET THAT...
YOU'RE MY PREY.

PANT
PANT

HUF
HUF
YOU WHO ARE STRONG... WHO ARE CALLED UCHIHA... WHO HAVE FRIENDS...
AND HAVE A PURPOSE... JUST... LIKE ME...

BY KILLING YOU...
I'LL ERASE ALL OF THAT...
AND THEN I WILL TRULY EXIST...
PULSE

AND I CAN FEEL ALIVE!!
PULSE

READ
THIS
WAY

...!!

...UGH...!
THUNK
THUNK

!

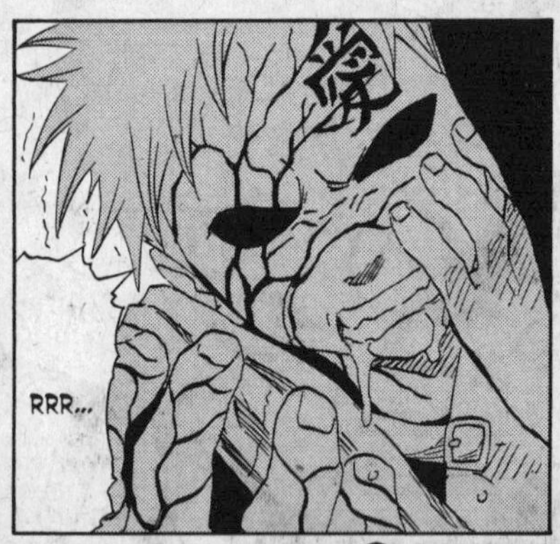
RRR...

...!!

THROB
AARGH-
ROWL...

GRR...

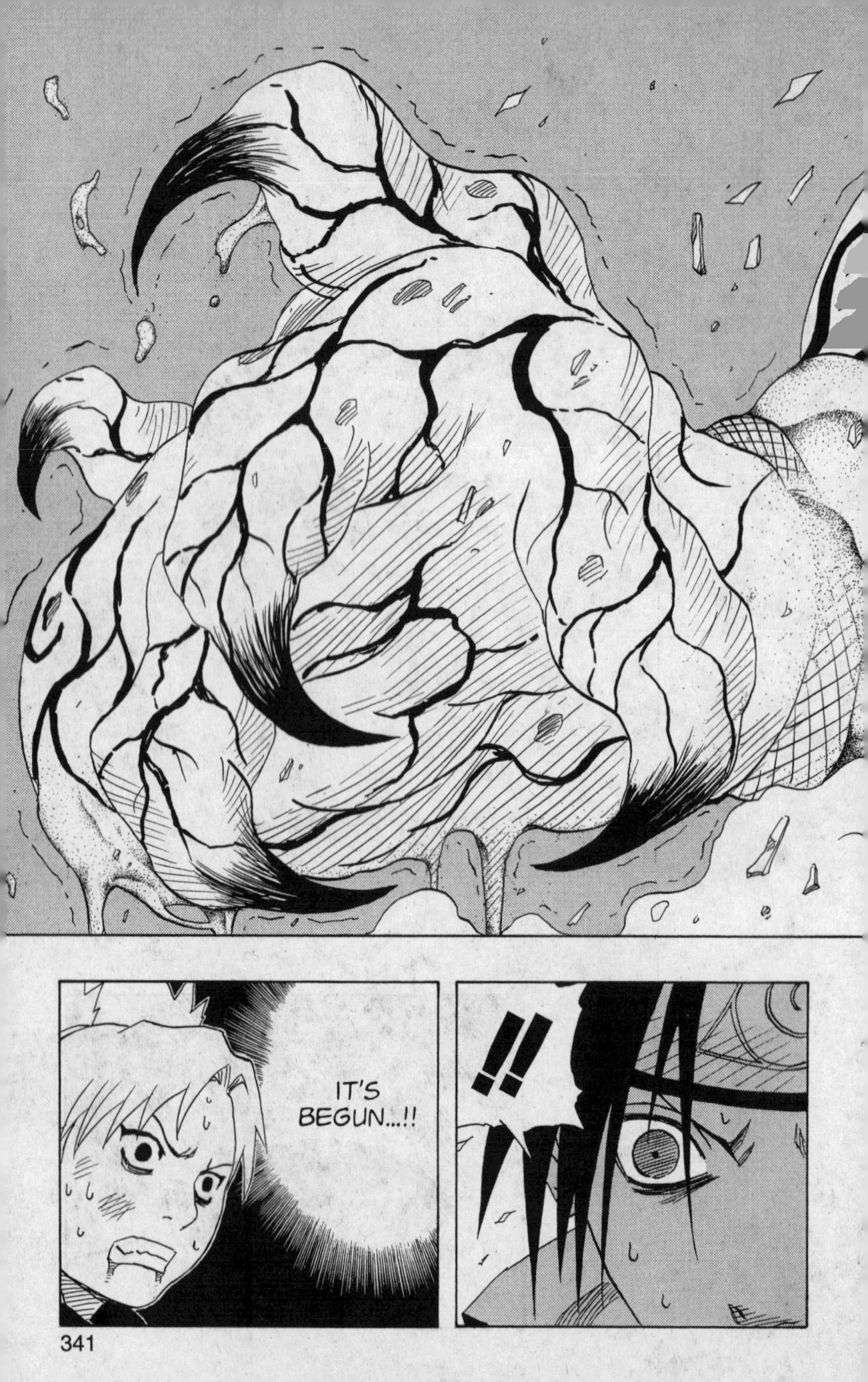

!!

IT'S BEGUN...!!

BURBLE
BUBBLE
HUF
HUF
HUF
GRR...

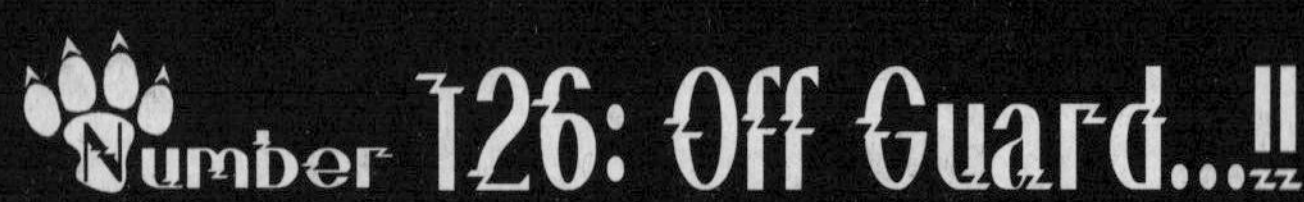

Number 126: Off Guard...!!

SHINO...
...I DON'T THINK I'LL BE FINISHED BEFORE YOU COME TO HELP ME, AFTER ALL...

CLACK

BOOOOM
KSSH
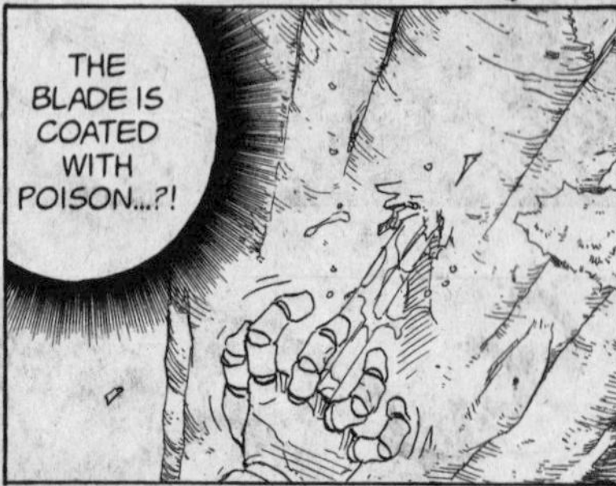
THE BLADE IS COATED WITH POISON...?!

!
CLOP

TWEAK

SPRING
SPRING

THOCK
THOCK

READ THIS WAY

!

SWOOOSH
!

...

GOOD MOVE, MAKING A DOPPELGANGER USING YOUR BEETLES...
AND THEN CIRCLING BEHIND ME!
SPROO
YOU'RE A PUPPET-USING MID- TO LONG-DISTANCE FIGHTING TYPE.
I JUDGED YOU TO BE WEAK AT CLOSE-RANGE BATTLES.
THAT PUPPET MASTER TECHNIQUE OF YOURS REQUIRES YOU TO CONCENTRATE ON OPERATING THE PUPPET...
...MAKING IT EASIER FOR OPENINGS TO BE FOUND IN THE MASTER'S DEFENSES...

YOU'RE PRETTY SMART...! KNOWING A PUPPET MASTER'S WEAK POINT!
HOWEVER, I'M NOW GOING TO SHOW YOU THE FUNDAMENTAL BATTLE TECHNIQUES USING THIS NINJUTSU!
NOW YOU'LL SEE WHAT KARASU CAN REALLY DO!
CLOP
!
BLAM
ZWOOSH
BOOF

!
...THIS IS A POISON SMOKE BOMB...!!

POP
I'VE INHALED A BIT...

I SEE... AND THE CASTER HAS NOW HIDDEN HIMSELF, HUH...

REEEE

CLACK
...

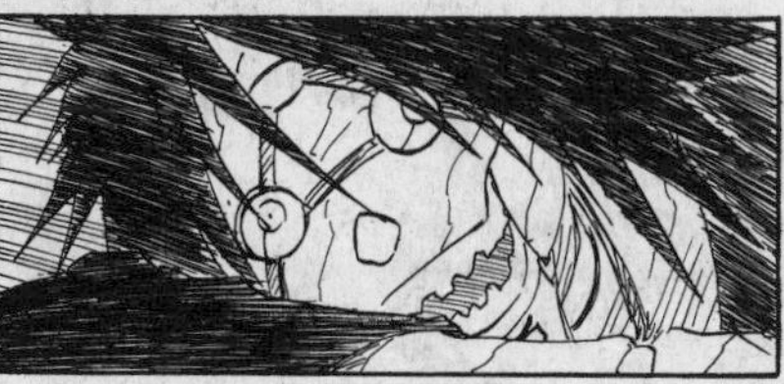

ZGASH

FWIP
FWIP

SKKRAPE

HACK

HUF
HUF

TREMBLE
TREMBLE

THIS CAN'T BE IT... I'VE COME SO FAR...?
...
HUF

...ARE YOU SAYING... I DON'T EVEN HAVE ENOUGH STRENGTH...
...TO PULL OUT HIS SOUL...?

THAT THIS AGED BODY... IS TOO DECREPIT, EVEN THOUGH I HAVE RESOLVED TO DIE...?!

IF YOU HAD BEEN EVEN JUST 10 YEARS YOUNGER... YOU MIGHT HAVE BEEN ABLE TO KILL ME... HEH HEH...

SHUFFLE
SHUFFLE

LISTEN UP...
ALL OF YOU, EVEN IF ENEMY SHINOBI SHOW UP, DO NOT PANIC. JUST KEEP PROCEEDING QUICKLY TO THE INNER SHELTERS!
SHF
YOUR JÔNIN AND CHÛNIN INSTRUCTORS WILL PROTECT YOU, EVEN AT THE COST OF OUR OWN LIVES!!

HUNH?!

!!

CRACK!!

A FISSURE SPLITTING ACROSS THE THIRD HOKAGE'S STONE PORTRAIT...
...HOW OMINOUS...

...GRANDPA...

READ THIS WAY

CREEEEEEAK

UGH... I CAN'T MOVE HIM... THAT FELLOW MUST HAVE PACKED HIS BEETLES INTO KARASU'S JOINTS...
TREMBLE
TREMBLE

CREEEAK

SCUTTLE

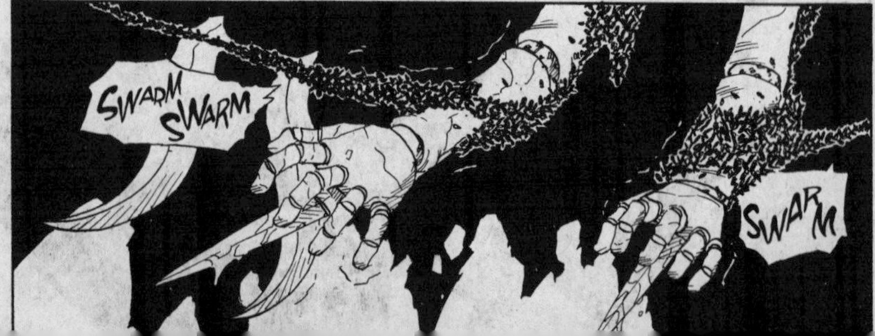
SWARM SWARM
SWARM

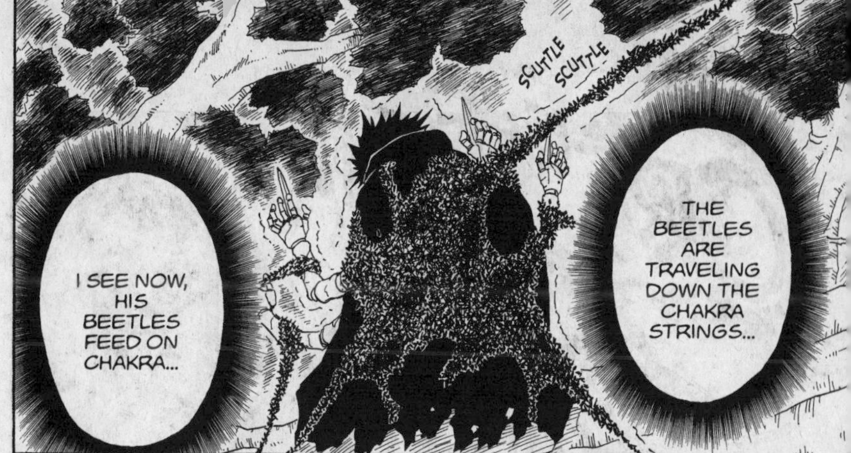
SCUTTLE SCUTTLE
THE BEETLES ARE TRAVELING DOWN THE CHAKRA STRINGS...
I SEE NOW, HIS BEETLES FEED ON CHAKRA...

UGH... AT THIS RATE, MY LOCATION WILL BE REVEALED...!
SNIP
SNIP

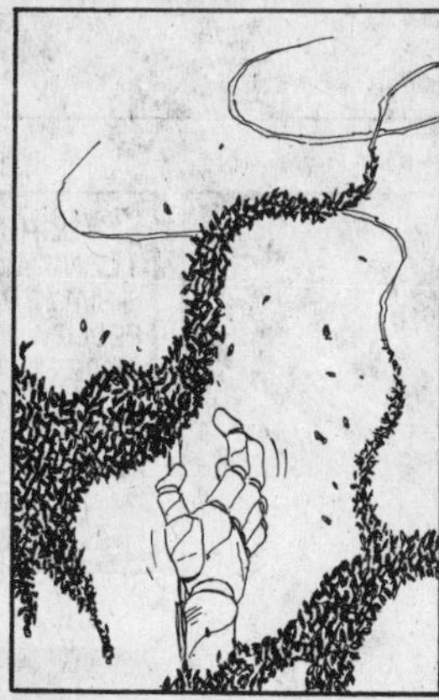

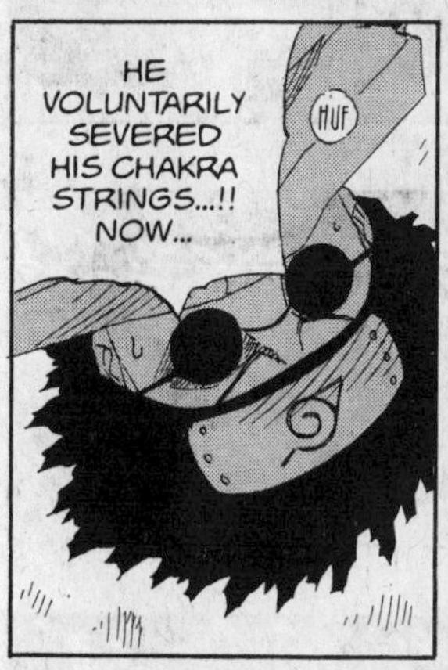
HE VOLUNTARILY SEVERED HIS CHAKRA STRINGS...!! NOW...
HUF

POP

WHAT THE...?!! HOW... WHERE DID ALL THESE BEETLES COME FROM...?!!
SWARM

HUF
HUF
YOU'RE THE ONE WHO DROPPED HIS GUARD... THE BEETLES CRAWLING DOWN YOUR CHAKRA STRINGS WERE DECOYS SO THAT YOU DIDN'T SEE THE OTHERS CREEPING UP BEHIND YOU...
THEY'VE BEEN ON THE MOVE THIS WHOLE TIME... AIMING FOR YOUR HEADBAND...

...WH- ...WHAT?!
SCUTTLE
SCUTTLE

THAT FIRST SWING I TOOK AT YOU... YOU THOUGHT I MISSED...
HUF
HUF
BUT I WAS ATTACHING A BEETLE TO YOU...

BUT... HOW WERE YOU ABLE TO TELL MY LOCATION FROM JUST THIS ONE BUG...?
I HATE EXPLAINING THE SAME THING OVER AND OVER.

SWOOOOSH
!

READ THIS WAY

FAP

READ THIS WAY

!
HUF
HUF

HEH... CAUGHT YOU OFF GUARD! IT'S MERE CHILD'S PLAY FOR A FIRST-RATE PUPPET MASTER TO REATTACH SEVERED CHAKRA STRINGS.
... EACH AND EVERY PART OF HIS BODY FROM HEAD TO TOE... HAVE WEAPONS CONCEALED WITHIN THEM--HE'S A RIGGED PUPPET!!
TWEAK

CLOP
KAKLINK

THE NEEDLE'S COATED WITH POISON...

DIE!!
WHOOM

!!
HUF

READ THIS WAY

!!
...DON'T TELL ME...
SCUTTLE
SCUTTLE
SCUTTLE
BEFORE YOU LEFT THE ARENA, I HAD MY BEETLES MARK YOU WITH A FEMALE SCENT.
EVEN THOUGH IT IS ALMOST ODORLESS...
...THE MALE OF THE SAME SPECIES CAN STILL DETECT IT...
SCUTTLE
SCUTTLE

THEN... THIS BEETLE ON MY HEADBAND...

THAT'S RIGHT...
SHE'S A FEMALE...

BUCKLE

IT'S THE POISON FROM THE SMOKE BOMB...
...IT LOOKS LIKE I WON'T BE ABLE TO GO HELP YOU... SORRY...
SLUMP

...UCHIHA SASUKE...!!

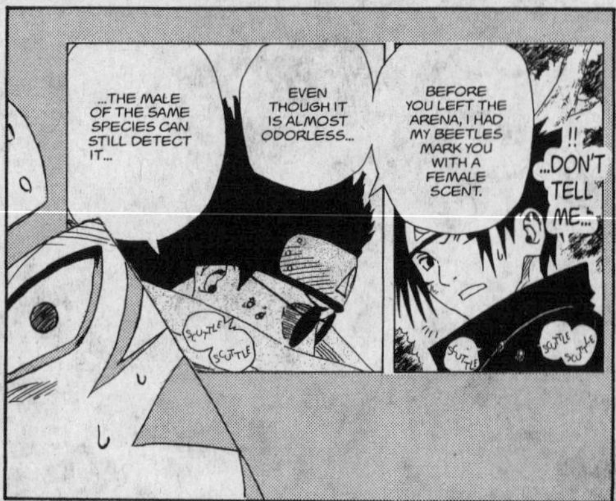

NARUTO

岸本斉史

I'm starting to run out of things to write for this "Author's Comments" section...
Since going to the movies is practically my only hobby, I guess I'll write about movies...
Hmm. Some movies I've seen recently are...
...Oh man! I've been so busy recently that I haven't gone to the movies--!!
I want to see movies...

—Masashi Kishimoto, 2002

NARUTO

SHONEN JUMP MANGA

STORY AND ART BY
MASASHI KISHIMOTO

CHARACTERS

Sasuke サスケ

Naruto ナルト

Guy ガイ

Sakura サクラ

Neji ネジ

Rock Lee ロック・リー

Tenten テンテン

Shikamaru シカマル

Kiba & キバ&

Akamaru 赤丸

Hinata ヒナタ

Gamabunta ガマブン太

Ino いの

Choji チョウジ

Shino シノ

The Story So Far…

Twelve years ago a destructive nine-tailed fox spirit attacked the ninja village of Konohagakure. The Hokage, or village champion, defeated the fox by sealing its soul into the body of a baby boy. Now that boy, Uzumaki Naruto, has grown up to be a ninja-in-training, learning the art of ninjutsu with his teammates Sakura and Sasuke.

Naruto and company take on the Chûnin Selection Exams but suffer a sudden attack from Orochimaru in the Forest of Death. Orochimaru leaves a curse mark on Sasuke's body and vanishes…

Then, during the finals of the Chûnin Exams, Orochimaru, disguised as Kazekage, takes the Hokage hostage and erects a barrier shield. *Operation Destroy Konoha* is under way as Naruto chases after Sasuke and Gaara, who have both disappeared.

NARUTO

VOL. 15

NARUTO'S NINJA HANDBOOK!

CONTENTS

Number 127: To Feel Alive...!!

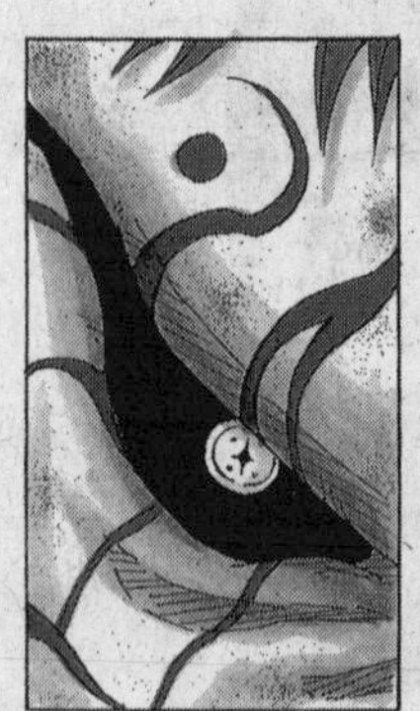

UZUMAKI NARUTO
UCHIHA SASUKE

GAARA OF THE SAND
Number 127:
To Feel Alive...!!

NARUTO
-ナルト-

SHUDDER
...IT'S THE SAME EYE...
...AS EARLIER...!!

QUIVER
QUIVER

CROUCH

!!

RRRROAR!!

愛

KABOOM

SPLINTER
ROCK

...HE... REALLY IS A MONSTER ...
HWOO HWUFFF

DO YOU FEAR ME?
愛

UCHIHA... SASUKE!

...

DO NOT FORGET ...

YOU ARE MY PREY.

...WAIT!

!

WHY... ARE YOU OUT TO GET ME?

YOU'VE GOT EYES THAT KNOW REAL ISOLATION...
!!
...
...AND...
...EYES THAT RECOGNIZE IT AS THE GREATEST PAIN IN THIS WORLD...

READ THIS WAY

I THOUGHT I TOLD YOU. YOU HAVE EYES LIKE MINE...
...EYES SEEKING STRENGTH, SPILLING OVER WITH HATRED AND INTENT TO KILL...

JUST LIKE ME...
...EYES ITCHING TO KILL THOSE WHO DROVE YOU INTO THE TORTURE CALLED SOLITUDE...
...

THAT'S IT, THOSE ARE THE EYES...
ALL RIGHT, HOLD IT RIGHT THERE...
GAARA, RIGHT...?
!
...!
I DON'T KNOW HOW YOU THINK YOU KNOW ALL ABOUT SASUKE, BUT...
...YOU SHOULDN'T TALK LIKE YOU'VE SEEN THROUGH HIM ENTIRELY.
NOW, WHAT IN THE WORLD DID YOU WANT TO SAY TO HIM, TRACKING HIM ALL THE WAY DOWN HERE BEFORE THE FINALS?
...!
A BATTLE IS A GAMBLE...
...WHERE ONE PITS ONE'S EXISTENCE AGAINST ANOTHER'S...

READ THIS WAY

AND YOU TRY TO KILL EACH OTHER...

AND WHERE ONLY THE VICTOR GETS TO SAVOR THE WORTH OF HIS EXISTENCE.
...IN OTHER WORDS, WHAT YOU'RE SAYING IS...
"LET'S FIGHT A DEATH MATCH" AS OPPOSED TO JUST A MATCH, HMM?

UCHIHA... I KNOW... YOU ACTUALLY DESIRE IT TOO...
DEEP INSIDE YOUR HEART...

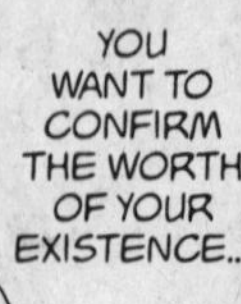
YOU WANT TO CONFIRM THE WORTH OF YOUR EXISTENCE...
YOU'RE WONDERING, "AM I REALLY AS STRONG AS I THOUGHT?"

"AM I TRULY STRONGER THAN THE OPPONENT I FACE WITH THESE HATE-FILLED EYES OF MINE?"

...

WELL, WHAT'S THE MATTER ...?!
ARE YOU AFRAID OF ME?

...

UMF

HAVE BOTH YOUR HATRED AND YOUR INTENT TO KILL... WAVERED BECAUSE OF YOUR FEAR?
IS THIS THE PITIFUL EXTENT OF YOUR EXISTENCE?
愛

IF YOU WANT AN ANSWER...

COME ON!!

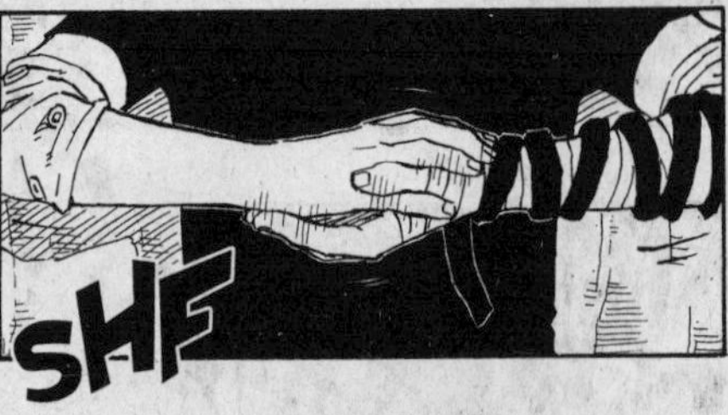

SHF

GRNCH
I WAS LEFT ALIVE...
...INTENTIONALLY... ALL BY MYSELF... FOR WHAT PURPOSE?!

!
CHIRP
CHIRP

CRACKLE
NAH... I KNOW THE REASON...
CRACKLE

CRACKLE CRACKLE
HE LEFT ME ALIVE SO HE WOULDN'T BE TORMENTED BY THE GUILT OF ANNIHI-LATING THE ENTIRE CLAN...

CHIRP CHIRP CHIRP CHIRP CHIRP
BIG BROTHER ITACHI CHOSE ME AS HIS AVENGER...
...AS THE ONE WHO WILL EVENTUALLY DESTROY HIM!

!!

LAUNCH

RRRRRROAR

LAUNCH

AAAARGH!!

...

...!!

TAP
THUMP

...?!

A-HA...
A-HA HA HA HA HA HA HA HA HA!
愛

Number 128:
Exceeding One's Limits...!!
SASUKE

A-HA HA HA HA HA HA HA HA HA!

A-HA HA HA... I SEE!
...SO THAT'S WHAT THAT WAS!

NO WAY...
SASUKE WAS ABLE TO MATCH AND COUNTER GAARA'S ENHANCED STATE ATTACK?!

...I JUST REALIZED...
WHY... I'M ENJOYING MYSELF SO!

?!
HUF
HUF

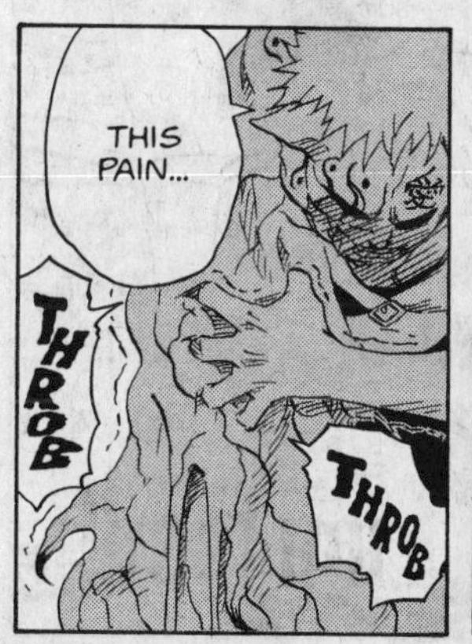
THIS PAIN...
THROB
THROB

IF I CAN DEFEAT ONE STRONG ENOUGH TO WOUND ME, ROB HIM OF ALL THAT HE IS...
HA HA HA HA
...I'LL FEEL EVEN MORE ALIVE THAN EVER!

...
HUF
HUF

SASUKE'S MANAGED TO WOUND GAARA TWICE NOW... GAARA, WHO HAD NEVER EVEN BEEN SCRATCHED BEFORE...
IS HE... A MONSTER TOO?

NAH... THE REAL MONSTER IS INSIDE GAARA...
BUT ONLY HIS RIGHT ARM TRANS-FORMED...

HA, HA, HA! MORE, I WANT MORE!
SLITHER SLITHER

SLITHER
ARGH!!!

!!

!!

HUF
HUF
HUF

READ THIS WAY

ONE AFTER ANOTHER ...
...WHAT IS HE?!!

READY FOR ME?!!
CLENCH

HE'S EVEN FASTER THAN BEFORE!

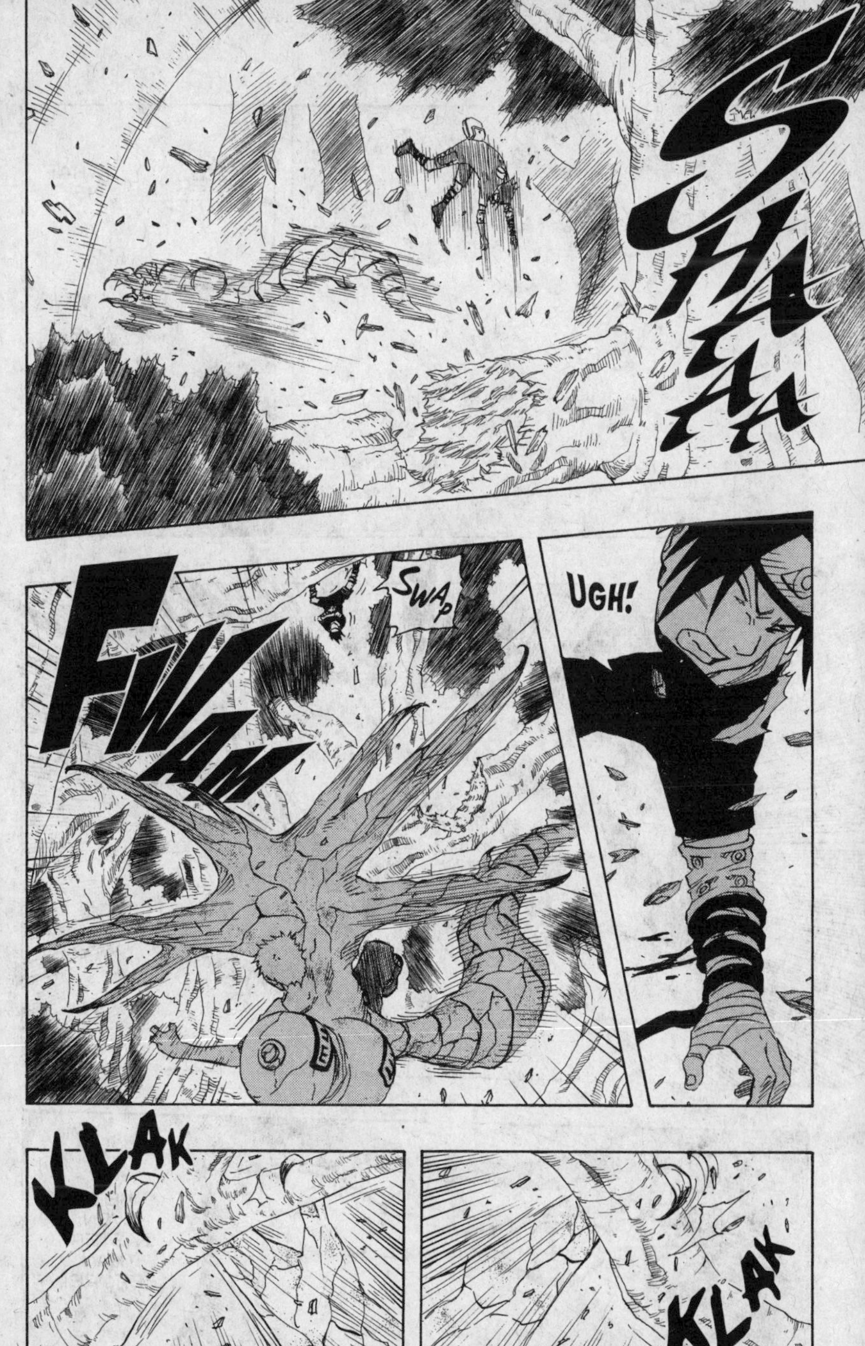
SHAAA
UGH!
FWAM
SWAP
KLAK
KLAK

STRETCH

I CAN'T EVEN DODGE HIM WITHOUT TAKING TIME TO PREDICT HIS MOVES...

WITHOUT THE SHARINGAN, I'D ALREADY BE DEAD...

WHOOM!
BUT... SINCE I ALREADY USED IT ONCE IN THE MATCH... AND AGAIN JUST NOW...
...I CAN'T USE THE CHIDORI ANYMORE...
FWIP
HUF
FIRE STYLE...

GÔKAKYÛ NO JUTSU! FIRE STYLE! FIREBALL TECHNIQUE!!
!!!
SKA
RINK
DIE!
I GUESS FIRE IS INEFFECTIVE AGAINST SAND...
...THE JUTSU JUST ISN'T POWERFUL ENOUGH...
FAMP
I GUESS...
... CHIDORI'S MY ONLY CHOICE.

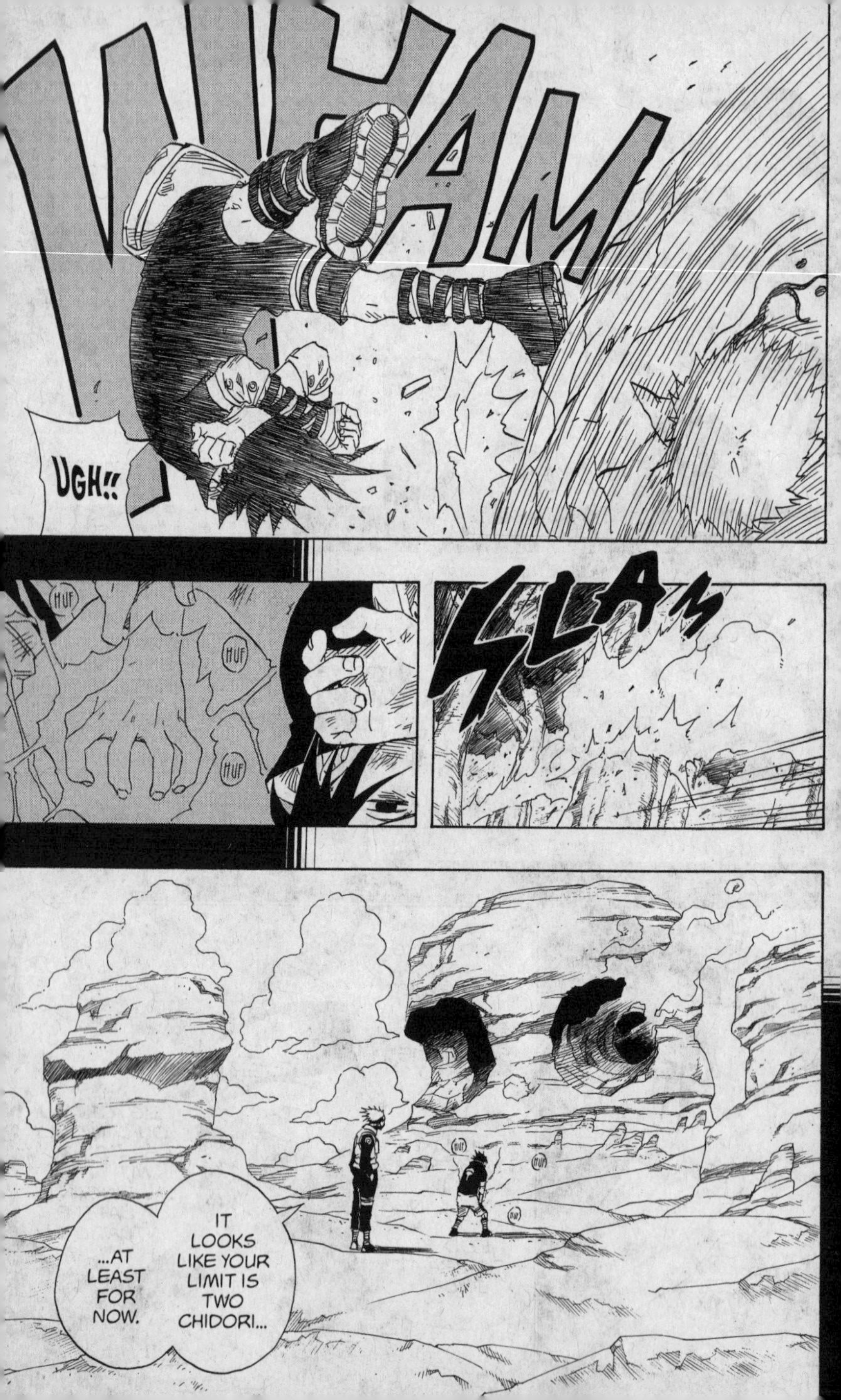
WHAM
UGH!!
SLAM
HUF
HUF
HUF
HUF
HUF
HUF
IT LOOKS LIKE YOUR LIMIT IS TWO CHIDORI...
...AT LEAST FOR NOW.

!!
ARGH...!
CRACKLE CRACKLE FIZZ...
HUF
HUF
HUF
TWITCH
HUF
HUF
HUF
HUF
RIGHT NOW, YOU ONLY HAVE ENOUGH CHAKRA TO EMIT TWO CHIDORI A DAY.
HUF
HUF
CHIDORI...
...IS A JUTSU YOU CAN ONLY USE JOINTLY WITH THE SHARINGAN IN A BATTLE SITUATION...
AND USING SHARINGAN AND OTHER JUTSU AT THE SAME TIME...
...IS LIKE COMBUSTING AND EXPENDING ALL OF YOUR BODY'S CHAKRA AT ONCE...
...
HUF
HUF
HUF
FIZZLE FIZZLE

READ THIS WAY
BUT! YOU'RE STILL AMAZING...
EVEN I...
IF I USE FOUR CHIDORI OR RAIKIRI IN THE SAME DAY, I'LL USE UP ALL OF MY CHAKRA...
...
WHAT WOULD HAPPEN...
...IF I TRY TO PUT OUT MORE THAN TWO?
...
THE THIRD ONE WON'T START... AND LISTEN CAREFULLY!
IF YOU TRY TO FORCIBLY INITIATE THE JUTSU...
NOT ONLY WILL THE JUTSU NOT WORK, BUT YOUR CHAKRA WILL BE DRAINED TO ZERO...

AND IF YOU'RE NOT CAREFUL, YOU'LL DIE.

EVEN IF YOU SURVIVE IT... I GUARANTEE THAT IT WON'T BE GOOD FOR YOU.
...ESPECIALLY FOR YOU...

HUF
HUF
HUF

IS THIS ALL YOUR EXISTENCE IS WORTH?
LET ME TELL YOU...

YOU'RE WEAK!!

FWUMP

READ THIS WAY

'CUZ YOU'RE NAÏVE...
AND YOUR HATRED IS NOT STRONG ENOUGH.

...

THE STRENGTH OF ONE'S HATRED IS THE STRENGTH OF ONE'S WILL TO KILL...
AND THE STRENGTH OF ONE'S WILL TO KILL IS THE STRENGTH OF VENGEANCE.

...

YOUR HATRED WILL NEVER MATCH MINE!!

SHUT UP...

DO YOU UNDER-STAND ME...?

ZAP
IT MEANS...
YOU ARE WEAKER!!
LAUNCH
!
THROB
FIZZ...

CLASH

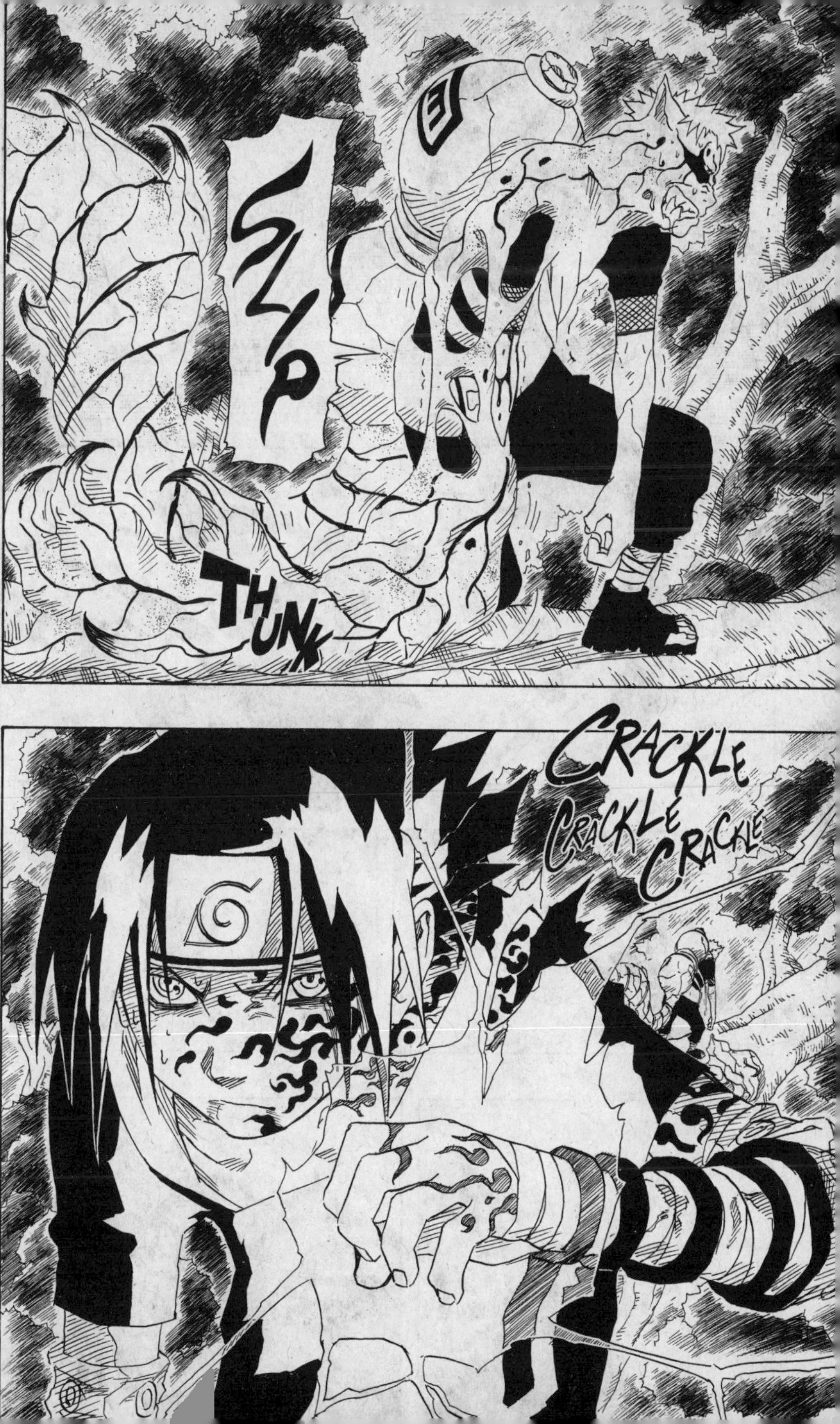

SLIP

THUNK

CRACKLE

CRACKLE CRACKLE

READ THIS WAY

UGGGGH...!!

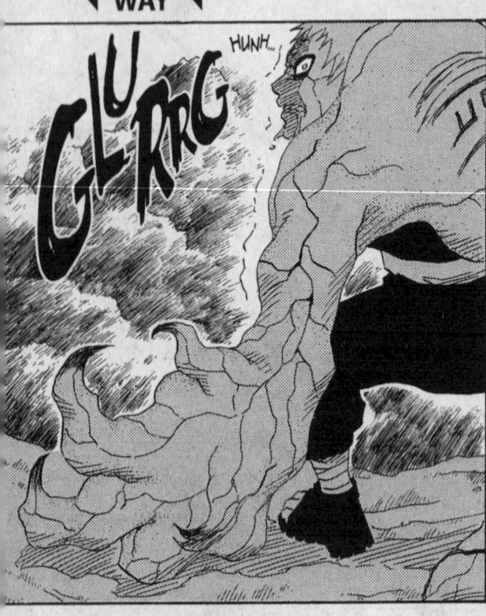
GLURRG
HUNH...

SLITHER

THUD
UGH!

THROB
...THE CURSE MARK, AGAIN...

RRRROAR!!
WHOOSH

!!
AGH...! MY BODY, CAN'T MOVE...

VWA
!!!
WHAM!

FUMP

KER
THWACK

TUMP

SASUKE!!
TAP

HUF
HUF
HUF
TMP

!

...
HUF
HUF

Number 129: To Hurt...!!

UNH... UGH...

WE WERE ONE STEP TOO LATE.
UNH...

...THEY'RE...

UGH...
YOU ALL...

HE WAS PROBABLY FIGHTING RECKLESSLY... JUST LIKE THAT TIME!!
AND MASTER KAKASHI TOLD ME I DIDN'T HAVE TO WORRY ABOUT THE MARK!
ARGGGGH..

TH... THIS IS...

S... SAKURA...?
SAKURA!

WHAT IS IT!!

WHO'S... THAT?!!

!
GRRRR

READ THIS WAY

HE'S THE ONE... WHO KNOCKED SASUKE DOWN...

HIS APPEARANCE MAY HAVE CHANGED...
BUT IT'S THAT FELLOW, GAARA!
SNIFF SNIFF

!

I TOOK THE LIFE OF THE WOMAN I WAS SUPPOSED TO CALL MOTHER IN THE PROCESS OF BEING BORN...
IN ORDER TO BECOME THE WORLD'S STRONGEST SHINOBI... AN INCARNATION OF SAND WAS IMPLANTED INSIDE OF ME...

I WAS BORN...
...A MONSTER!

SO THAT'S... THAT "MONSTER," EH...

I'M NOT A BATTLE TYPE NINJA DOG, SO DON'T COUNT ON ME!!
HARRUMPH!
I CAN SEE THAT!!

UGH... UNNH.
IN ANY CASE, WE'VE GOT TO GET THROUGH THIS CRISIS...
...AND SOMEHOW GET SASUKE TO MASTER KAKASHI...!!

UGH... UNNH...

EVEN IF YOU SURVIVE IT... I GUARANTEE THAT IT WON'T BE GOOD FOR YOU.
...ESPECIALLY FOR YOU...
...YOU MEAN THE CURSE MARK...?
...

IF YOU GIVE IN TO HATRED AND RELY ON THE POWER OF THAT CURSE MARK...
...YOUR MATURATION WILL STOP RIGHT THERE.

AND THEN... YOU WON'T BE ABLE TO WIN AGAINST ITACHI.
HUF
HUF

...I'VE GOT TO SUPPRESS THE MARK...!
HACK!!

SASUKE!!

...

...YOU'RE... ONE... I DIDN'T GET TO KILL!
!

I WOULD FIGHT ONLY FOR MYSELF AND LOVE ONLY MYSELF.
...FOR AS LONG AS THERE ARE PEOPLE OUT THERE FOR ME TO KILL...

...THEN I WILL NOT CEASE TO EXIST.

L...LET'S RUN!!
C'MON!!
WHIRL

!
HUH?
UCHIHA SASUKE!!
DIE!
!

SWOOSH

SAKURA!

THWACK
AIEEE!!
KLIP
ARGH!!
SLAM

TAK

THROB
UGH!

SWF
ZOOM

...THAT GIRL TRIED TO STAND UP TO GAARA...!

SAKURA!!

READ
THIS
WAY

DARN!
DARN!
WHAT AM I
SUPPOSED
TO DO?!!

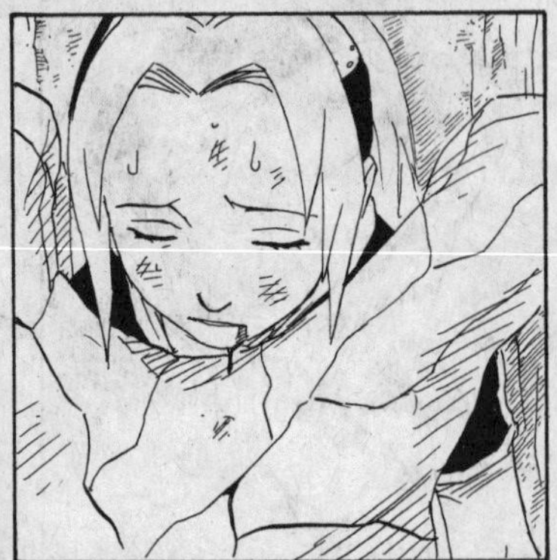

I DON'T
KNOW IF I
CAN HANDLE
THIS GUY...
...NOW,
HELP ME
FEEL
ALIVE.
GULP

...!

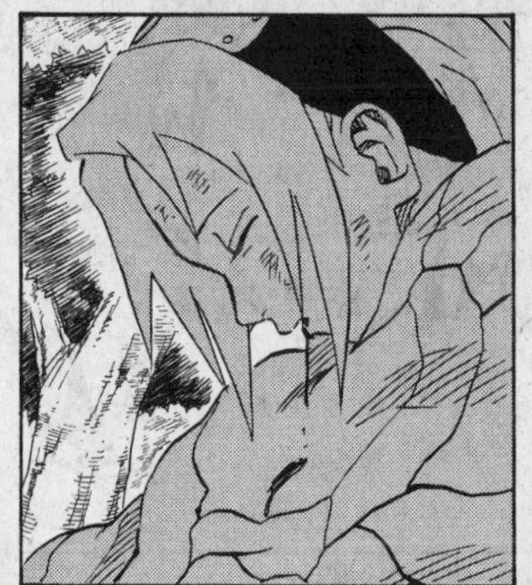

UNH...
UNH...

WHY...?

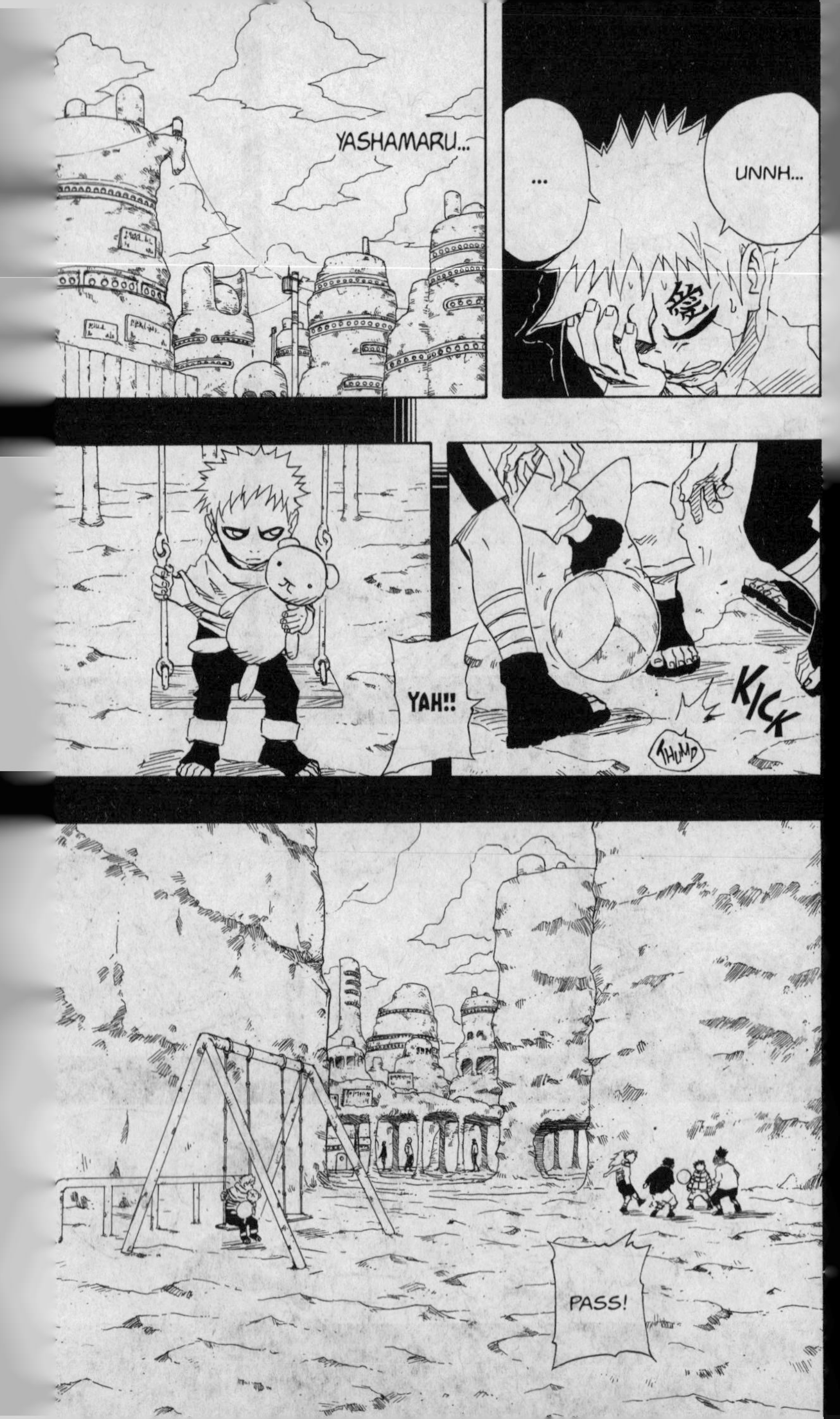

UNNH...
...
YASHAMARU...
KICK
THUMP
YAH!!
PASS!

OH--! MAN!
WHAT ARE WE GONNA DO?!
NONE OF US CAN DO THE WALL-CLIMBING TECHNIQUE...
!
SHOOO...
SHOOO
!!
Y... YOU'RE...!

READ THIS WAY

SHF
I...IT'S GAARA!
GAARA OF THE SAND...
R...
!
RUN--!
WAAAAH--!!
DASH
DASH
WAIT!
DON'T GO AWAY!!

SLAM
WAAAH!
SLAM
HELP--!
I DON'T WANT TO BE ALONE ANYMORE
...
SNAP
AAAAH!
NO!
RUSH
BLOCK
UGH!!
LORD GAARA, PLEASE CALM YOURSELF!!

U...UNH...

LIFT
SLOOSH...
THE SAND PROTECTS ME...
...IT'S STILL USELESS ...
SLITHER SLITHER...
SLOOSH
!
LORD GAARA...

READ THIS WAY
I MIGHT NOT LOOK LIKE IT, BUT I AM STILL A MEMBER OF THE MEDICAL CORPS CHARGED BY LORD KAZEKAGE HIMSELF TO SEE TO YOUR SAFETY AND WELL-BEING.
PLEASE DO NOT ENGAGE IN SUCH BEHAVIOR IN FRONT OF ME.
...EVEN IF THE SAND PROTECTS YOU AS WELL...
...
...YASHAMARU...
I'M SORRY.
YOUR WOUND...
DOES IT HURT?
OH, THIS?
WELL, JUST A BIT...
BUT IT'S ONLY A SMALL SCRATCH. IT'LL HEAL IN NO TIME.
YASHAMARU...?
HMM?
WHAT DOES IT MEAN...
TO HURT?

THE WORLD OF KISHIMOTO MASASHI
MY PERSONAL HISTORY, PART 21

IN MY SECOND YEAR OF COLLEGE, AFTER I GOT TO KNOW MY TWO MANGA-DRAWING UPPERCLASSMEN, I SELECTED THE TRADE PUBLICATIONS I WANTED TO WORK FOR, AND STARTED TO DRAW MANGA AIMED TOWARD THOSE MAGAZINES' CONTESTS.

EVEN AMONG THE NEWCOMER MANGA AWARDS, THERE'S A LOT OF VARIATION.

EACH MAGAZINE HAS A DIFFERENT STYLE OR THEME, AND IF YOU DON'T MATCH YOUR WORK TO THOSE THEMES, IT'S MORE DIFFICULT TO GET SELECTED.

FOR EXAMPLE, IF YOU DREW AND SUBMITTED A HOT-BLOODED BATTLE ACTION MANGA WITH ONLY STRAPPING MALE CHARACTERS TO A SHOJO MANGA MAGAZINE CONTEST, THE MOMENT THEY OPENED YOUR ENVELOPE AND SAW YOUR COVER ILLUSTRATION, THEY WOULD PUT IT BACK IN THE ENVELOPE, SEAL IT, AND EITHER THROW IT IN THE TRASH OR SEND IT BACK TO YOU. WELL, THAT MIGHT BE A RATHER EXTREME EXAMPLE, BUT UNLESS YOU REALLY TRY TO UNDERSTAND A MAGAZINE'S FLAVOR, YOU'LL JUST BE LABELED A "POOR MISGUIDED FOOL."

WHERE IT ESPECIALLY GETS TRICKY IS THE DIFFERENCE BETWEEN SEINEN AND SHONEN MAGAZINES. BECAUSE THEY ARE SOMEWHAT SIMILAR IN TASTES, IT'S VERY EASY TO GET THEM CONFUSED. I WAS A CASE IN POINT MYSELF. I OFTEN DREW HALF-AND-HALF MANGA THAT COULD HAVE QUALIFIED AS EITHER SEINEN OR SHONEN. THE REASON IS THAT THE MANGA THAT HAD INFLUENCED ME WERE THE SHONEN TITLE *DRAGONBALL* AND THE SEINEN TITLE *AKIRA*. THUS, I ACTUALLY WENT THROUGH A PERIOD WHERE I DEBATED WHICH FLOW I SHOULD GO WITH, AND EVEN IF I CHOSE ONE, ELEMENTS OF THE OTHER WOULD CREEP IN. BESIDES, BEYOND ANY SUPERFICIAL SIMILARITIES, THE ART DESIGN, DIALOGUE, TENSION, THEME, AND REPRESENTATION ARE QUITE DIFFERENT, SO (IN MY CASE!) I HAD TO DECIDE WHICH TYPE I WAS GOING TO DRAW AND GO WITH JUST ONE.

THUS, I MADE MY CHOICE, WHICH AT THAT TIME WAS TO AIM FOR SEINEN MAGAZINES. AT THE TIME, THE *AKIRA* INFLUENCE WAS GREATER IN MY ART STYLE AND NAME [OUTLINE/STORYBOARDS], AND I THOUGHT THAT MY PERSONALITY WAS MORE SUITED TOWARD SEINEN MAGAZINES AS WELL. HOWEVER, WHEN I TRIED TO DRAW SEINEN-AIMED MANGA, I JUST COULDN'T GET RID OF THE FEELING THAT SOMETHING WASN'T RIGHT, AND IT DIDN'T GO WELL... I REALIZED I HAD TO CONTEMPLATE WHAT I WANTED TO DRAW A LOT DEEPER, AND THE MORE I ANALYZED IT, THE "THING" THAT HAD PERMEATED THE DEPTHS OF MY HEART KEPT RISING TO THE SURFACE. IT WAS THAT INVINCIBLE MASTERPIECE OF SHONEN MANGA... *DRAGONBALL*... (AND YOU KNOW FROM *NARUTO* WHAT'S HAPPENED SINCE ☺).

Number 130: Love...!!
...WHAT DOES IT MEAN...
...TO HURT?
...I... I'VE NEVER EVEN BEEN INJURED, SO...
I WAS WONDERING WHAT IT FELT LIKE...
...
...
WELL... I'M NOT SURE HOW TO DESCRIBE IT...
IT'S KINDA PAINFUL... KINDA UNBEARABLE...
IN SHORT, I GUESS YOU COULD IMAGINE... BEING HIT OR CUT AND YOU CAN'T HOLD IT IN OR BE YOURSELF ANY LONGER...
I CAN'T REALLY DESCRIBE IT...
IT'S NO FUN, DEFINITELY...

...
YASHA-
MARU...
!
...THEN...
YASHAMARU,
DO YOU...
...HATE
ME?
...

READ
THIS
WAY

HUMANS LIVE THEIR LIVES HURTING OTHERS AND BEING HURT IN RETURN.
BUT EVEN DESPITE ALL THAT...
...PEOPLE STILL LOVE MORE THAN THEY HATE...

...THANKS, YASHAMARU...
MAYBE I AM STARTING TO UNDERSTAND... WHAT IT MEANS TO HURT, NOW.
...IS THAT SO...?
...
SO... COULD I BE INJURED TOO?
JUST LIKE EVERYONE ELSE...

?!

IT... ALWAYS HURTS.
...!

...

IT DOESN'T BLEED...
BUT IT HURTS RIGHT HERE.
SKRCH
...

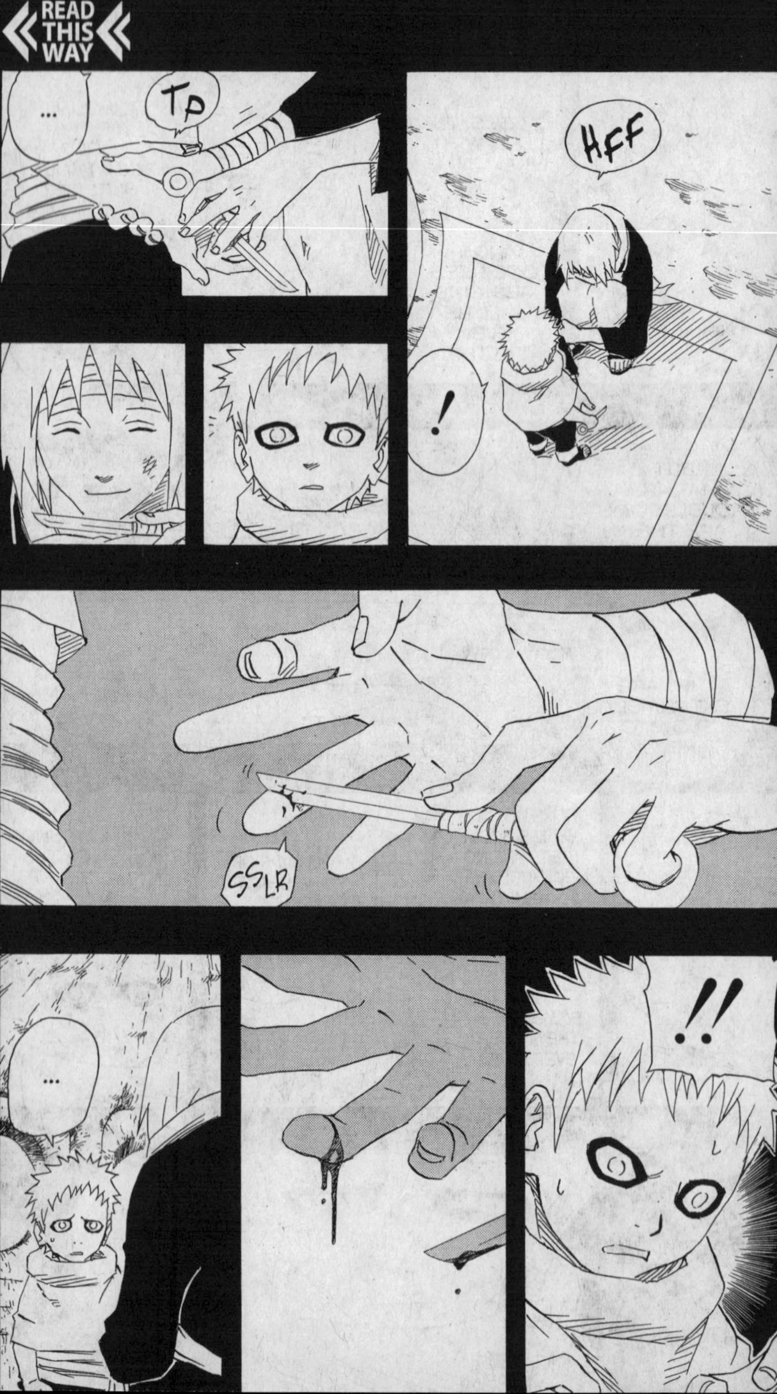
READ THIS WAY
HFF
!
TP
...
SSLR
!!
...

A WOUND OF THE BODY CERTAINLY BLEEDS...
AND CAN APPEAR PAINFUL.
BUT AS TIME PASSES, THE PAIN WILL FADE ON ITS OWN...
AND IF ONE USES MEDICINE, IT WILL HEAL EVEN FASTER.
...!
TAP
...BUT WHAT ARE TROUBLESOME ARE THE WOUNDS OF THE HEART...
THEY ARE EXTREMELY SLOW TO HEAL.
...WOUNDS OF THE HEART?
WOUNDS OF THE HEART ARE A BIT DIFFERENT.
UNLIKE WOUNDS OF THE BODY, THERE ARE NO MEDICINES THAT CAN HELP THEM GET BETTER...
AND SOMETIMES, THEY NEVER EVER HEAL.
...
...

READ THIS WAY
THERE IS JUST ONE THING...
...THAT CAN EASE THE WOUNDS OF THE HEART.
...
...?
UNFORTU-NATELY, IT'S A BOTHERSOME CURE...
...FOR YOU CAN ONLY RECEIVE IT FROM ANOTHER.
...
...WHAT IS IT?
LOVE.

LOVE?
YES.
...
...B...BUT, SO HOW CAN ONE RECEIVE IT?
YOU HAVE ALREADY RECEIVED SOME, LORD GAARA.
I HAVE?
LOVE IS...
...THE FEELING THAT MAKES YOU WANT TO STRIVE FOR AND PROTECT THOSE AROUND YOU WHO ARE PRECIOUS TO YOU.
...JUST LIKE ELDER SISTER...

...
I TRULY BELIEVE ELDER SISTER LOVED YOU VERY DEEPLY, LORD GAARA.
SHUKAKU OF THE SAND IS SUPPOSED TO BE A WRAITH USED FOR OFFENSIVE ASSAULTS.
WHEN THE SAND TRIES TO PROTECT YOU, I BELIEVE IT'S AN EXPRESSION OF MATERNAL LOVE.
I THINK THAT YOUR MOTHER'S WILL HAS SEEPED INTO THAT SAND.
...
ELDER SISTER...
...MUST HAVE WANTED TO PROTECT YOU...
...EVEN UNTO HER DEATH...

YASHAMARU, THANK YOU FOR YOUR HELP...
WHAT DO YOU MEAN?
FOR STOPPING ME.
OF COURSE.
OWW...
YOU ARE VERY PRECIOUS TO ME, LORD GAARA!
...THEN... YASHAMARU ...?
MAY I ASK YOU FOR A FAVOR...?
WHAT IS IT?
I WANT SOME WOUND OINTMENT.

READ THIS WAY
KNOCK
KNOCK
!
CLATTER
I'M SORRY ABOUT EARLIER... IT MUST HAVE HURT...
HERE'S SOME WOUND OINTMENT, PLEASE TAKE...
...GO HOME, MONSTER...
...

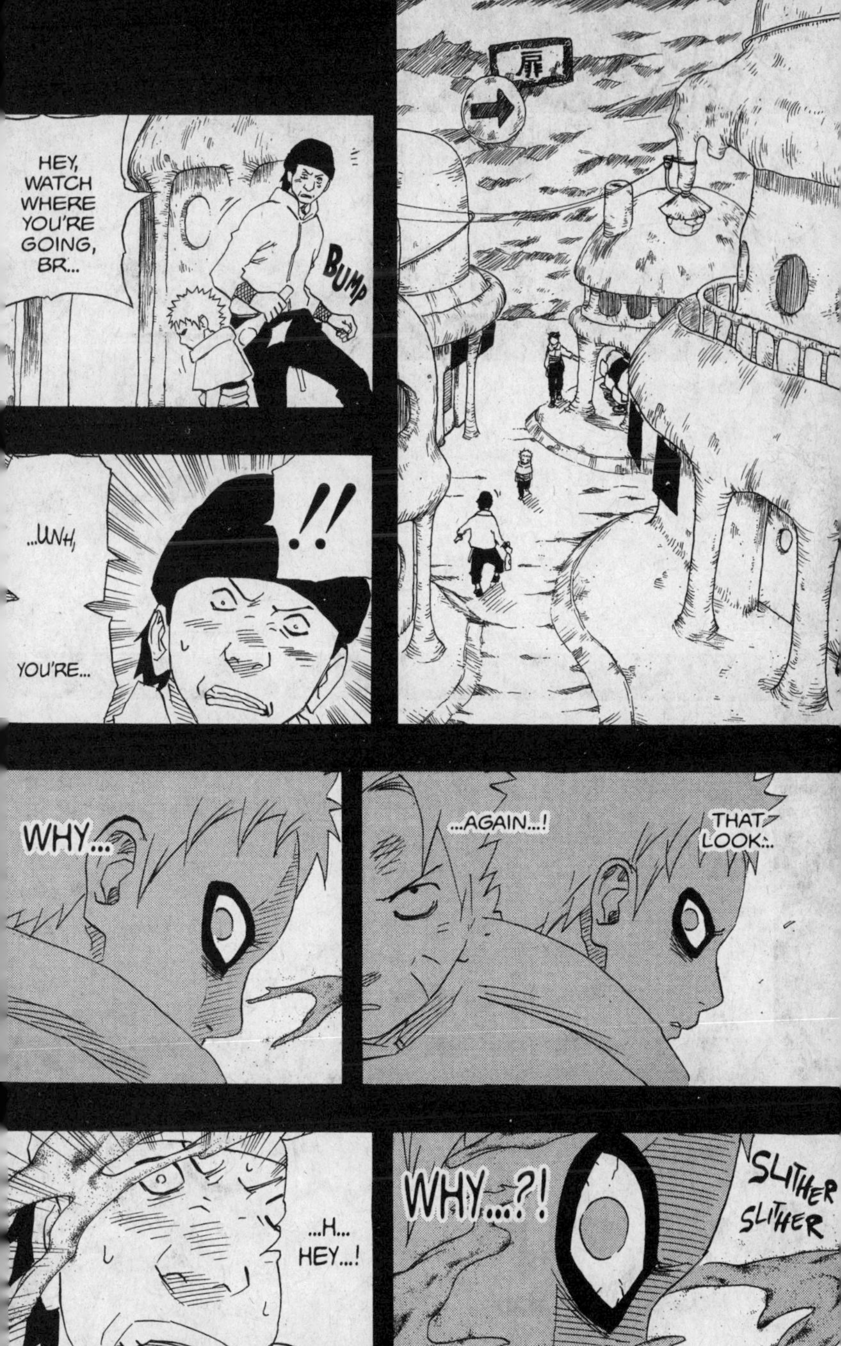
BUMP
HEY, WATCH WHERE YOU'RE GOING, BR...
!!
...UNH,
YOU'RE...
THAT LOOK...
...AGAIN...!
WHY...
SLITHER SLITHER
WHY...?!
...H... HEY...!

SMASH
WAAAAAH!!

WH...WHAT HAPPENED?!
I...IT WAS GAARA!
H...HEY, HE... HE'S DEAD!!

PLOD
PLOD

I GUESS...
IT STILL DOESN'T WORK...
WHY... AM I SUCH A MONSTER?!
WHAT... AM I...!?
SKREEEE
THERE IS JUST ONE THING THAT CAN EASE THE WOUNDS OF THE HEART.
LOVE.
...
...YASHAMARU...

!!
SHOOOM
THOCK
THOCK
THOCK
HUH?
THUNK
VMMM
VMMM
VMMM
VMMM
VMMM
!!
...WHAT?!
...WHY?!
WHY ME...?!!
ALWAYS ME!!

FWSH
THOOM
SLITHER SLITHER
!!
THOCK THOCK
THONK THONK
CLE NCH
SQUELCH

READ THIS WAY
CHAK...
WHO...?
WHY...?
...

YOU TRULY ARE IMPRES-SIVE...
LORD GAARA...
...YASHAMARU...
DANG
SKRENCH

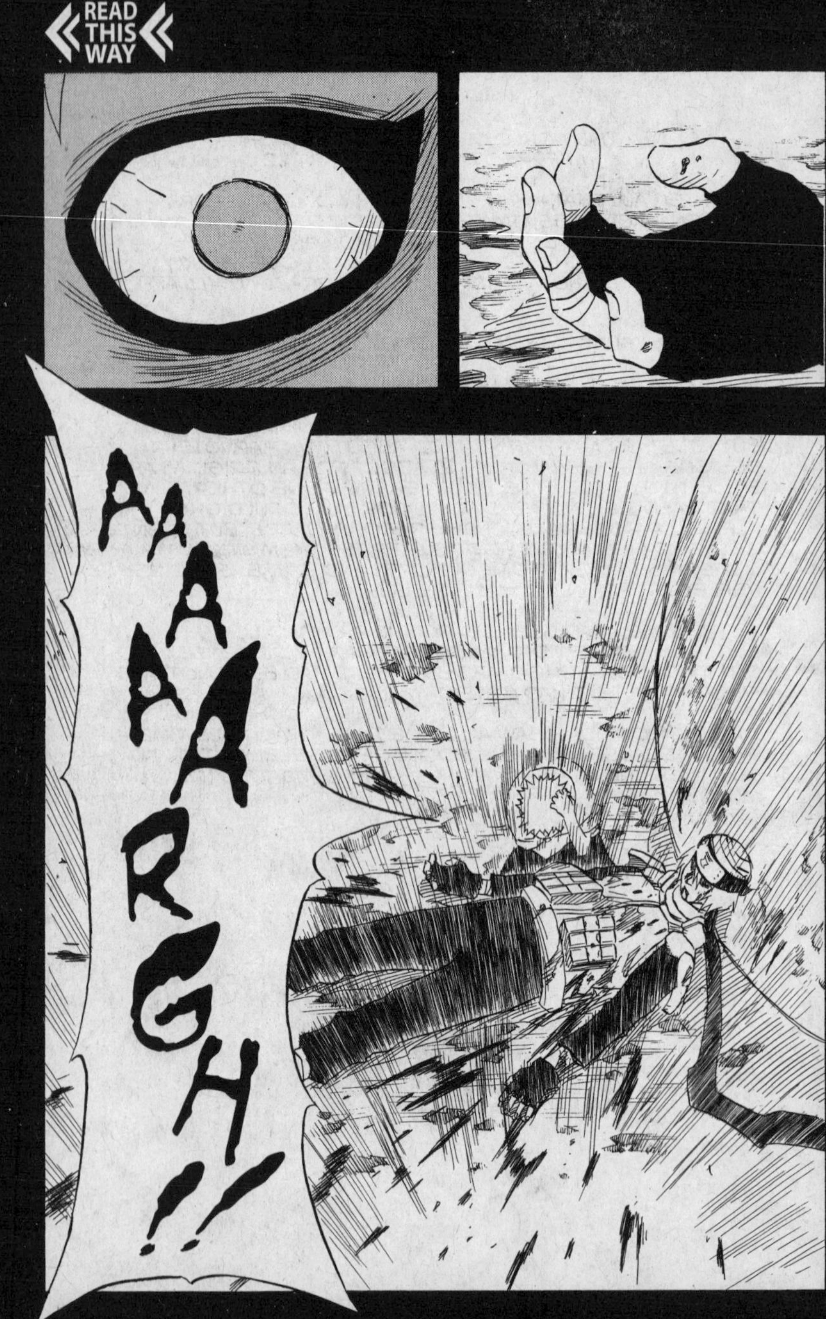
READ THIS WAY
AAAAARRGH!!

THE WORLD OF KISHIMOTO MASASHI
MY PERSONAL HISTORY, PART 22

SO AFTER ALL THAT, HAVING DECIDED I WOULD AIM FOR SHONEN MAGAZINES, I IMMEDIATELY CHOSE WITHOUT ANY HESITATION THE SPECIFIC SHONEN MAGAZINE WHOSE CONTEST I WOULD ENTER. OF COURSE, I CHOSE *WEEKLY SHONEN JUMP*, THE MAGAZINE IN WHICH *DRAGON BALL* APPEARED.

HOWEVER, I SUDDENLY RAN RIGHT INTO A WALL...

BECAUSE I HAD INITIALLY BEEN AIMING FOR SEINEN MAGAZINES, MY ART STYLE WAS NO LONGER SHONEN. WELL, TO A CERTAIN EXTENT, I COULD STILL DRAW SHONEN-LIKE STYLE, BUT I JUST COULDN'T GET CRAZY ABOUT MY CHARACTER DESIGNS. I HAD BEEN GROPING ABOUT FOR AN ORIGINAL ART STYLE THIS WHOLE TIME, BUT THERE WAS ONE OTHER THING THAT WASN'T GOING WELL AT ALL FOR ME. I COULD DRAW PLENTY OF ROUGH SKETCHES OR STORYBOARDS, BUT THEN I COULDN'T FIGURE OUT HOW TO EXPRESS THEM WELL WITH LINES; IN SHORT, HOW ONE DISTORTS AND EXPRESSES LINES REFLECTS THAT INDIVIDUAL'S SENSE.

AT THE TIME, I HAD BEEN SEARCHING HIGH AND LOW WITHOUT SUCCESS FOR NEW DRAWINGS THAT HAD GOOD SENSE IN ADDITION TO BEING GREAT ART, BUT THERE HAD BEEN NOTHING SINCE *AKIRA* THAT HAD CAUGHT MY EYE.

AND THEN ONE DAY, I SAW AN ANIME THAT TOTALLY BLEW ME AWAY... BECAUSE IT CONTAINED ALL OF THE ELEMENTS I HAD BEEN SEEKING. THAT ANIME WAS *HASHIRE MEROSU* [RUN, MELOS].

Number 131: The Name Gaara...!!

AAAAARGH!!

CHATTER CHATTER
CHATTER CHATTER
WH... WHY...
WHY...?
WHY...?!
WHY YOU... YASHAMARU...
WHY...?!

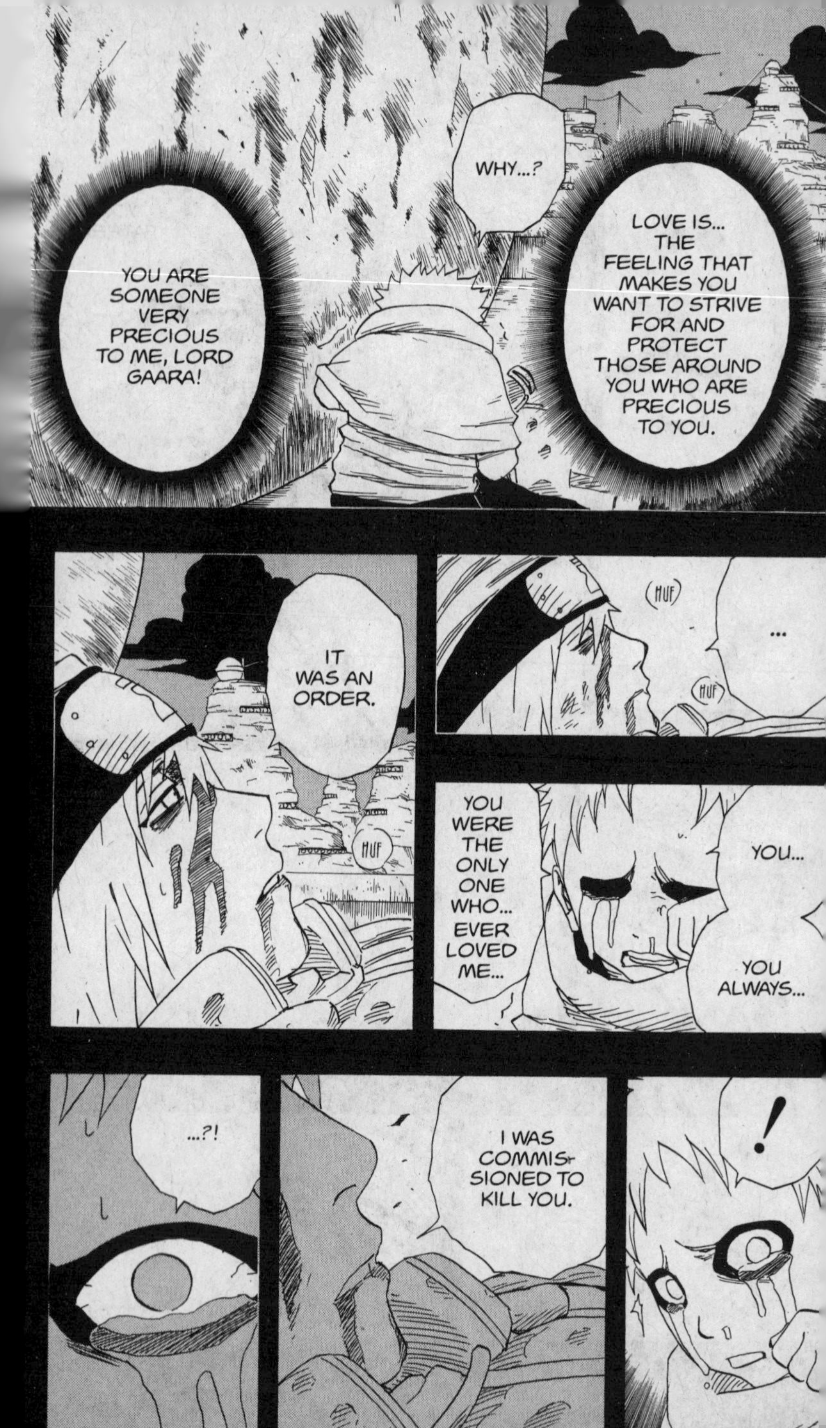
LOVE IS... THE FEELING THAT MAKES YOU WANT TO STRIVE FOR AND PROTECT THOSE AROUND YOU WHO ARE PRECIOUS TO YOU.
WHY...?
YOU ARE SOMEONE VERY PRECIOUS TO ME, LORD GAARA!
(HUF)
...
(HUF)
IT WAS AN ORDER.
HUF
YOU...
YOU ALWAYS...
YOU WERE THE ONLY ONE WHO... EVER LOVED ME...
!
I WAS COMMIS-SIONED TO KILL YOU.
...?!

BY YOUR FATHER...
LORD KAZEKAGE...
!!
FATHER DID...?
CLAP
ULP!
GAH...!!
GACK
...
HUF
HUF

WHY...
...WHY WOULD...
WHY WOULD FATHER...?
HUF
YOU, LORD GAARA... IN WHOM THE SHUKAKU WAS IMPLANTED WHILE YOU WERE STILL IN THE WOMB...
...HAD BEEN WATCHED OVER AND GUARDED UNTIL NOW AS AN EXPERIMENTAL SUBJECT.
HOWEVER, IF YOU CANNOT LEARN TO CONTROL THE SAND THAT IS THE POWER OF THE SHUKAKU WRAITH...
...YOU WILL EVENTUALLY BECOME TOO DANGEROUS FOR THE VILLAGE, LORD GAARA...
SO IT WAS DECIDED...
HUF
HUF
...
...
THEN...
...THEN YOU DIDN'T HAVE A CHOICE, YASHAMARU...
YOU HAD TO CARRY OUT ATHER'S ORDER ...

NO...
...THAT'S NOT ENTIRELY TRUE...
!!
I CERTAINLY DID... RECEIVE AN ORDER FROM LORD KAZEKAGE.
... HOWEVER ...
I PROBABLY COULD HAVE REFUSED IT IF I HAD THOUGHT TO...
...!
...
BUT LORD GAARA ...
DEEP DOWN INSIDE... I THINK I...

...RESENTED YOU...
...FOR STEALING THE LIFE OF MY MOST BELOVED OLDER SISTER WITH YOUR BIRTH...
...
I TRIED DESPERATELY TO LOVE YOU... EVEN IF ONLY AS A MEMENTO OF MY OLDER SISTER...
...BUT IN THE END, I COULDN'T ...
MY OLDER SISTER DID NOT WANT YOU...
SHE WAS SACRIFICED FOR THE VILLAGE AND DIED CURSING THIS PLACE...

AND SINCE THAT DAY...
UNLIKE WOUNDS OF THE BODY, THERE ARE NO MEDICINES THAT CAN HELP THEM GET BETTER... AND SOMETIMES, THEY NEVER EVER HEAL.
I THINK I HAVE CARRIED A WOUND OF THE HEART THAT WILL NEVER HEAL...
...
ELDER SISTER...
...GAVE YOU YOUR NAME, YOU KNOW.
"THIS CHILD'S NAME SHALL BE GAARA...
"A SHURA, A DEMON, WHO SHALL LOVE ONLY HIMSELF..."
"LOVE ONLY YOURSELF... AND FIGHT ONLY FOR YOURSELF...
"...SO BY DOING THAT, YOU WILL BE ABLE TO KEEP EXISTING..." THOSE WERE THE THINGS SHE WISHED FOR YOU.

HOWEVER... ELDER SISTER DID NOT NAME YOU THUS...
...BECAUSE SHE LOVED OR WORRIED ABOUT YOU...
SHE GAVE YOU THAT NAME SO THAT YOU WOULD SURVIVE AND BE A REMINDER TO THE WORLD ...
...A REMINDER OF HER HATRED, OF HOW SHE WENT TO HER DEATH LOATHING AND CURSING THE WORLD... REMIND THEM... AND SHOW THEM ALL...!
NO, YOU WERE NEVER LOVED...!
...
YANK
AND NOW...
PLEASE DIE WITH ME...

KA
BOOM
CLUNK
I TRULY BELIEVE ELDER SISTER LOVED YOU VERY DEEPLY, LORD GAARA.
...
LOVE...?

WHEN THE SAND TRIES TO PROTECT YOU, I BELIEVE IT'S AN EXPRESSION OF MATERNAL LOVE.
I THINK THAT YOUR MOTHER'S WILL HAS SEEPED INTO THAT SAND.
...UNH... ...AAH...
LOVE.
AAAAH --!!
RRRRROAR!!!

"LOVE ONLY YOURSELF...
"AND FIGHT ONLY FOR YOURSELF...!"
SO THAT'S GAARA.
ME...
I FINALLY UNDERSTAND...
I AM ALONE.
I WON'T TRUST ANYONE ELSE ANYMORE... WON'T LOVE THEM... I'M ALONE...
HEH HEH... THAT'S RIGHT...
I'M ALL ALONE...

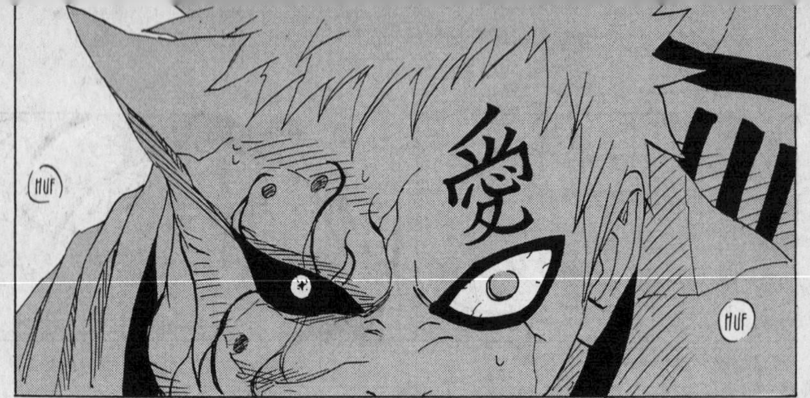
HUF
HUF

...OH... IT'S THAT LOOK...!!

GULP

...

WHAT'S THE MATTER...?
I THOUGHT YOU WERE GOING TO RUN AWAY?
!!

...SASUKE...

...NARUTO...

!!

UGH...

WHO ARE THEY TO YOU?

TH...THEY'RE MY FRIENDS!
IF YOU TRY TO TOUCH THEM AGAIN...
I'LL SLAUGHTER YOU!!

...
愛

PRESS
AIEEE!!

!!

...!!

WELL... WHAT'S THE MATTER? I THOUGHT YOU WERE GOING TO SLAUGHTER ME?
愛

UGH...
COME ON, THEN.

DARN!
LEAP
!
THWA
G
SLA
M
...!!
...DARN!

READ THIS WAY

...
...HE'S NOT HIS USUAL SELF...
...DID SOMETHING... HAPPEN... BETWEEN THE TWO OF THEM?

IN ANY CASE... IN ANY CASE!
I'VE GOT TO RESCUE SAKURA!!
BUT HOW?

THAT'S RIGHT... IN THIS SITUATION...
HMM~~!
!
EVEN THOUGH IT USES UP A LOT OF CHAKRA...

!

FWUP
MY ONLY CHOICE IS TO SUMMON THAT TOAD!!

SLAP

KUCHIYOSE! SUMMONING!!

BOOF

WHAT THE?! YOU'RE JUST A BRAT!!
IF YOU WANT MY HELP, GIVE ME SOME MUNCHIES!
OR ELSE I WON'T PLAY WITH YOU!

READ THIS WAY

Y'KNOW, I REALLY!! I REALLY REALLY HATE YOU FROGS!!!
WHAT?! DON'T YOU DARE MOCK AMPHIBIANS!!! EH!!!

ARGH...
GRRRR
THIS ISN'T THE TIME OR PLACE TO BE PLAYING AROUND, MINI-WART!
FWP

DARN! WHY IS IT...
WHAT WAS ALL THAT TRAINING FOR? AT THIS RATE, THERE ISN'T...

愛
FRIEND...?! WHAT A LAUGH...

LOOOOM
I FIGHT...
...ONLY FOR MYSELF!!

THE WORLD OF KISHIMOTO MASASHI
MY PERSONAL HISTORY, PART 22 (CONTINUED)

HASHIRE MEROSU [RUN, MELOS] REALLY AMAZED ME! THE MUSCLES AND BONE STRUCTURE WERE REPRESENTED WITH NEW LINE TECHNIQUES, AND THE DESIGNS FELT REALLY FRESH. NOT TO MENTION REALLY COOL. I IMMEDIATELY BECAME INTERESTED IN THE CHARACTER DESIGNER AND ANIMATION DIRECTOR OKIURA HIROYUKI, AND AS I RESEARCHED HIS FILMOGRAPHY AT THE LOCAL VIDEO RENTAL STORE, I STARTED NOTICING THAT SOME OF THE ANIMATORS' NAMES APPEARED AGAIN AND AGAIN IN MANY OTHER FILMS. "OH! THIS GUY, HE WORKED ON THIS FILM TOO. OH! THIS GUY TOO!" ...ALONG THE WAY, I GOT INTO ALL SORTS OF ANIME, AND STARTED MEMORIZING THE NAMES OF VARIOUS ANIMATION DIRECTORS AND ANIMATORS. AT THAT TIME, WHEN MANGA WERE MADE INTO ANIMATION, THE ANIME OFTEN HAD BETTER ART, SO I HAD STARTED FEELING THAT ANIMATORS WERE BETTER ARTISTS. AND THAT IS WHEN MY ENCOUNTER WITH A CERTAIN TITLE AND A CERTAIN ANIMATOR IMMENSELY INFLUENCED ME.

THAT TITLE WAS JUMP'S FAMOUS *NINKŪ*, A NINJA MANGA JUST LIKE MINE. AND THE ANIMATOR WHO INFLUENCED ME WAS NISHIO TETSUYA, THE CHARACTER DESIGNER AND ANIMATION DIRECTOR FOR THE ANIMATED VERSION.

Number 132:

The Two... Darkness and Light

RRRRROAR!!
RIPPLE RIPPLE

HE... TRANSFORMED AGAIN...

SLIP

SNIP

UNLESS YOU TAKE ME DOWN, THE SAND AROUND THAT GIRL WON'T DISSOLVE.
IN FACT, IT WILL SLOWLY CONSTRICT, EVENTUALLY SMOTHERING AND CRUSHING HER!
SWIP...

READ THIS WAY

UGH...!
SAKURA...

...HE HASN'T INITIATED THE TANUKI NEIRI NO JUTSU – THE PLAY POSSUM TECHNIQUE – YET, BUT...
BUT AT THIS RATE... EVEN I...

...HE'S SLOWLY APPROACHING PERFECT POSSESSION...

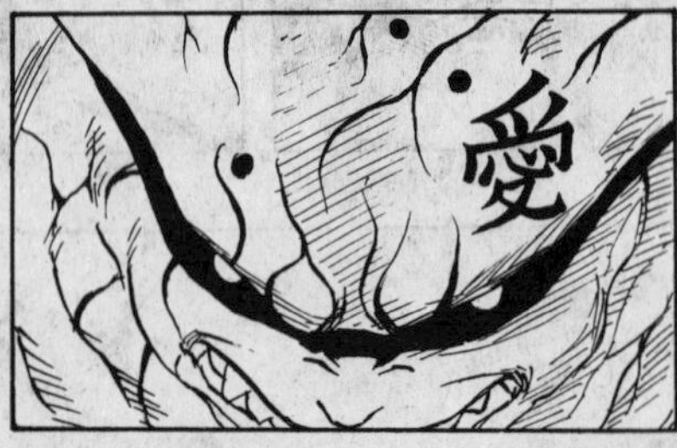
愛

...
...THAT LOOK...

SSHF
CCREEAK
SSHF

VOOSH

SAND SHURIKEN!!

SLAM
UGH!!

!

UGH...

THUD
THUD
THUMP
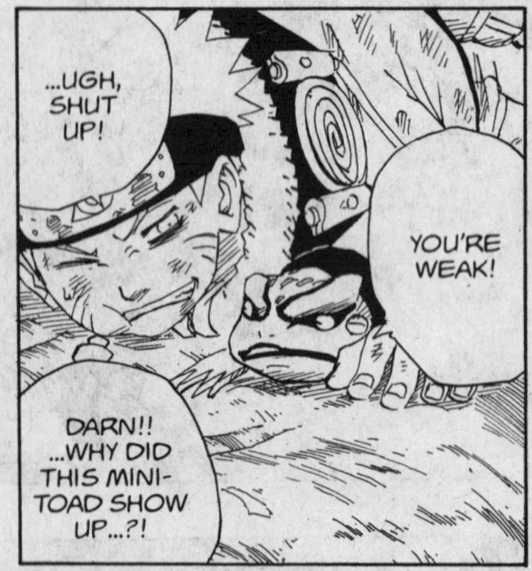
YOU'RE WEAK!
...UGH, SHUT UP!
DARN!! ...WHY DID THIS MINI-TOAD SHOW UP...?!

!! BUT WHAT IN THE WORLD IS THAT THING?

!

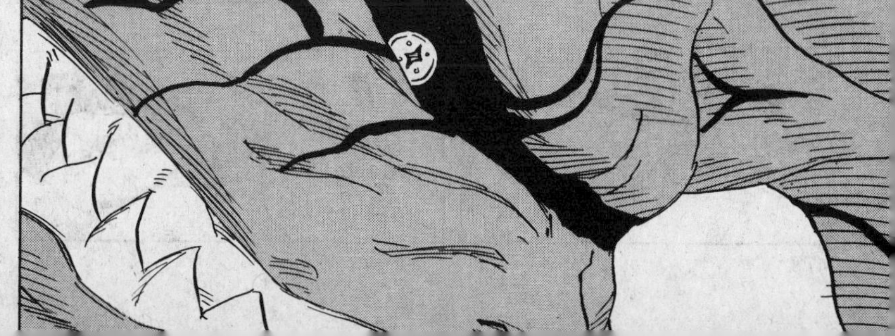

READ
THIS
WAY

H...HE'S
GOT SUCH
LONELY
EYES...
...

VERY...
SOLITARY
EYES...

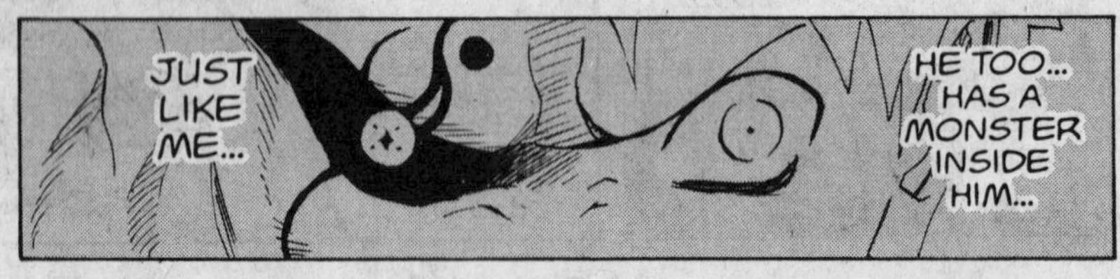
HE TOO...
HAS A
MONSTER
INSIDE
HIM...
JUST
LIKE
ME...

...

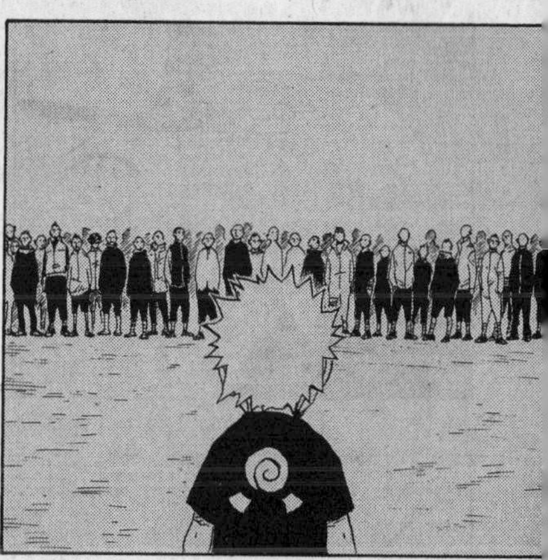

...I HATED ALL OF THEM...
...I DIDN'T KNOW WHO OR WHAT I WAS TO DESERVE TO BE HATED SO MUCH, OR WHY I EXISTED...

IN OTHER WORDS, YOU...
...ARE THE NINE-TAILED FOX SPIRIT THAT DESTROYED THE VILLAGE!!
DIDN'T YOU THINK IT WAS STRANGE? TO BE SO DESPISED EVERYWHERE YOU WENT?

EVER SINCE I FOUND OUT I HAD THE NINE-TAILED FOX INSIDE ME, EVERYONE'S EYES SEEMED EVEN MORE CALLOUS...
IT WAS SO PAINFUL...

...
...BUT...

NARUTO! IT'S BEEN A WHILE, WANT TO GO EAT RAMEN?!
YAY! HEY! HEY! I WANT EXTRA PORK TODAY!!

HUMPH! YOU IDIOT... IF YOU WANT TO WIN AGAINST ME, TRAIN HARDER.
SHUT UP! I WON'T LOSE TO YOU!!

HEY-- NARUTO! WHAT DID SASUKE SAY ABOUT ME?
HE DIDN'T REALLY SAY ANYTHING. BUT HEY! HEY! DON'T YOU WANT TO KNOW WHAT I THINK ABOUT YOU?

HMM--... NARUTO, IF YOU KEEP EATING JUST RAMEN AND RED BEAN SOUP, YOU REALLY WILL DIE. ♡
IF YOU'RE GOING TO BE A NINJA, YOU NEED TO EAT VEGETABLES. HERE'S A DELIVERY.
Eat your veggies! Kakashi
WHAT--?! BUT I HATE VEGGIES!

I STARTED MEETING FOLK WHO WOULD ACKNOWLEDGE ME...
SO ...

EVEN THOUGH I HAD A FOX DEMON INSIDE ME, AND PEOPLE LOOKED COLDLY AT ME, I GOT USED TO IT.

CUZ...
I WASN'T ALONE ANY-MORE!!

THAT'S WHY WHEN I THINK ABOUT THE PAST, IT MAKES ME SHUDDER.

...THAT PAIN WASN'T JUST ANYTHING... IT WAS JUST PITCH BLACK.

THAT'S WHY I REALLY DO UNDER-STAND IT.

TO THEM, I AM NOW A RELIC OF THE PAST THAT THEY JUST WANT TO ERASE AND FORGET.

SO FOR WHAT PURPOSE DO I EXIST, WHY AM I ALIVE?

SO THIS IS WHAT I CAME UP WITH...

"I EXIST TO KILL ALL HUMANS OTHER THAN MYSELF."

I DON'T KNOW WHAT ACTUALLY HAPPENED TO HIM, BUT...
I KNOW HE'S BEEN ALONE THIS WHOLE TIME, CONTINUING TO SUFFER... WITHOUT ANY RELIEF, HE STILL... CAN ONLY TRUST HIMSELF...! HE'S STILL FIGHTING INSIDE THE DARK...
愛

...THAT'S RIGHT... IN HIS EYES, SOME-ONE LIKE ME, WHO HAS OTHERS THAT ACKNOWLEDGE HIM... MAY SEEM LIKE A COWARD WHO LIVES IN A CAREFREE, SUNNY WORLD...

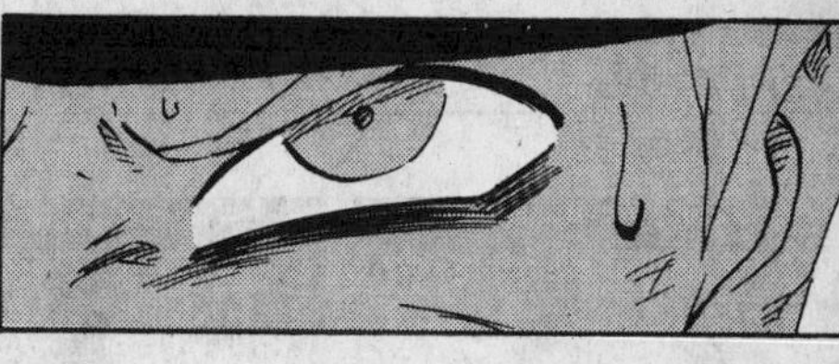

UNH...
WRRSH

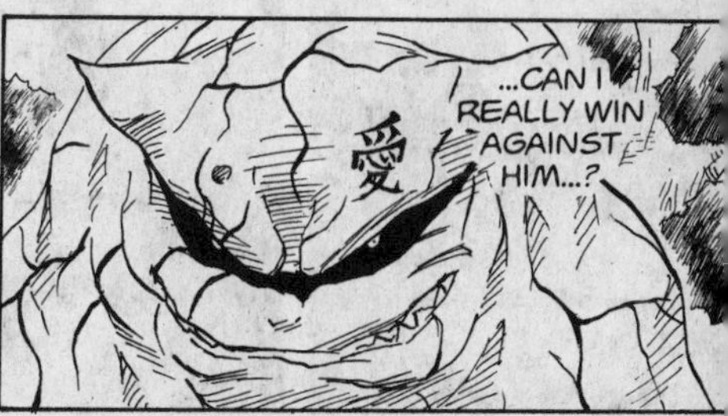
...CAN I REALLY WIN AGAINST HIM...?
愛

READ
THIS
WAY

...UGH!

WHAT'S THE MATTER... ARE YOU SCARED OF ME?
!

WHETHER YOU FIGHT FOR YOURSELF...
...OR FOR OTHERS...

UGH...

YOU SHOULD ONLY LOVE YOURSELF!
ONLY FIGHT FOR YOURSELF!
THAT'S THE DEFINITION OF THE STRONGEST ONE!!
愛

...

NOW! FIGHT ME!!
SHOW ME YOUR POWER, JUST LIKE WHEN YOU TOOK DOWN HYUGA!
KLAKK
I'LL GRIND THAT POWER INTO NOTHING-NESS!!

...

WELL?! WHAT'S THE MATTER!
IF YOU DON'T FIGHT ME, I'LL KILL THAT GIRL!

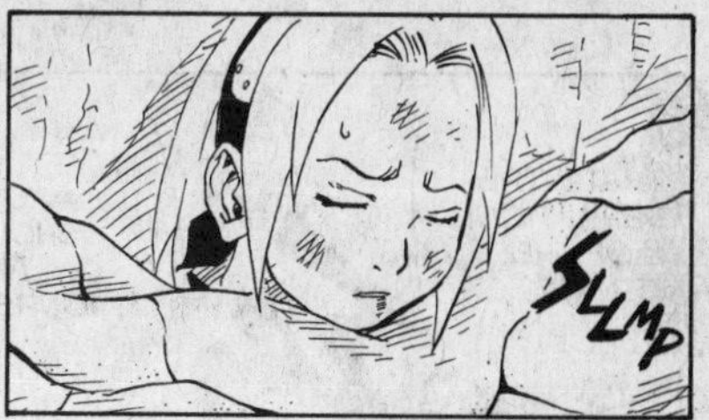
SLUMP

...UGH...
HUF
HUF
FSSH

DARN!
LEAP

WIND STYLE: MUGENSAJIN DAITOPPA! INFINITE SAND DEVAS-TATION!!

WAAH!!

BOOM...

BUT YOU WON'T ESCAPE.
FIRST, I'M GOING TO PLAY WITH YOU WITHOUT LETTING YOU DIE.
I WANT TO SEE HOW LONG IT TAKES FOR YOU TO GIVE UP ON YOUR FRIENDS AND TRY TO RUN AWAY.

YIKES... THAT REALLY HURT...
UGH...

THUD
THUD

HUMPH...

SHF
...

READ THIS WAY

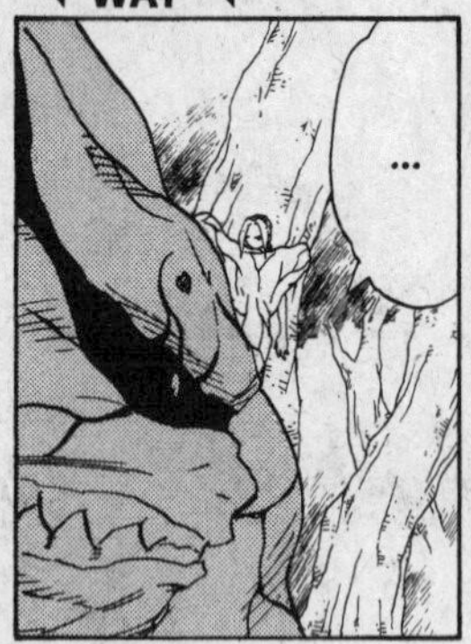

...

...ARGH...
SAND SHURIKEN!!
SLASH

SHF
...
WHY...DO I FEEL LIKE THIS...

GAH!!
WHOOOOOM

...!

...DARN...
...DARN...
SLUMP

...HE...
...
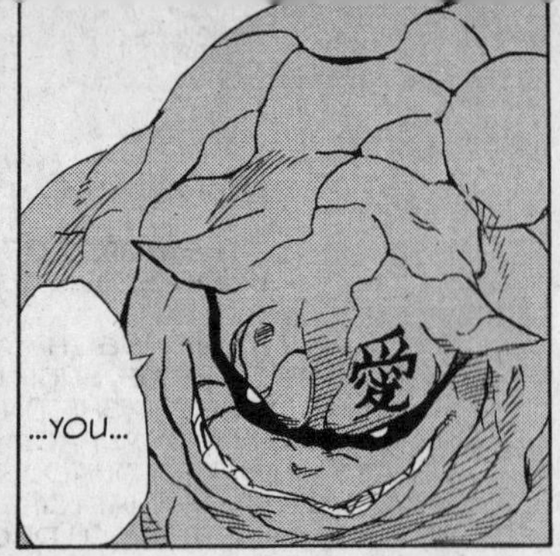
...YOU...
愛

...
...WHAT IS IT...
...THIS FEELING WELLING UP...?

...FOR WHAT-EVER REASON ...
STAGGER...
...JUST... JUST AGAINST THIS GUY...

GRAAA

I DON'T WANT TO LOSE TO HIM EVEN IF I END UP DYING!!

THE WORLD OF KISHIMOTO MASASHI
MY PERSONAL HISTORY, PART 22 (PART 3)

REGULARLY MIMICKING THE ART STYLES OF MY FAVORITE ANIMATORS AT THE TIME, SUCH AS OKIURA-SAN AND MORIMOTO KOUJI-SAN, STARTED SHIFTING MY STYLE TOWARD SEINEN MAGAZINES AND AWAY FROM SHONEN MAGAZINES AGAIN. ...THAT'S WHEN I FORTUITOUSLY SAW IN MY TARGET MAGAZINE THAT THE SERIES THAT I LIKED EVEN AS A MANGA, *NINKÛ*, HAD BECOME ANIMATED, SO I DECIDED I WOULD WATCH IT WHILE EATING A SALMON BENTO AND PREPARED MY MEAL AND SAT MYSELF DOWN IN FRONT OF THE TELEVISION. THE MOMENT I STUCK THE DISPOSABLE CHOPSTICKS IN MY MOUTH TO SPLIT THEM APART, THE *NINKÛ* ANIME STARTED, AND I GOT DRAWN RIGHT INTO THE OPENING SEQUENCE WITH THE STILL UNBROKEN CHOPSTICKS FORGOTTEN IN MY MOUTH.

IT MADE SUCH AN IMPACT ON ME! FOR IT CONTAINED NEW DISTORTIONS, HAD GREAT SENSE, EVEN BETTER ART, AND ON TOP OF IT ALL, JUST INDESCRIBABLE, REALLY REFRESHING LINE TECHNIQUE THAT SEEMED LIKE A MIX OF SEINEN AND SHONEN STYLES. IN SHORT, IT WAS THE IDEAL ART STYLE THAT I HAD BEEN SEEKING.

"THIS IS IT!" I THOUGHT TO MYSELF.

SINCE THEN, I STARTED MIMICKING NISHIO-SAN'S DRAWINGS, AND IT PRETTY MUCH WAS THE BASIS FOR THE ART STYLE OF THIS CURRENT *NARUTO*. AND AS SOME OF YOU MAY KNOW, AMONG ONE OF THE CHARACTER DESIGNERS FOR THE *NARUTO* ANIME IS NISHIO TETSUYA-SAN HIMSELF. I AM A LUCKY MAN. THE MAN THAT I RESPECTED AND RECEIVED SO MUCH INFLUENCE FROM IS DOING DESIGNS FOR ME! IT WAS A REALLY HAPPY MOMENT FOR ME WHEN I HEARD THIS, LIKE ONE OF MY DREAMS HAD COME TRUE (AND IN THAT INSTANT, I INVOLUNTARILY PUMPED MY FISTS IN THE AIR.) PLUS, ANOTHER ONE OF THE CHARACTER DESIGNERS IS SUZUKI HIROFUMI-SAN. HE IS AN AWESOME FELLOW WHO HAS WORKED ON SOME OF MY FAVORITE ANIME. THEY ARE SUCH GREAT ARTISTS THAT I'M EMBARRASSED THAT THEY LOOK AT MY MANGA.

Number 133: Those Who Are Strong...!!

HUF

HUF

HUF

HUF

HUF

TREMBLE...

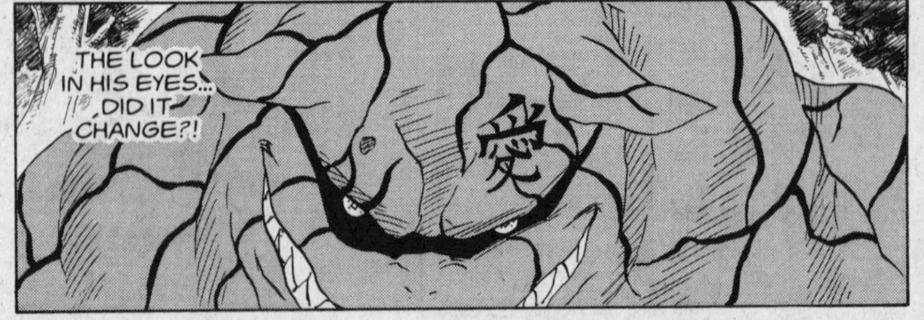
THE LOOK IN HIS EYES... DID IT CHANGE?!
愛

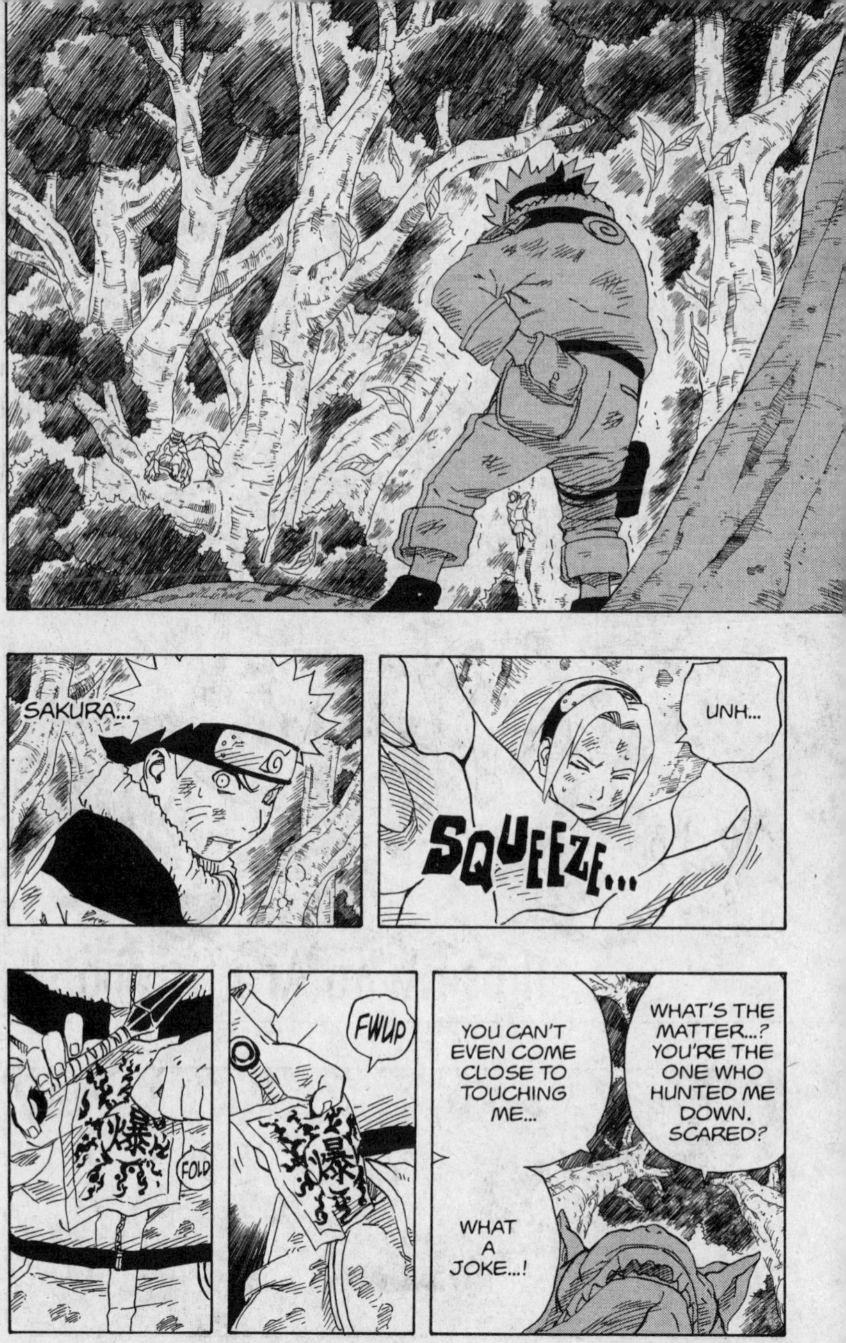

UNH...
SQUEEZE...

SAKURA...

WHAT'S THE MATTER...? YOU'RE THE ONE WHO HUNTED ME DOWN. SCARED?
YOU CAN'T EVEN COME CLOSE TO TOUCHING ME...
WHAT A JOKE...!

FWUP

FOLD

I'M GONNA GIVE IT EVERY-THING I'VE GOT!!
FWUP
FWUP

...I DON'T KNOW HOW FAR I CAN GO OR HOW MUCH I CAN DO, BUT...
SHOMP

BOOF BOOF BOOF BOOF
ART OF THE SHADOW DOPPEL-GANGER !!!

LADIES AND GENTS, WE NOW PROUDLY BRING YOU A MOST SECRET AND SPECIAL TECHNIQUE!! THE UZUMAKI NARUTO...

HERE WE COME!!

BUNSHIN TAIATARI! DOPPEL-GANGER BODY SLAM!!
KRSH
SWOOSH

GO!!!!
ZOOM
SHMP

GRAB
BOOF
SPIN SPIN
KAGEBUNSHIN NO JUTSU! ART OF THE SHADOW DOPPEL-GANGER!!
!
ONE MORE! ART OF THE SHADOW DOPPEL-GANGER!!
BOOF
ZOOM

TAKE THIS!!
MASTER KAKASHI'S SPECIALTY... KONOHAGAKURE VILLAGE'S MOST SACRED TECHNIQUE!!

UGH!

ONE THOUSAND YEARS OF DEATH!!
POKE

...
...

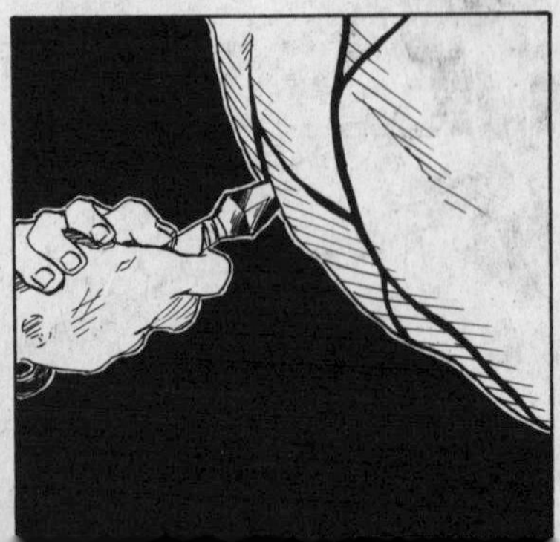

WHAM
!
SIZZLE
SIZZLE
KABOOM
...KABOOM.

ARGH!!

UGH!!

THUD

SHMP

SLAM

!
WHAT A BRILLIANT MOVE! AND... EVEN IN HIS CURRENT CONDITION, SASUKE MANAGED TO CATCH NARUTO!

...
...D...DID HE KILL HIM?

...UGH... HE MANAGED TO TARGET THAT LETTER BOMB RIGHT AT MY WEAKEST SPOT—UNDER MY TAIL...
GRRR...
I CAN'T ABSORB ALL OF THE IMPACT...

HUF
HUF
... SASUKE ...!

HEH... YOU'RE FINALLY SHOWING YOUR STUFF...
...BUT AFTER ALL THAT... JUST ONE BLOW?
HUF
HUF

...YOU GOTTA TRY HARDER... 'CUZ THIS TIME... I CAN'T HELP YOU... LIKE I DID IN THE LAND OF WAVES...
...IDIOT.
SH...SHUT UP...

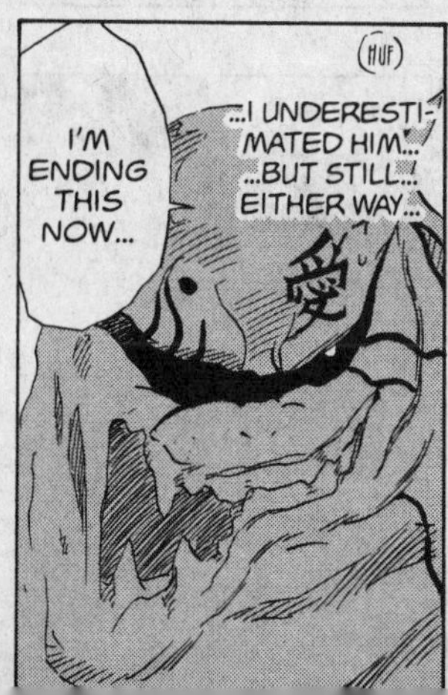
HUF
...I UNDERESTIMATED HIM... ...BUT STILL... EITHER WAY...
I'M ENDING THIS NOW...
愛

READ THIS WAY

YOU...
...BETTER RESCUE SAKURA, NO MATTER WHAT!
HUF
HUF

U... UNH.
...I TRUST YOU TO BE ABLE TO DO IT...

...AND THEN... ONCE YOU FREE HER...
TAKE HER... AND GET THE HECK OUT OF HERE...
... SASUKE... WHAT...?

...EVEN IN THIS STATE... I CAN AT LEAST... DELAY HIM A LITTLE...
IT'S OVER. THAT'S ALL I CAN DO.
STRUGGLE...

...NO MORE ...

I'VE ALREADY LOST EVERYTHING ONCE BEFORE... I DON'T EVER...
...WANT TO WATCH MY **PRECIOUS COMRADES** DIE IN FRONT OF ME AGAIN...

...!

...PRECIOUS... COMRADES...

...

SHUNK

...
...RIGHT...

I WILL NEVER LET MY COMRADES DIE!

...
YOU'RE ABSO-LUTELY RIGHT...

!

...I THOUGHT OF HIM AS STRONG...
'CUZ LIKE ME, HE GREW UP WRAPPED IN LONELINESS AND SADNESS...
...AND YET HE KEPT FIGHTING FOR HIMSELF FROM INSIDE THAT CORE OF SOLITUDE...
RISE

!
HUF
HUF
... NARUTO ...

...BUT THAT'S NOT WHAT IT TAKES TO BE TRULY STRONG, IS IT...
YOU CAN'T REALLY GET STRONG JUST FIGHTING ONLY FOR YOURSELF...

...DO YOU HAVE...

...ANYONE SPECIAL IN YOUR LIFE?

WHEN PEOPLE... ARE PROTECTING SOMEONE TRULY PRECIOUS TO THEM...

...

CROUCH

...THEY TRULY CAN BECOME AS STRONG AS THEY MUST BE!

... NARUTO ...

!

愛

YOU WILL GET STRONGER...
AAAAAAAAH!!
HAAAAAA!
FSSH
ZAP ZAP
WH...WHOA, HE'S SUMMONING UNBELIEVABLE AMOUNTS OF CHAKRA... IS...IS THIS REALLY...
SHK
UNH...?!
NARUTO?!
I SWEAR, I'LL PROTECT ALL OF YOU!!

TAJÛ KAGE-BUNSHIN NO JUTSU! ART OF THE MULTIPLE SHADOW DOPPEL-GANGERS!!!
HE'S GOOD!
!!
!
!
!!

BO
SORRY FOR THE WAIT, FOLKS!!
WE NOW BRING YOU NARUTO'S WHIRLING SWIRLING NINJA HANDBOOK!!

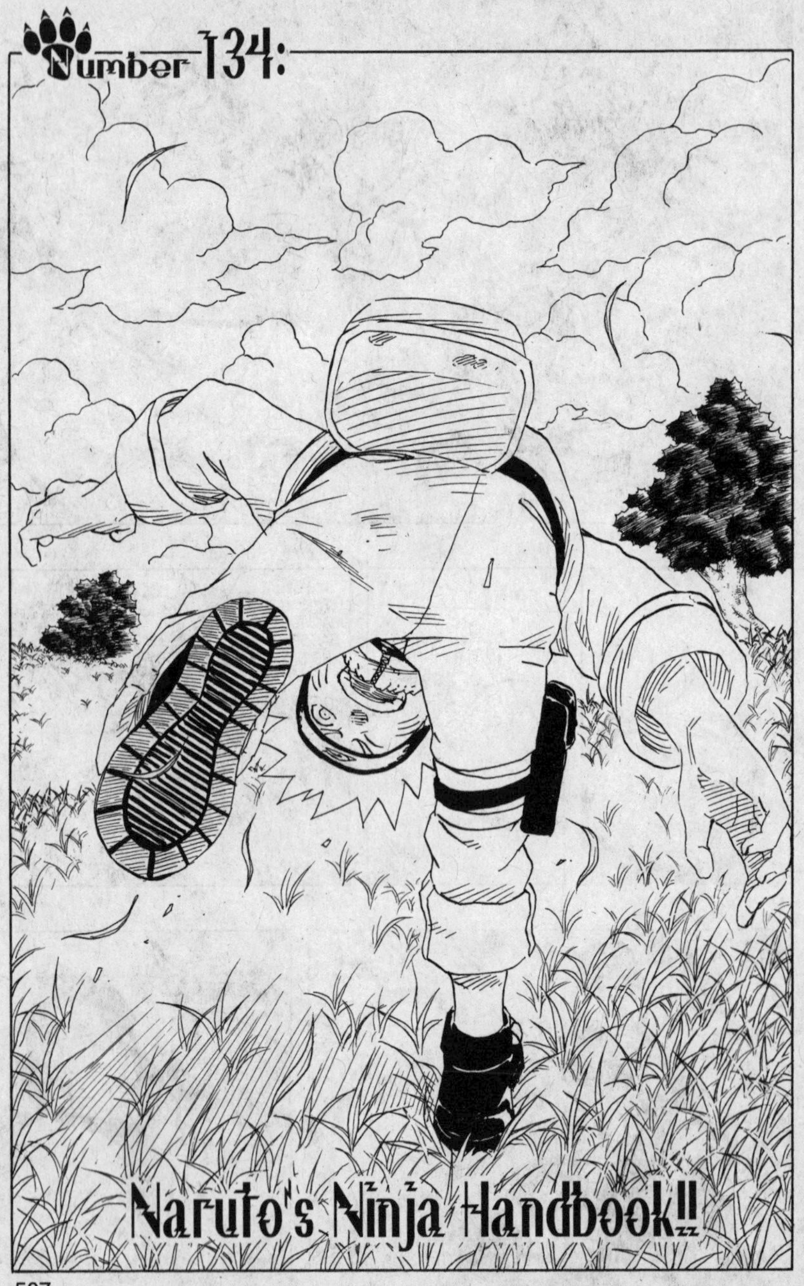
Number 134:
Naruto's Ninja Handbook!!

WH...WHAT THE... HOW MANY DOPPEL-GANGERS DID HE CREATE ...?!

WH... WHAT IS THIS?!

...WH...WHOA... INCREDIBLE ...

...
YOU... THIS...

SASUKE, RELAX.
LEAVE THE REST TO ME!

ALL RIGHT, Y'ALL!!
TIME TO MOVE!!

HUF
HUF

...
THIS...
HUF

THIS IS NARUTO?!

!!

GO!!
SH
AA

NARUTO'S NINJA HAND-BOOK!

!!
I HAVEN'T RECOVERED FROM THAT LAST ATTACK...
I CAN ONLY SHIELD MYSELF WITH THE SAND!!

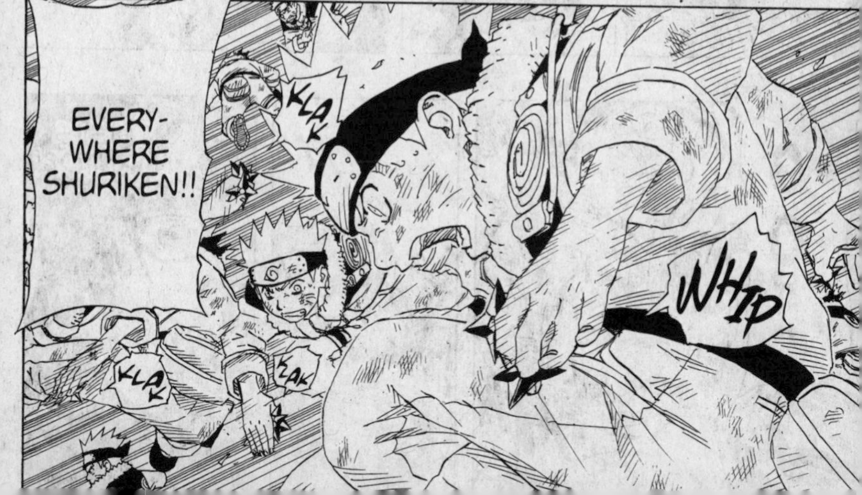

SHOOF
SHOOF
SHOOF
THOCK
THOCK
THOCK
THOCK
THOCK
THOCK
THOCK
!!
U!
ZU!
MA!
KI!

NARUTO'S 2000 BLOWS...

READ THIS WAY

!

... BARRAGE !!

THUD

SLAM

UGH... WH...WHAT IS HE...
ALL OF A SUDDEN ...

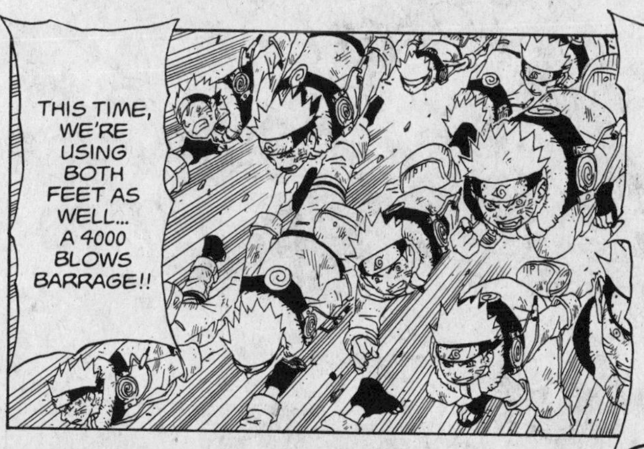
YEAH!!
IT AIN'T OVER YET! THERE'S MUCH MORE TO COME!!
THIS TIME, WE'RE USING BOTH FEET AS WELL... A 4000 BLOWS BARRAGE!!

NO WAY... HE'S REALLY GOT GAARA CORNERED...

THERE'S NO WAY... I...I CAN'T...

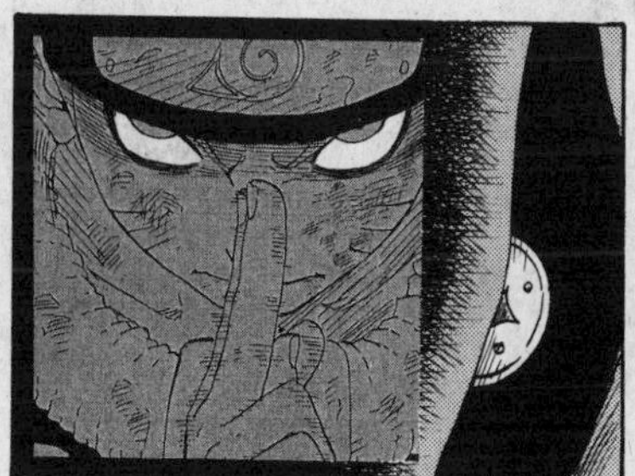

I WILL NOT LOSE TO SOME-ONE LIKE YOU!
ROOOOOOAR!!
O...OH NO, DON'T TELL ME... IT'S FINALLY HAPPENING?!
KA BOOM
POP POP POP POP

SHUDDER
WH...WHAT IS THAT...?

...!

CROAK!
HIS OPPONENT IS QUITE GOOD!

IT...IT'S FINALLY EMERGED?

PERFECT POSSESSION!!

SO THAT'S... THE MONSTER THAT'S INSIDE HIM, HUH...
HUF
HUF
HUF
HUF
IT'S HUGE...

SWISH

SNAP SNAP

!!
SWIRL
HUF
HUF

WAAAAH!!
SQSH

SLITHER
SLITHER
DARN IT... I USED UP MY CHAKRA WITH THOSE DOPPEL-GANGERS JUST NOW...

!
NARUTO!!

!!

...

SLITHER
SLITHER

CRUNCH

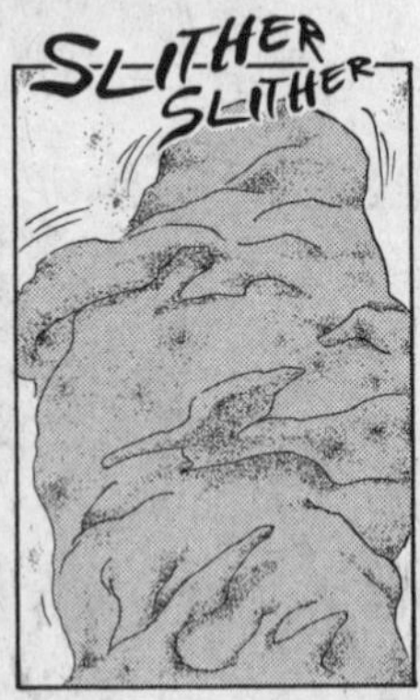
SLITHER
SLITHER

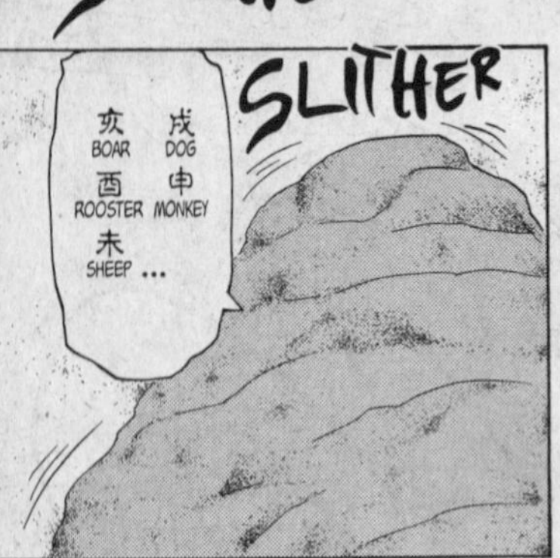
SLITHER
亥 BOAR 戌 DOG
酉 ROOSTER 申 MONKEY
未 SHEEP ...

DARN! CAN'T GET UP...!!
THROB
CREAK
THROB

I CAN'T BELIEVE I WAS FORCED TO REVEAL MYSELF... BUT IT'S ALL OVER NOW...
SABAKUKYÛ! THE COFFIN OF CRUSHING SAND!

SABAKU-SÔSÔ! IMPLODING SAND FUNERAL!
KUCHIYOSE NO JUTSU! THE ART OF SUMMONING!!
POP

THE TRAINING'S FINALLY PAYING OFF! AWESOME! I CAN DO IT!!
PUMP
WHAT IS IT THIS TIME ?!
WHAT THE–? YOU AGAIN...?

I SWEAR... TO PROTECT SAKURA!!

OH MY...
...!
HEH HEH... HE'S AN ENDLESS SOURCE OF ENTERTAINMENT...
UZUMAKI NARUTO... WHAT... THE HECK IS HE...
HEY, CHIEF TOAD, SIR! FIGHT WITH ME, PLEASE, WILL YA?!!
I'M REALLY COUNTING ON YA, CHIEF!!
HUF
IF I'M NOT MISTAKEN... THAT'S SHUKAKU, THE SAND SPIRIT...

SHIVER SHIVER
...
...NARUTO... WHAT... HAVE YOU BEEN UP TO...

...NO THANKS!!

WHAT ?!!

WHAT DO YOU MEAN!!
I THOUGHT YOU SAID YOU WERE GONNA MAKE ME YOUR HENCHMAN!!
RAGE RAGE

AND A BOSS HELPS HIS HENCHMEN WHEN THEY'RE IN TROUBLE, RIGHT!
THAT'S CALLED HONOR-BOUND DUTY!!
WHAP
WHAP

INDEED, I DID SAY I WOULD MAKE YOU MY HENCHMAN... BUT I HAVEN'T EVEN EXCHANGED SAKÉ CUPS WITH YOU YET...
AND WHY SHOULD I GO OUT OF MY WAY TO FIGHT THAT CREATURE...? HOW IDIOTIC.

HOP
HOP
YOU GOT TO BE KIDDING! I'M STILL A KID!
I CAN'T DRINK!!

SQUISH
!

PA!!
EH?!
PA?!

DON'T BE SO STUBBORN, AND HELP THIS KID, WILL YA!
AFTER ALL, HE PROTECTED ME!

WHAT IN THE WORLD ARE YOU DOING HERE...
...GAMA-KICHI?!

I HAD NOTHING BETTER TO DO, SO I CAME OUT TO HAVE SOME FUN.
BUT HIM OVER THERE, HE TRIED TO BULLY ME!

EH? HUH? HE'S REALLY YOUR DAD?
YUP!

CLICK
...KID... I'LL ACKNOWLEDGE YOU AS MY HENCHMAN!
AND I'LL SHOW YOU PLENTY OF HONOR-BOUND DUTY!!

GLARE
WHAT~~?!

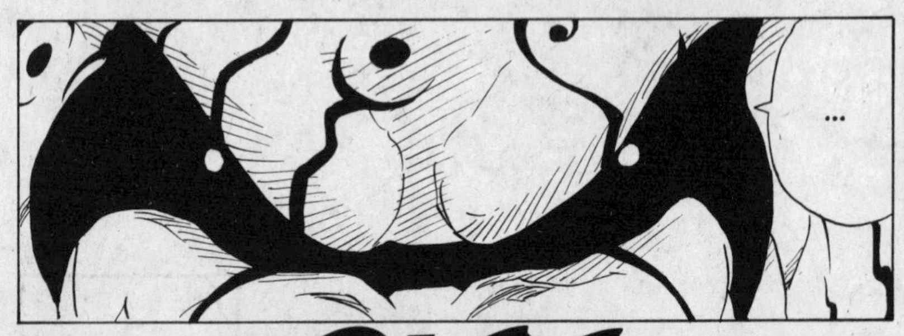
...

SLOOSH
I'M GOING TO SETTLE THIS SCORE... YOU LACKEY!

HE'S
GOOD!

Number 135:
The Gale-Like Battle...!!

!

STOMP

SWAY
WHOA!

ZOOM
HOLD ON TIGHT!

TRAP

!

GAMA DOSUZAN! TOAD SLASH!!

SHWOOM
WHAT A TOUGH FELLOW... HE'S SO SOLID I BARELY MANAGED TO PULL OUT THE SLASH...!
W... WOW...
CRASH
BOUNCE

SLAM
SSSHH
THUD
GAH!
WAAH!!
WHOA!

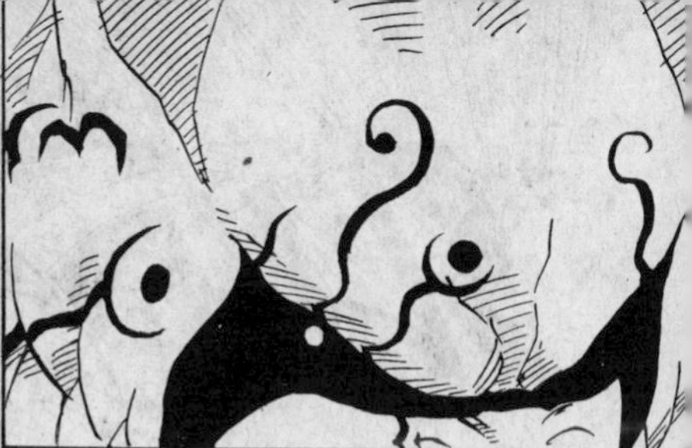

...
IF I DON'T GET RID OF HIM QUICKLY, THE WHOLE LAND-SCAPE'S GOING TO CHANGE...

HEY, CHIEF!
SAKURA'S OVER IN THAT DIRECTION, SO WE CAN'T GO THAT WAY!! CAN YOU LURE HIM OVER HERE?!!
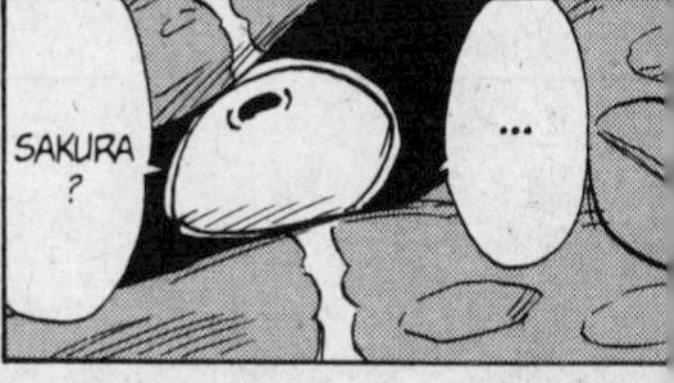
...
SAKURA ?

WE'VE GOT TO TAKE HIM DOWN!
OTHERWISE, WE CAN'T SAVE SAKURA!

...

SHE'S HIS GIRL...
...PA.

FASCINATING! THIS IS GETTING FUN!!
UZUMAKI NARUTO!!

HUH...

...!
TH... THAT'S...!

SHF

CRRK

...SO THAT'S THE HOST, HUH...

!!
SH...SHOOT, GAARA'S PLANNING TO GO ALL THE WAY...! I'VE GOT TO GET OUT OF HERE...!

KSSSSH

IN GRATITUDE FOR GIVING ME SUCH A GOOD TIME SO FAR...
...I'LL SHOW YOU THE TRUE STRENGTH OF THE SAND SPIRIT.

...

THOSE WHO BECOME POSSESSED BY THE DEMON SHUKAKU STOP BEING ABLE TO TRULY SLEEP SOUNDLY...
...OUT OF FEAR!

?!

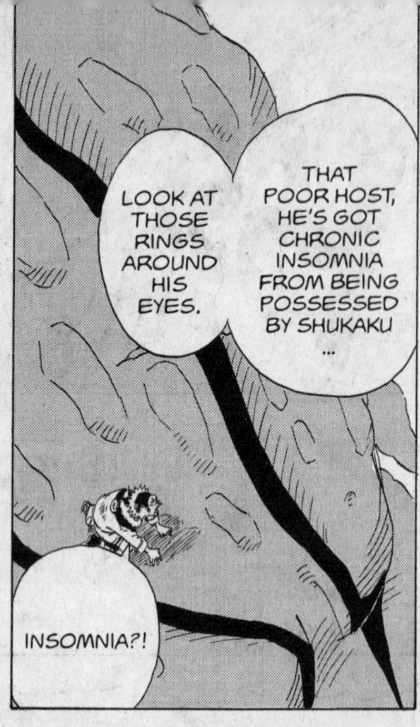
THAT POOR HOST, HE'S GOT CHRONIC INSOMNIA FROM BEING POSSESSED BY SHUKAKU ...
LOOK AT THOSE RINGS AROUND HIS EYES.
INSOMNIA?!

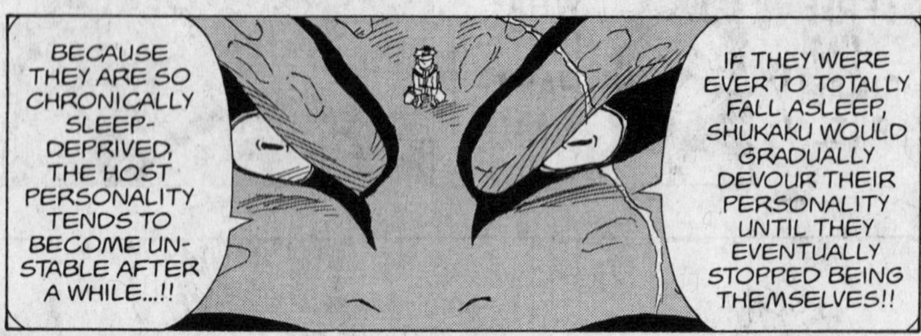
IF THEY WERE EVER TO TOTALLY FALL ASLEEP, SHUKAKU WOULD GRADUALLY DEVOUR THEIR PERSONALITY UNTIL THEY EVENTUALLY STOPPED BEING THEMSELVES!!
BECAUSE THEY ARE SO CHRONICALLY SLEEP-DEPRIVED, THE HOST PERSONALITY TENDS TO BECOME UN-STABLE AFTER A WHILE...!!

...

NORMALLY... WHILE THE HOST IS AWAKE...
... SHUKAKU'S TRUE STRENGTH IS SUP-PRESSED... BUT...

IF THE HOST VOLUNTARILY ENTERS SLEEP...

FSSS
SSSS
TANUKI NEIRI NO JUTSU! THE ART OF PLAYING POSSUM !!

SLUMP
SWAY SWAY

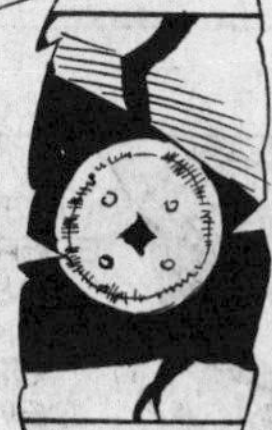
WHA-HAHA-HAHA-HAA!!

FREE, I'M FINALLY FREE!!

!
YEAH!
OOH, STRAIGHT OUT THE GATE, I SEE SOMEONE I WANNA SLAUGHTER !!

WIND STYLE...!
FWUMP

I'M GONNA LEAP!!
SLAP
RENKÛDAN! AIR BULLETS!!

SKOOSH
WATER STYLE...!
SKOOSH
WAAH!
LIQUID BULLETS!!
VOOM
ZOOMM
ZOOMM
AIR BULLETS!!
THOOT
THOOT

SHA-WOOM

PLOOSH

PLOOSH
THIS IS LIKE A HURRICANE...
WHAT A BATTLE...

WATCH OUT, CHIEF!!
THERE'S STILL ONE LEFT!

UGH!!

KA-BOOM
CRASH
WHEE! I DID IT!
I KILLED 'EM, I KILLED 'EM!!
!
WHOMP
OWW, THAT HURT! THAT LITTLE BALL WAS PACKED WITH AN UNBELIEVABLE AMOUNT OF CHAKRA!!

THE MOST IMPORTANT THING THERE IS! WE'VE GOT TO CLOBBER THAT HOST BRAT AWAKE!!
THEN THE JUTSU WILL COME UNDONE!!
FWIP

EVEN SOMEONE LIKE ME CAN'T TAKE MANY MORE OF THOSE LITTLE BALLS!
SO WHAT ARE WE GONNA DO?!!

HOW?!

WE NEED TO GET UP CLOSE AND STOP THAT FOOL'S MOVEMENTS!
THAT'LL GIVE US THE OPENING TO STRIKE!!

AGAIN, HOW?!

I'M A TOAD, I DON'T HAVE THE FANGS OR CLAWS TO HOLD HIM STILL!!

SO I'M GOING TO USE THE ART OF TRANS-FORMATION TO MORPH INTO SOMETHING PREDATORY!!

GRRR...!

TRANSFOR-
MATION
ISN'T MY
STRONG
SUIT!
I NEED YOU
TO WEAVE
THE SIGNS
FOR ME...
AND I'LL
LEND YOU MY
CHAKRA!!
IT'LL BE A
COMBO
TRANSFOR-
MATION!!

'CUZ YOU USED
UP THE LAST OF
YOUR CHAKRA
TO SUMMON
ME, RIGHT?!!
SHF

EH?!! SOME-THING WITH FANGS AND CLAWS...
UHH! UHH!

HERE WE GO!!
WAIT! OH, NO!

BOOF

GRRAR

SLAM

GRAB

CHOMP

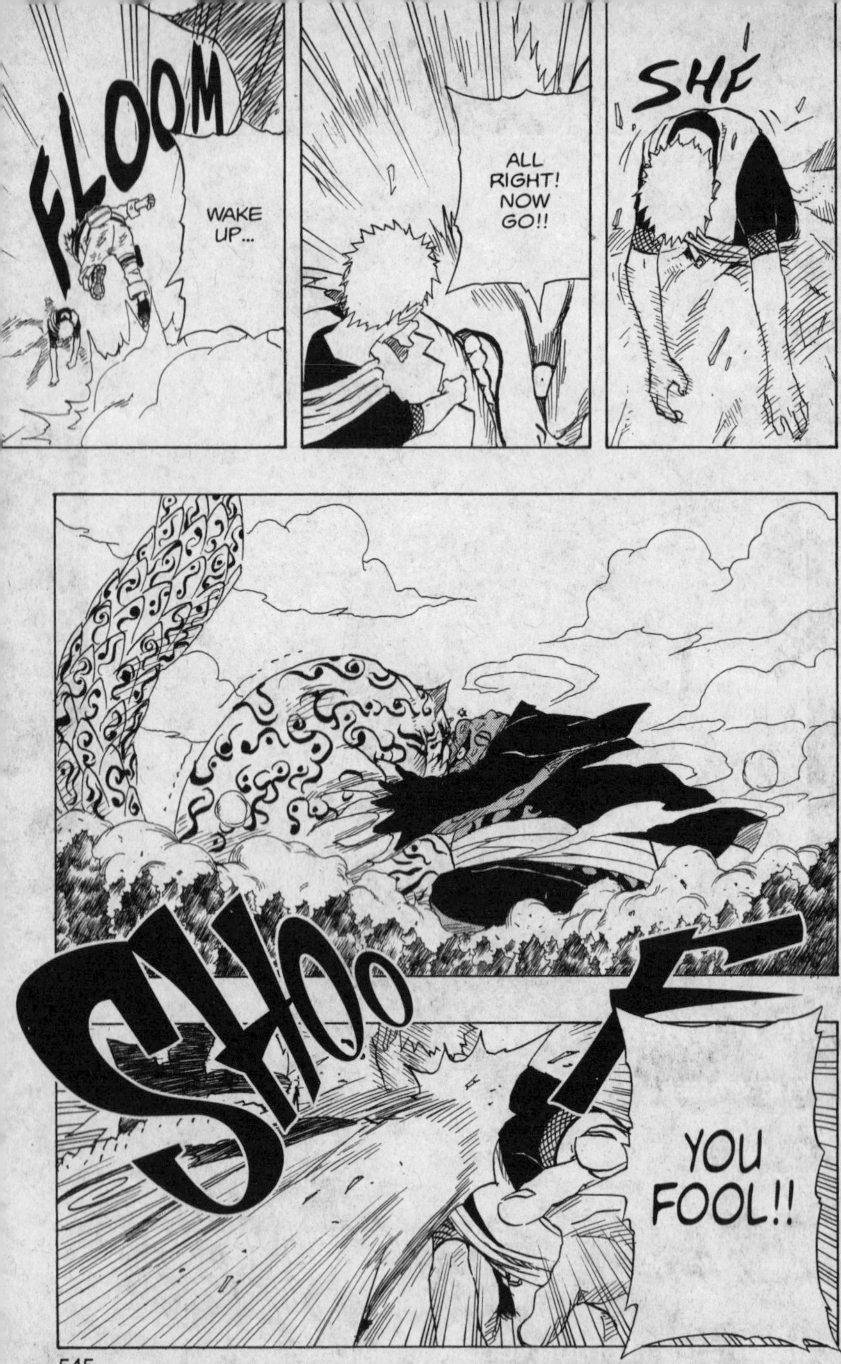

SHOO

YOU FOOL!!

IN THE NEXT VOLUME...

THE WAGER

Not everyone has survived Orochimaru's attack on the village. When a long-lost ninja returns with a dangerous entourage, Naruto finds his life in more danger than ever before. Who is Uchiha Itachi and what does he want with Naruto and Sasuke? Meanwhile, Jiraiya attempts to train Naruto to push beyond his limits while Orochimaru uses threats to coerce a legendary kunoichi into helping him. But will her tragic past play a part in destroying Naruto's future?

Watch Naruto...

SHONEN JUMP NARUTO

© 2002 MASASHI KISHIMOTO

All Day...

SHONEN JUMP NARUTO SHIPPUDEN

©2002 MASASHI KISHIMOTO / 2007 SHIPPUDEN All Rights Reserved.

Everyday... for FREE!

Watch thousands of anime episodes officially on

neonalley.com

TV 14

SEE INTO THE SOUL
OF BLEACH
WITH THE MANGA,
PROFILES AND ART BOOKS
RATED
T
FOR
TEEN
ratings.viz.com
viz media
www.viz.com

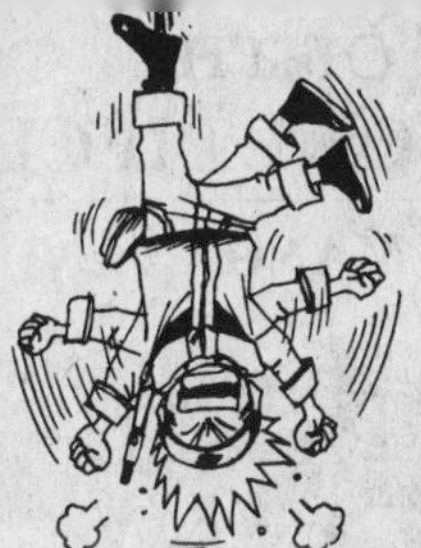

You're Reading in the Wrong Direction!!

Whoops! Guess what? You're starting at the wrong end of the comic!

...It's true! In keeping with the original Japanese format, **Naruto** is meant to be read from right to left, starting in the upper-right corner.

Unlike English, which is read from left to right, Japanese is read from right to left, meaning that action, sound effects and word-balloon order are completely reversed...something which can make readers unfamiliar with Japanese feel pretty backwards themselves. For this reason, manga or Japanese comics published in the U.S. in English have sometimes been published "flopped"—that is, printed in exact reverse order, as though seen from the other side of a mirror.

By flopping pages, U.S. publishers can avoid confusing readers, but the compromise is not without its downside. For one thing, a character in a flopped manga series who once wore in the original Japanese version a T-shirt emblazoned with "M A Y" (as in "the merry month of") now wears one which reads "Y A M"! Additionally, many manga creators in Japan are themselves unhappy with the process, as some feel the mirror-imaging of their art alters their original intentions.

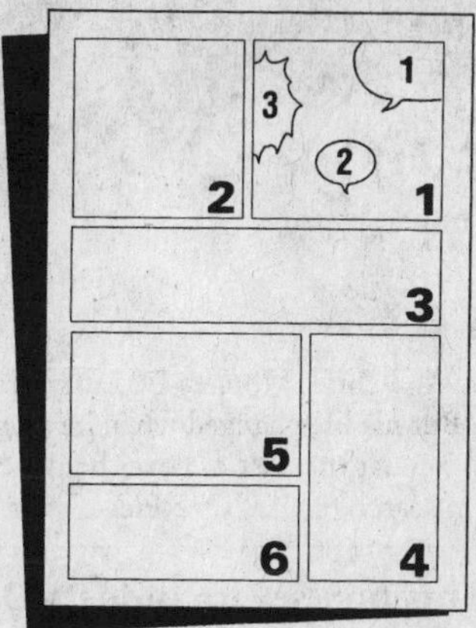

We are proud to bring you Masashi Kishimoto's **Naruto** in the original unflopped format. For now, though, turn to the other side of the book and let the ninjutsu begin...!

—Editor